The Threadbare Buzzard

A MARINE FIGHTER PILOT IN WWII

Second Lieutenant Thomas M. Tomlinson, USMCR (1942)

The Threadbare Buzzard

A MARINE FIGHTER PILOT IN WWII

THOMAS M. TOMLINSON

ZENITH
PRESS

*This book is dedicated to a large group of very young men
that shared a narrow range of age. They also shared the soaring
freedoms, terrors, joys, and, all too often, the final fate that
were the handmaidens of their profession.*

*Those were the only common denominators.
They were saints, sinners, cowards, heroes, mountebanks,
and men of high integrity. They were the washed and
unwashed, the blessed and the damned.
May they live forever in our memories.*

First published in 2004 by Zenith Press, an imprint of MBI Publishing
Company, Galtier Plaza, Suite 200, 380 Jackson Street, St. Paul, MN
55101-3885 USA

ISBN 0-7603-2055-1

Cartography by Phil Schwartzberg
All photos from the author's collection unless otherwise noted

Printed in the United States of America

Contents

Prologue

One of the dandy little fringe benefits of flying in World War II was the right of every participant to assign himself the rank of eagle. There were Screaming Eagles, Eagle Squadrons, and just plain Eagles. There were even some lady eagles. A person operating a flying machine could soar like an eagle, have the eyes of an eagle, or, in fact, have a beak like an eagle. Of course, there were the real bald eagles of this context who were the aging fliers of earlier days whose careers as eagles as well as sexual predators were coming to a close despite creative hair combing and shoe polish.

This eagle stuff came to be, in no small part, because the eagle had been designated the national bird on June 20, 1782, over the strenuous objections of one of the nation's most illustrious and horniest founders, who would certainly know of these matters. Mr. Benjamin Franklin held out some rather compelling reasons. He was quoted as saying, "For my part I wish the bald eagle had not been chosen as the representative of our country. He is a bird of bad moral character; he does not get his living honestly; you may see him perched on some dead tree, where, too lazy to fish himself, he watches the labor of the Fishing Hawk and when that diligent bird has at length taken a fish, and is bearing it to his nest for the support of his mate and young ones, the bald eagle pursues him and takes it

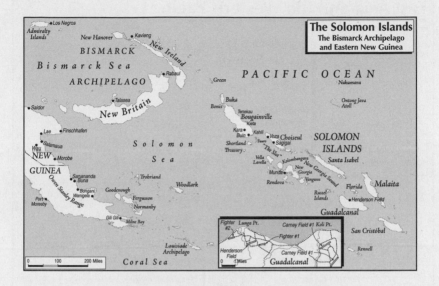

from him. With all this injustice, he is never in good case, but, like those among men who live by sharping and robbing, he is generally poor, and often very lousy." Strange counsel from a politician, until it is recalled that Old Ben held out for the wild turkey.

However, the eagle was not protected in the Lower Forty-eight until 1940 and not until 1952 in Alaska, where it can be seen feasting on the garbage dumps when not being intimidated by competing crows, U.S. protection or not.

In Poverty Flats, Montana, it is recognized that the scream of an eagle pursued is like the yelp of a mongrel pup chased by a testy cat. However, crows cannot intimidate buzzards. Hence, there is nothing to abridge the right of a flier from Poverty Flats to emulate the honorable buzzard. This formidable bird recognizes carrion in its true and undigested state.

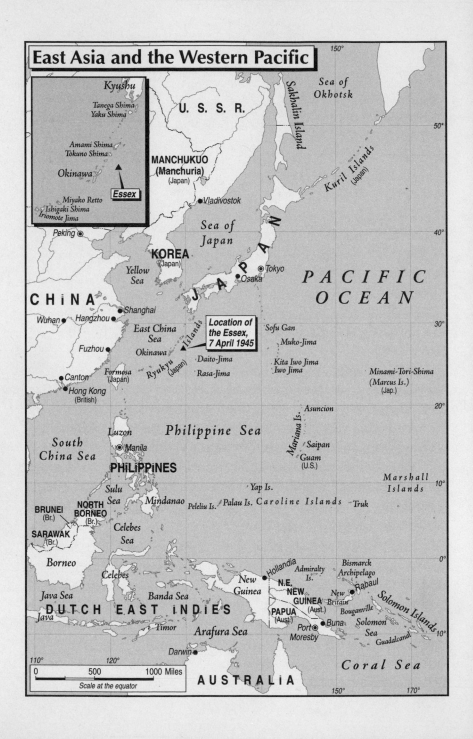

East Asia and the Western Pacific

150°

Kyushu

Tanega Shima
Yaku Shima

U. S. S. R.

Sea of
Okhotsk

50°

Amami Shima
Tokuno Shima

MANCHUKUO
(Manchuria)
(Japan)

Sakhalin Island

Kuril Islands
(Japan)

Okinawa

Essex

● *Vladivostok*

Miyako Retto
Ishigaki Shima
Iriomote Jima

Sea of
Japan

40°

Peking ◉

KOREA
(Japan)

J
A
P
A
N

PACIFIC
OCEAN

C H I N A

Yellow
Sea

● *Tokyo*
● *Osaka*

Wuhan ● ● Hangzhou

● Shanghai

East China
Sea

**Location of
the Essex,
7 April 1945**

Sofu Gan

30°

Fuzhou ●

Ryukyu Islands

Okinawa ▲

● *Muko-Jima*

Kita Iwo Jima
Iwo Jima

Minami-Tori-Shima
(Marcus Is.)
(Jap.)

Canton ●

Formosa
(Japan)

(Japan)

Daito-Jima

Rasa-Jima

Hong Kong ●
(British)

20°

*South
China Sea*

Luzon

Philippine Sea

Mariana Is.

Asuncion

◉ Manila

PHILIPPINES

● *Saipan*

Guam
(U.S.)

*Marshall
Islands*

10°

*Sulu
Sea*

Mindanao

Yap Is.

Peleliu Is. *Palau Is.* Caroline Islands ● *Truk*

BRUNEI
(Br.)

NORTH
BORNEO
(Br.)

*Celebes
Sea*

SARAWAK
(Br.)

Borneo

0°

Celebes

Hollandia

*Admiralty
Is.*

*Bismarck
Archipelago*

Java Sea

Banda Sea

New
Guinea

N.E.
NEW
GUINEA
(Aust.)

New
Britain

● Rabaul

Solomon Islands

Java

DUTCH EAST INDIES

PAPUA
(Aust.)

Bougainville

*Solomon
Sea*

Timor

Arafura Sea

Port ◉
Moresby

● Buna

Guadalcanal

10°

Darwin ●

Coral Sea

110°

120°

0   500   1000 Miles

Scale at the equator

AUSTRALIA

150°

170°

I

On the western fringe of Poverty Flats (not its given name), Montana, there was a factory that produced sugar by reducing the big, red sugar beets to basics. The chief byproduct was the pungent beet pulp that permeated the area with a more virulent stench than that of rotting fish. This was at its worst during the frigid winter nights when the hunger moon sailed overhead, and, if the freight trains weren't fighting their way up the frozen grade, the only sound was the lonesome howl of a starving coyote in the forbidding hills.

The beet pulp attracted another disgusting industry. The parsimonious ranchers discovered that this revolting biomass added a lot of weight to beef cattle at a very low cost. As a consequence, vast feed pens were located there. Here, the sad-faced steers contemplated their future in a Kansas City steak house while sloshing around in their own byproducts in a disgusting re-enforcement of the beet pulp.

The local schoolrooms afforded no escape, since they were crowded by the offspring of the impoverished Russian-Germans who were refugees from the dusted-out wheat farms of eastern Montana and the Dakotas. Their cure for any physical complaint was raw garlic, and this smell in an airless classroom surrendered no points to the aroma of the beet pulp and feeding pens.

However, Poverty Flats in the last days of the Great Depression was not a totally despicable place. When the icy winter had loosened its grip, the climate became quite palatable, with the snow disappearing rapidly from the lower ranges of the surrounding mountains and down in the valley under the welcome caress of the Chinook winds. These winds were dry westerlies, which happily took the moisture from the snow along with them on their easterly passage and spared the denizens a lot of grief with mud.

With the greening of the grass, the prairie-dog town on the flats became hyperactive with the barking rodents emerging from their holes to greet the warming sun and the stream of Flathead Indians coming down through Paradise from the reservation. The Indians' horses would be drawing the travois loaded with the baggage with which to pitch their lodges and spread the deerskins to dry the roots of the profusely flowering bitterroots. These roots were prized for the medicinal tea and dietary supplement that the Indians required. The men rode, and the women walked.

Other flora and fauna bestirred themselves as the season progressed into the hot summer. At the old army fort it was time for maneuvers, and the mule-drawn caissons would come stampeding out of the gate in clouds of dust with the officers on horseback, the sergeants cursing, and the infantry heel-and-toeing it.

Once, in the days of glory, some of the chaps from the fort had participated in the excitement stirred up when Chief Joseph was kicking the U.S. Army's rump over in the Big Hole Valley. On a sortie to Fort Fizzle (its true name), one gallant second lieutenant shot himself in the foot, thereby becoming the only casualty ever suffered in action by the post. This Fort Fizzle was only a hastily constructed log breastwork jointly manned by the military and some civilian volunteers. These hardy pioneers, having heard all of the military bull-bleep they required, decided to walk off despite the threat of being shot by the army officer in command. Meanwhile, the wily Chief Joseph had no trouble circumnavigating this mess.

East of town was Hellgate Canyon, named for its history as a place where one particular tribe would ambush other warhoops going east for the buffalo before the white man appeared. In the white man's time, in a bitter winter, a bunch of incensed ranchers from around the diggings at Bannock and Virginia City, Montana, rode down a band of brigands in this place despite the fact that the snow was ass-deep on a tall Indian. These lads had been murdering folks for their gold, and in the time-honored tradition of politicians, the local sheriff at the mines was the leader. A rope and a pole gate brought this episode to a satisfactory, albeit frigid, conclusion.

Local denizens were proud of the fact that if one were traveling west he could pass through Hellgate on the way to the aforementioned Paradise—which it wasn't, really.

There wasn't a whole lot of action in Poverty Flats, and it was no place for a restless youth to rot. The grinding depression had little to offer besides hard work and a rather tacky school system whose staff and management's collective IQ hovered right around room temperature.

True enough, Mr. Franklin Delano Roosevelt was in the process of undoing the chaos of Mr. Herbert Hoover's disastrous administration. Mr. Roosevelt was not popular in an area where the rule was "One cow, one vote." He had made the fatal blunder of supplying the bucolic bumpkins with rural electrification. This was reducing the reproduction rate of the strong sons needed to wet-nurse the cows by allowing the agrarian population to stay out of the sack later in the evening to read the Holy Bible with the newfangled 'lectrik light.

This 'lectrik light also allowed escape for a discontented youth to read voraciously, tales of derring-do. The travels of all the great adventurers and explorers right down to Richard Halliburton were perused and finally the aerial exploits of the World War I flyers were discovered. This was the real goods, but seemingly impossible of attainment. However, there was a glimmer of light at the end of the tunnel, and it wasn't the headlight of an onrushing train.

In this unlikely circumstance there were some adventurous local chaps utilizing elderly Ford Tri-Motor and Travelaire airplanes to haul Forest Service freight to fight fires. When the lightning strikes set the forests ablaze, the sun would become only a coppery disk in a smoke-obscured sky. Then, the pleasing odor of burning pine filled the air, and the flying machines were kept very busy.

Since Lindbergh had recently flown the Atlantic, flying was accounted a glamorous undertaking. This aerial firefighting operation also presented the opportunity for an adventurous youth to learn how to fly. Unfortunately, being of such a tender age, possessing this skill would not really have solved anything had it not been for an incredible stroke of good fortune. Europe went up in flames, and World War II was underway.

Since the United States wasn't participating yet, there was no way for anyone so young to get to fly in the U.S. service. Anyway, the U.S.A. then ranked nineteenth in military might, right behind Holland and Portugal. This prohibition did not apply to Merry Olde England, whose desperation made it insensitive to whom they got killed, and they had developed an insatiable appetite for aviators of any persuasion, nationality, or age—even the contemptible Yanks.

Opportunity knocked. Besides, the short summer was ending, and it was time to travel.

II

I t was a long ride on a ramshackle bus from Poverty Flats to the Canadian border at Sweet Grass, Montana, and Coutts, Alberta. This flight from hearth and home was accomplished one jump ahead of a father sentimentally loath to lose a cheap laborer in his construction business. He was reinforced by the county sheriff.

This was a close-run affair, and the bureaucracy at the port of entry caused me a near-fatal delay. This was my first, but hardly the last, encounter with the "Sanctimonious Ass" school of "His Majesty's Civil Servants." While the customs office on the U.S. side of the border at Sweet Grass was housed in a neat little brick building staffed with very decent officials, such was not the case a few yards away on the dreary prairie. A ratty little frame building housed the Canadian customs and immigrations at Coutts. The official in charge had the typically thin nose, ratty mustache, and close-set eyes of the English. He wore a frowzy uniform, and as was the custom of the Brit, be he doorman, railway conductor, bellhop, collector of slops, or any other lackey wearing a uniform, he had his service ribbons from the First World War proudly displayed on his narrow chest to support his insufferably superior attitude.

Although it was obvious that no attempt would be made to dissuade any suckers headed for His Majesty's Service, the chance to demonstrate superiority over a Yank, especially if he were a somewhat defenseless seventeen-year-old, was irresistible. The lads from Poverty Flats had no great admiration for the Brits, and when His Majesty's representative undertook to remove a U.S. comic book as contraband, which posed a threat to *empire*, he got a sarcastic evaluation of the royal imperative. However, the wise words of the Oracle of Poverty Flats were recalled just in time to avoid a fatal confrontation. The applicable parable stated that "One does not engage in a pissing match with a skunk." A verbal retreat was initiated and the flight into the unknown North was resumed.

Fortune smiled, and a ride on a sheep truck was secured as far as Lethbridge, Alberta, where it was supposed one could offer his all to the Royal Canadian Air Force (RCAF). That was not true, and since night was falling and no allowance had been made in a very slender budget for hotel accommodations, the local Mounted Police rode to the rescue. They provided a blanket and space on a judge's desk for the night. They determined that the cells were too bloody lousy for an aspiring hero. They further arranged another ride, upgraded to a cattle truck this time, to Calgary, where a great dissimulation ensued. Although the proof of qualifications were in the form of an American pilot's license and log book, courtesy of Johnson Flying Service, it was allegedly illegal to enlist Americans at that time due to the neutrality acts forced on the U.S. president by the isolationist Congress. This promptly resulted in a magical change of birthplace from Wisdom, Montana, to Vancouver, British Columbia. At this juncture the imitation British Officer in charge advised, "And now, old boy, toddle on home and we will determine where best to use your experience and notify you." It didn't seem a bit odd to them that a citizen of Vancouver would be returning to Poverty Flats, Montana, to await his orders.

By now, beginning to get hungry, it was back to Poverty Flats, where food was available and a general attitude of good riddance prevailed in the household. In a short time, the Royal Canadian Air Force sent orders to report to Moose Jaw, Saskatchewan, for flight duties.

They did not specify what these duties might be or any set time to report. Reference to a map located Moose Jaw far to the east of Lethbridge, Alberta, and it was going to be a long lurch by bus over the lamentable roads of the day.

All went well after departing Lethbridge, as a bus, even more decrepit than the Montana version, banged and rattled over the potholed gravel highway. The endless prairie under overcast skies with scattered snow flurries was cold and dreary-looking. After the stop at Medicine Hat, a veritable metropolis with two grain elevators and not much else, the road got worse and only one other passenger remained. The snow was seriously increasing as dark came down, and the driver was having difficulty keeping track of the road. Then the engine failed and the bus ground to a halt. With the silence it was noted that the other passenger, being a sensible Canadian, was roaring drunk and being in good voice was repetitively singing, "I'll never say never again."

This was a first lesson in the self-reliance of the basic Canadians. The driver determined, after a frigid, knuckle-busting investigation, that it was a fuel problem. In an area where farmers were regularly found frozen to death between house and barn, it was essential to get the engine running to supply heat. To this end the driver drained gas from the tank into a can. He raised the engine hood, which fortunately was an interior one, and with the siphon hose running to the carburetor, power was regained. There were only two problems remaining. The first was that the sober passenger had to hold the gas can in a most uncomfortable position above the noisy engine as the vehicle jolted on its merry way. The second was that the gas in the small can would last for only a limited time. This required going out in the now raging blizzard to siphon more gas from the main tank in the bitter cold. During this silent period, the second passenger continued to supply the entertainment, singing, "I'll never say never again." This was the condition when a snowplow dispatched from Swift Current, another two-grain elevator metropolis, came on scene just before dawn.

This didn't appear to be a noteworthy event in those parts. After some sketchy repairs and the debarkation of the vocalist, the bus continued on to Moose Jaw, where the RCAF failed to deliver much of an impression. In fact, the installation was only a primitive dirt field now being covered with snow, and the buildings (two) were not much better. A small hangar and a shack with a ready room were it. There were a few shabby Fleet biplanes and a couple of Tiger Moths, which were also biplanes. Some of the Fleets were equipped with skis. The roundel insignia of the RCAF on their fuselages and wings comprised the only military manifestations in evidence.

The personnel matched the physical plant; they didn't wear uniforms, but rather whatever pieces of flying gear or clothing were handy, to repel the cold. It turned out that it was a place where people with previous flying time could begin their training to become flight instructors. If they made it through here, they would finish up at the big training base at Trenton, Ontario. Despite the sarcastic greeting given the new arrival, "What the hell did you do to get sent here?", it was a fine place to start a career in the glamorous field of aviation—especially with a background of Poverty Flats.

Along with his buddy, my instructor was a veteran of the Spanish civil war. Naturally, these two somewhat hard characters were from Texas. The entire company, which was miniscule, lived in the YMCA in town and took their meals at a Greek restaurant. They were ferried to the field by taxi. By then all flight training for the British Empire was done in Canada. This prevented a harassed flying instructor in a Tiger Moth from having a Messerschmitt on his tail in the traffic pattern of a training base in the beleaguered British Isles. Things were so tough over there that it was reported that the frightened king and queen had a ship standing by in order to abandon their subjects when the feared Germans invaded.

It is hard to realize the immense advantages to be had when entering a war at that stage and in that manner. Nobody was going to get washed out short of total incompetence, and as far as taking any direction from drill instructors, it didn't exist. This led to a lifelong inability to march or to properly "knuckle the forelock" (salute). Learning how to conceal contempt for authority and maintain personal integrity are valuable tools for a youth operating in the intellectual wasteland of the regular military.

Checkout in all the available types of aircraft was a short formality, and the real business was taken in hand. This was chiefly concerned with "patter," a system that was unique to the British training program. (Grudgingly, it must be admitted that it was far superior, to the system subsequently encountered within the U.S. Navy. Unfortunately, then and now, the U.S. Marines depended upon the navy for pilot training.)

The patter system required the instructor to make every maneuver with the airplane while describing it over a primitive speaking tube, called a gosport, to the student in a very standardized and logical sequence. This whole patter had to be memorized. It was somewhat galling, but with practice it reduced flying to an automatic reaction. While it was not appreciated at the time, it surely proved to be a lifesaver later in the war when the high stress of combat and other undesirable circumstances demanded instant responses not available to the inadequately trained.

Lessons in flying and instructing were not the only items on the menu. The other members of this school were a raffish collection of former Canadian bush pilots, former U.S. wing walkers, and former smugglers of everything from Prohibition booze to Chinese nationals. Although some were on the run from miscellaneous mischief in other lands, they were fine fellows and took in their newest and youngest member with good will. They arranged for a room for the Threadbare recruit at the local YMCA and a meal ticket on credit at the Greek's. All debts were to be paid when the first check arrived.

The check did not arrive, and that required a trip to the provincial capital at Regina to meet the air force officer responsible for this airborne dog and pony show. Not a pilot, he was a "wingless" squadron leader, a real "Colonel Blimp" type and carbon copy of the officious ass manning the customs house at Coutts. He did, however, have a better uniform and a larger mustache.

This was a little more frightening, since it developed that the RCAF was just as screwed up as other military services I've encountered over the years. With no paperwork from Calgary, it was "Col. Blimp's" contention that the young lad in front of him didn't exist and probably was some sort of criminal posing as a student at their fine flying school. He was also staring at the overshoes of his victim, which were not buckled up and were flapping open. Although sloppiness like this was considered very sophisticated among the youth of Poverty Flats, this sartorial gaffe impelled the officer to comment that all Yanks were "bloody savages."

Fortunately, the wise words of the Oracle of Poverty Flats were recalled, and the applicable parable for this case was: "If you want to work that horse you better feed him something he likes." Therefore, he was humbly advised that all of the folks in the States were not enthusiastic about the British war, but some of the youth were frothing advocates and secretly made their militant loyalty to England known to each other by leaving their overshoes unbuckled. The breathtaking gullibility of these Canadian hicks would have left their Poverty Flats contemporaries gasping.

Very shortly there were official papers, a much needed check, a sincere handshake, and a ride back to Moose Jaw. The papers restated the myth that Vancouver was the point of origin of the new hero, despite the squadron leader's rather accurate assessment of Yanks.

The YMCA was a swinging place then, since the personnel from the field were great patrons of Canadian whiskey, song, and waitresses from miles around. Across the snowplowed street was a great natatorium or indoor swimming pool; these were not all that uncommon at the time. The jolly Greek at the restaurant was most relieved to get paid, and his chow was better than most of the military garbage encountered later.

All in all, it was a rather merry life, and the flying, although desperately cold, provided many happy adventures, experiences, and lessons. One great lesson was how to manage an old biplane on snow skis in a brisk cross wind on the ground. These skis also made the crates somewhat tricky while doing aerobatics, which was the preferred way to fly. The Canadians, in their desperation, had bought up all manner of weird airplanes from all over the world, and some of these would have been ideal for wing walking had it not been for the awful cold of the season.

The performance of one model (whose maker will not be identified) proved to have a bad habit in an inverted spin. When an actual instructor was not available, it was the custom for one student to act as the instructor and another student to get in the back seat and respond to the patter. Once, when a "student-pilot" was being talked through an Immelman Turn by a "student-instructor," he applied too much forward stick on top, causing an inverted stall. A violent inverted spin ensued. The student-pilot was a chunky ex-bush pilot who wasted no time in releasing his Sutton Harness as the student-instructor hysterically screamed at him over the gosport. With the student-pilot's weight tumbling off into space, the flying machine underwent a drastic change in trim and fell into a docile dive.

Funny thing about that endless prairie: there was one tree all by its lonesome out there, and damned if that isn't where he wound up, tangled in his chute. Unable to extricate himself before rescuers arrived, and due to all of the excitement, he had responded to a call of nature and was in a foul mood when untangled. Remarkably, he bore no animosity and insisted on profusely thanking his frightened student-instructor for telling him to get out. May the god of Icarus be praised.

Between flights there was time for reaction training. This was accomplished in the shack that represented the pilot's lounge. A large iron stove fueled by chunks of coal tenuously held the frost at bay. A diligent student perusing his "Patter Book" would be rudely alerted by the shout, "Incoming!" If he were agile enough he could avoid the large chunk of coal aimed at him. When the student was fully trained, he could intercept the missile and return it with devastating results.

As a substitute for foxes, coyotes were another subject of our study. There were plenty of them out on the desolate prairie, which was only occasionally divided by primitive split-rail fences. When a coyote in his white fur coat was located against the snowy white prairie, it was "Tallyho!" and the chase was on. The coyote was best observed from the Tiger Moth aircraft at as close to the coyote's altitude as possible. A lesson learned from this research was that a coyote at flank speed can get under a split-rail fence and a Tiger Moth cannot. The only official question asked of the student who flew into the fence was, why, when faced with "engine failure," he couldn't have chosen a stretch of the abundant prairie without a fence in it? There were also some questions about the dependable little Gypsy engine failing to begin with. There didn't seem to be any point in burdening officialdom with unnecessary details, and it certainly was true that that engine had died as surely as a gunshot can cause a heart to fail. Anyway, that engine wasn't going to run again anytime soon.

With these many amusements, the time sped by, and soon the fledgling Buzzard, who had also learned that he had no interest in becoming an instructor, matriculated. The next phase would be at the permanent RCAF base at Trenton, Ontario, onward and upward. Spring was beginning to show unmistakable signs of coming to the prairie.

III

The leave taking from the Moose Jaw YMCA called for a splendid party, with many townspeople present. It would appear that the chaps were marching off for combat in the front lines, with the many toasts to the empire and patriotic ballads. "Pack Up Your Troubles in Your Old Kit Bag" and "It's a Long Way to Tipperary" come to mind.

Early in the morning, enjoying generally low visibility, I boarded the great Canadian Pacific train. Oh joy, this fine contrivance had a dining car, an observation car, and genuine Pullman berths. Literally these trains had been built for royalty, as had their associated hotels in the major cities. What a grand exit from Moose Jaw this was, in contrast with my modest arrival on a broken-down bus in a state of insolvency. Some of the fellow Buzzards had traveled this route before and had laid in a good store of Canadian whiskey to ease the long journey and enhance the tales of flying.

This splendid train had sparkling white sheets for the berths, a jolly porter, and, wonder of all wonders, a fine dining car. Here the soup course was always jellied consommé to prevent the diners from getting drenched when the train encountered a stretch of frost-warped track at speed. The big locomotives pulled their cars across the flat lands, through Winnipeg, and on to the deep forests of the lake country.

Here there was an unscheduled stop when a mob of Royal
Canadian Mounted Police boarded the train surrounding some
escaped prisoners of war: a defiant German submarine crew. A
day or so later the train again stopped in the deep woods, and the
Germans were extracted from the baggage car where they had
been chained down. A really grim-looking prisoner of war camp,
whence they had escaped, again enfolded them. This was pretty
heady stuff, and joy was abroad in the land as every clickity-clack
of the wheels on the railroad track widened the gap from Poverty
Flats.

There was time to explore Toronto, which aptly illustrated the
observation that, after two hog callin's and a county fair, the like of
this had never been seen before. Soon it was on to nearby Trenton,
which was practically on the north shore of Lake Ontario. This was a
real air base, and the Harvard aircraft with their dominating, throaty
roar snarled off practically day and night. The Harvard was to become
the universal trainer of the allied world and known as the AT-6 and
SNJ among many other names. That was after the aircraft's stability
had been vastly improved by squaring off the wing tips and the designation changed from Mark I Harvard to Mark II Harvard in the
British service.

This airplane had an interesting postwar career. With the Rising
Sun insignia of the Japanese air force painted on wings and fuselages,
it was used to represent the fearsome Japanese Zero fighter in count-
less war movies. It looked about as much like a real Zero as Dick
Nixon looked like Marilyn Monroe.

One day, close to a satellite field used mostly for emergency landing practice, the British sergeant pilot instructor in the front seat of
a Mark I Harvard ordered his student to put the aircraft into a regular spin at a relatively low altitude. He added that whenever the student was frightened enough, he could recover. The student promptly
initiated that recovery procedure. The trouble was that the kite did-
n't respond. The instructor, cursing fearfully, seized the controls and
with increasing panic gunned the engine, dropped the flaps and land-

ing gear, and as a last resort jettisoned the hatch and went over the inside of the spin.

The impressionable student followed him, also on the inside of the spin, and jerked his ripcord when barely clear. One swing in the chute and a rude arrival with terra firma ensued. The former Mark I Harvard was blazing merrily not far off, and the former instructor and his unopened chute were about halfway there.

The school, in common with a lot of other RCAF activities, had what was known as a rumble fund. This fund was financed by fines for various dumb stunts, like ground-looping. Losing the ripcord while employing one of His Majesty's parachutes called for a substantial rumble-fund fine. The student was disturbed to find that in the excitement of the aforementioned fall he had thrown his away. The instructor's unused parachute had a ripcord that was just going to waste. It was only the chore of a moment for the student to secure it, causing this parachute to deploy with startling speed.

For the chaps in the parachute loft who packed the chute there was some trouble over this. Their distress was extremely touching, which prompted the student to give a full confession. There was, however, sufficient outrage over the instructor's conduct, which had led to the crash, that the perpetrator's parachute-opening crime was forgiven. In the confusion, the rumble-fund fine for the missing ripcord was also forgotten.

Full spring was blossoming, and the contrast with the desolate winter just past on the prairie was awesome. The station, with its white permanent buildings, military formality, and occasionally marching troops, flags, and bugle calls, formed an impressive background for the continuous flight operations.

The introduction to a more formal military environment was most illuminating. Since the very beginnings of organized warfare, sex has proved to be a vexatious problem and caused more than one commander to wish that his troops were neutered. A suspicion is always current among the troops that management is forever conspiring to blunt their appetite for such pleasures. In the RCAF it was supposed that saltpeter was introduced in the chow for this purpose. In the mess hall the daily rumor would have the saltpeter in the coffee or the pudding or wherever. That item would go begging, much to the chagrin of the mess sergeant.

At any rate, where there are boys the girls are sure to follow. Then in residence at Trenton was a famous American aviator. After washing out of U.S. Army flight training and before being shot down and becoming a prisoner of the dictator Franco, he had become an ace in the Spanish civil war. Franco uncivilly determined to have him shot. The press coverage of this drama was monumental and increased exponentially when his gorgeous fiancée raced from New York to Spain to plead for his life. Franco, who had never demonstrated much compassion before, proceeded to pardon him, raising other questions.

Given the naiveté of the times and the romance of flying, the aviator's welcome back in New York was tumultuous. Little noted afterward was the fact that his fiancée was a showgirl he had never met, and she was seeking stardom, not some tramp flier. Even less noted was the free ride accorded the hero to the Canadian border by the New York cops. It was determined at some higher level to spare massive embarrassment by not bringing up his many transgressions in the time between his brief stint in the U.S. Army and the Spanish caper. For a youth from Poverty Flats, getting to meet distinguished chaps of this caliber was certainly a heave ahead socially.

In fact, this high achiever continued operating even after a rather lackluster wartime career. Following World War II, he was in some difficulty for selling an RCAF airplane in South America. Later, as a pilot of a state-owned international airline, there was the interesting matter of the gold bullion that went missing on a flight he commanded.

Another impressive American at the Trenton air base was the epitome of the dashing Hollywood aviator. A very dapper number with a pencil line mustache, he made modest reference to his past vocation as a stunt pilot in his Texas drawl.

It caused somewhat of a stir when his girlfriend flew up to see him in her own airplane, which, in those days, was unheard of. Also unheard of was being out on bail for murder, which she was. She had allegedly helped a rich old Texan, to whom she was briefly wed, to saddle up for his journey to the Big Alamo in the sky. This crime was amply documented in an article in *True Detective* magazine, of which they were quite proud. Our fellow classmate was described as the piano-playing Don Juan in a roadhouse where romance had blossomed. The article's author was apparently in ignorance of the stunt-flying aspect of this fascinating epic.

The lady, a somewhat hard-looking case, ensconced herself in luxury in an upscale hotel in Bellevue with her dachshund, which was very pregnant. During the subsequent party for the stunt pilot Don Juan and his friends, the lady's mutt proceeded to whelp, spreading small dogs and afterbirth all over the fine bed and white sheets. This so traumatized the very proper hotel manager, who also sported a pencil line mustache, that he threw the whole lot out of his splendid establishment.

The flying instructor assigned at this time was a remarkably clean-cut young flying officer of the RAF, as opposed to the RCAF persuasion. He had been invalided out of the fighting and, despite navigating with a cane, was an extremely competent pilot. He loved violent aerobatics as much as his youngest and most enthusiastic student did. It was no difficult chore to enlist him in a scheme to get out of a future of instructing and the chance to strap on a fighter.

This led to my interview with a mournful-looking wing commander, whose nose bore ample testimony to his appreciation of the process of fermentation. He was also startlingly well informed on U.S. politics. He pointed out that the right-wingers in the U.S. government were more for Hitler than Britain and determined to keep President Roosevelt from coming to England's assistance. Among the most venomous were two beauties from Montana, of all places: Senator Burton K. Wheeler and the women's libber Representative Jeanette Rankin. This caricature of the gentler sex, who also was an enraged reactionary had voted against the United States entering World War I and would do the same in World War II. The wing commander observed that the world would soon be speaking German if these muttonheads and their cowardly ilk were not outfoxed. For a very young citizen from these worthies' state to wind up as a piece of bullet-ridden meat in the wreckage of a Spitfire would be counterproductive and was not going to happen.

When it was pointed out that this youth officially came from Vancouver, B.C., according to his papers, the wing commander uttered a word completely out of character for a British gentleman. In his cold roast beef manner, he offered that the best course, for now, was to continue as ordained. He added, with a trace of sadness, that the war was young and it wouldn't be long before there would be plenty of opportunity for all of the eager children to "get bloody well pranged," *pranged* being a self-explanatory English term.

This interview left the buzzard from Montana somewhat disappointed, but now being relieved of the duty of personally defeating Germany, he was determined to enjoy all opportunities to the fullest.

The flying was still fine, and it was interesting that the airspace over the town of Corbyville was forbidden lest the roar of aircraft engines disturb the gestation of the fine rye whiskey in the vats—mayhap another of the doleful wing commander's decisions.

This was a new kind of territory to be explored. The tameness of the landscape and the rather insipid character of the denizens, in contrast with the western reaches and peoples, were exciting to the wide eyes of youth. The war had brought a lot of excitement to the country. Uniforms, patriotism, and excited talk were plentiful. The trains were convenient and cheap. Even Niagara Falls was only a short train ride away. After the years spent surveying the falls' picture on the shredded-wheat boxes on the breakfast table, this was indeed an adventure. Again the student was matriculating, and this time with an unwanted instructor's rating. A grade of "Permanent Two" was assigned. This was supposed to be unheard of right out of school and was supposed to be awarded only after instructing for a considerable time. Still, the assigned flying school was EFTS 10 at Lethbridge, Alberta.

IV

Although an experienced traveler and man of the world by this time, I found that the long train ride was not an unattractive prospect. Canada, although with a thriving bush flying industry, was just as backward as everyone in those days, and their airline was government-owned and both limited and primitive. The aircraft were few and small. They would hold only a handful of passengers and were subject to the many delays of weather and mechanics. The dependable trains with their Pullman cars and great dining, despite the jellied consommé, were the only way to go. Though practically archaic today, this was, in retrospect, indeed an era of gracious transportation.

Not so gracious were the by-now familiar environs of Lethbridge. It was just a raw farm town on the prairie, and Elementary Flying Training School Number Ten was located on the outskirts at what passed for a municipal airport. It boasted a fairly large new hangar and all of the buildings required of a military base, with mess halls, barracks, administration building, and clubs—not to mention a great number of Tiger Moth biplanes. The only thing not entirely military was the lot of the flying instructors.

Classified as sergeant pilots on indefinite leave without pay, the flying instructors actually worked for civilian companies that ran the bases. This allowed them to be paid approximately four times the pay of their contemporaries in uniform and returned handsome profits to the politically oriented companies. The instructors dressed casually, and most of them lived in a ramshackle old hotel in town.

When the wind blew, as it frequently did on the open prairie, it had an interesting influence on flight operations. Not noted for its blinding speed, the Tiger Moth managed to cope with this unfortunate circumstance mostly due to the creative actions of the instructors. With a strong, steady wind, there would often be a line abreast of Moths right over the field like a school of fish facing upstream. They could be seen doing turns and other maneuvers as the instructors went through their patter. Occasionally one of them would dive and then pull up to do a loop or an Immelman Turn. As he climbed and the wind took him, he would suddenly race backward. Another tactic, the "elevator," was handy for landing. It required getting immediately over the desired landing spot and reducing speed to approximately the wind velocity and actually making a vertical descent. This also made it easier for the ground crewmen to grab handholds in the lower wingtips to control the airplane in the ferocious wind.

One instructor had been a well-known flying-circus pilot in the great barnstorming days in the States. Though many claimed this distinction, he was the genuine article. In addition to his flying skill, he was a formidable human being. Not to be outdone, he was actually making an approach going astern when an unfortunate pocket in the wind dropped him, the Tiger-Moth, and his student the last fifty feet. This didn't do the Moth much good, and our hero put his big feet right through the bottom of it. There was an impressive lack of mirth associated with this episode. He later disappeared from the local scene after chasing the managing director of the school and the mayor of Lethbridge all over the local golf course. They were spending a quiet Sunday morning out on this grim piece of real estate when the Tiger Moth appeared.

These times were only an extension of the early days of flying, and there were farmers within Tiger Moth-range of the field who had never seen an airplane up close. Some of the former barnstormers-turned-instructors afforded them a rare experience. They would land in a handy pasture and, leaving the student standing there, take the yokel for his first ride for a few bucks. This remunerative sideline was soon discovered, and these instructors also vanished.

The students were a mixed bag, with Americans strongly represented. Great numbers of these claimed to be from Texas and were replete with a suspicious accent and a pair of mail-order cowboy boots. Why anybody would want to pose as a manure-encrusted farm worker was a mystery to the Buzzard from Poverty Flats.

In Montana, some of the fierce locals had started their ranches with cattle taken from the trail herds of the Texans coming north. Texans were not given much respect in those parts. At any rate, there were so many of these worthies that the RCAF became known as the Royal Texas Air Force. They were also limping from the effects of trying to march in cheap high-heeled boots.

The English were the toughest to teach flying, since a lot of their mechanical background was acquired with a bicycle as opposed to the American's heritage in Model T Fords. The English, with centuries of the class system behind them, were well disciplined and subservient, which is scant recommendation for the embryonic pilot. They were all in the rank of leading aircraftsmen, or LACs, which was a step up from the entry rank of aircraftsman second class, or acey-deucey.

The acey-deuceys got a lot of drill, potato-peeling, and gate-guarding experience while awaiting assignment to flying school and the promotion to LAC. Joining the RCAF was considered quite romantic, and a minor Hollywood type was one of the acey-deuceys guarding the gate. However, he was married to a well-known star, famous for her round heels, which led the instructors to holler, "Boy, you must be *hung*," as they passed through the gate with the poor chap doing present arms at rigid attention.

When an acey-deucey was sent to flying school, he was not only promoted one rank, he was allowed to wear a white flash in his overseas cap to advise the females of his glamorous new status. This worked fine until disgruntled other ranks spread the rumor that the white flash designated the bearer of a venereal decease.

There were interesting places to fly while going about the boring and overworked business of being a teacher in an airplane. The Canadian extension of Glacier National Park offered spectacular vistas to buzz, and the Indian reservation had lots of horses to chase. Unfortunately, one student undertook this amusement on his own while out solo. The horse survived.

The wind finally put paid to the school at Lethbridge. Sometimes it would howl for days, confining many of the instructors to the old hotel where they lived. Life could be hazardous with golf balls whizzing down the corridors. This did little to clear the back load of students, and it was determined to relocate the operation, lock, stock, and windsock.

The town of High River, not far south of Calgary, was designated as the new home. One fine morning everybody with any faint qualification strapped on a Tiger Moth, and the disorganized gaggle straggled north.

The new field had a few of the old hangars from the peacetime RCAF, and the old-timers referred to these as the "Ciscan Fighter" hangars, whatever those were. All of the rest of the base was new and was the wonder of the two-grain-elevator town, which was tastefully arrayed on the railroad tracks and the banks of the Highwood River. All of this offered new fields to explore.

On rare time off, there was Calgary, then a super cow town, and the magnificence of Banff. The railroads had created some of the wonders when they opened the country and extended their facilities to the visiting royalty from Britain, who owned the whole shooting match.

Civilization in Canada was, with only a few exceptions, confined to a strip about fifty miles wide above the U.S. border. The Turner Valley oil fields out to the west of Calgary were a fine example of British dominance. Nationalistic Canadians, whose homeland merely enjoyed the status of a Dominion, would usually refer to the British Empire as "The Brutish Empire." This was to celebrate their arrogance and superior attitude.

All of these features were readily accessible, as well as other attractions. For instance, there was a large breeding ground for geese to the east of Calgary. This served to test the personal loyalty of a favorite student who had been washed out of the U.S. Navy and later became an ace in England. In fact, he reported that at Pensacola, his instructor, a snob of the regular navy, had informed him that some people could play the piano and others could fly airplanes. Perhaps he could play the piano. Actually, he was a splendid pilot and demonstrated his coolness under pressure and the ability to take the heat required of a fighter pilot.

The Tiger Moth was fitted with a Plexiglas "Coopy hatch," which kept the wind out and afforded a convenient frame for a hood that could be raised to restrict the student's view to the cockpit when practicing instrument flying. Instrument flying was very big in the RCAF, to prepare students for the weather they would encounter in the British Isles. This required at least ten hours "under the hood" in the airplane just in primary training and another ten hours in a Link Trainer, which was a ground-bound simulator.

On this particular day the nesting habits of geese were being studied, when one big bird took off and his course led him through the flying wires on the starboard side. After this substantial blow, the Moth still seemed willing to fly.

Turning to look back at the student, the instructor discovered that by some aberration of trajectory, the former goose had removed the rear portion of the Coopy hatch and festooned the student's features with his innermost workings. The student was wiping these accouterments from his brow while bending a somewhat resentful gaze upon his instructor. Back at the field, the chief flying instructor (CFI) was not buying the explanation that the student was under the hood doing his instrument flying at an altitude of about two thousand feet when the aircraft was assaulted by that miserable goose.

The student, when separately interrogated, bore sturdy witness to this hastily composed lie and did not crumble under pressure or threats. The CFI swore that he had flown in that area, man and boy, for God knew how long, and he had never seen a goose, at that season, above fifty feet in the air. That CFI could have been a role model in the highly competitive field of idiocy.

The assistant CFI was a friend and advocate, but unfortunately his position was mostly decorative due to his colorful past, as attested by a magnificent girth and robust complexion. A famous pilot in the First World War, he had spent the intervening years as a bush pilot in the northern reaches of Canada. He once described an interesting episode that required flying a corpse out of the far north. This was accomplished during the time of the perpetual twilight over the mysterious and lonely Barren Lands. The volume of the other freight left only enough room to put the corpse in the copilot's seat. On the long, dreary flight in the primitive aircraft of the day, it was necessary to change altitude periodically to conform to the terrain. When this would happen, there would be an eerie groan. However, when our hero's startled gaze would snap to his passenger, the chap remained slumped in his seat with his mouth still agape. Only later was it determined that the changing air pressure was acting like a bellows on the inactive copilot's interior. By the time this explanation surfaced, the assistant CFI was well into the rum.

Every year the Calgary Stampede, a genuine big-time rodeo, is held and, war or no war, was to go on. Rumor had it that this event had been canceled only once due to a miscalculation of the fair board. In their wisdom, they had decreed that the Indians, who were traditionally admitted free, would now have to pay to get in. This caused the Indians to initiate a rain dance. This was no more the season for rain than it was for geese to be flying at more than fifty feet. Nevertheless, the rains came, the fair board reconsidered, and the rain stopped. As the Oracle of Poverty Flats used to say, "Never underestimate the power of the aborigine."

A fortuitous day off permitted attending the first day of the stampede, and, like Toronto, it certainly fit the exclamation that after two hog callin's and a county fair, the likes of this had never been seen before. With appetite whetted but work to be done, there was room for a compromise. Following a conversation with another instructor, an arrangement was agreed upon to fly up with the students to look over the spectacle from the air while practicing a little formation flying, like loops and slow rolls, for instance. On the way home a tail chase developed with the other instructor in the lead. He must have looked back to check the pursuit at the wrong time while going between random farm houses and barns, and he really took down one of those pesky split-rail fences. The Tiger Moth wound up well crumpled in a field but did not burn. The field was, fortunately, level and permitted landing when there was no sign of life from the wreckage. The control stick through the instructor's middle had permanently erased his exuberance, and general damage had been done for the student.

The instructor was a young Canadian from a small farming community some distance north of Calgary, where he was the local hero due to being an aviator. It was determined to give him full military honors in his hometown, and the aviation school would supply the pallbearers from the ranks of his fellow instructors. The student came from Los Angeles, California, and was returned there without comment.

The undertaker at High River was straight out of central casting. He was a cadaverous ghoul dressed in black with long white hands. He was inclined to go through the motions of washing these hands while gazing benignly down upon any flying instructor he managed to corner on the muddy main street. When he finished his work, the coffin was sent by truck to the hometown of the deceased. The instructor pallbearers departed very early the next morning in one of their cars for the long lurch over the potholed gravel roads of the day.

This was dusty, dry country and required large quantities of a refreshment called a Calgary Pink Lady to survive. This party arrived somewhat unsteadily at the barren farm town in the burning midday heat. In the local pub a Royal Canadian Army sergeant major and his burial detail were encountered. Over a lot more refreshments, he outlined his scheme for the ceremony.

With this taken care of, the party adjourned to the victim's home. The home was a small clapboard affair on the outskirts of town. It was no better nor worse than the other houses in the depressing town, and the coffin was open for viewing on the rickety front porch. The whole town was assembled with weeping women and weathered men looking grim in worn black suits, with their large knuckled hands protruding from the inadequate sleeves. Some even boasted celluloid collars.

This was the first sight of the former instructor since viewing him in the wreckage of the Tiger Moth, and it was highly unnerving. The mortician had managed to put a vicious snarl on his usually placid features, and it was a distinct relief when they nailed down the lid. The coffin was placed on a wagon drawn by a team of horses. The pallbearers marched beside this, and immediately ahead was a platoon of RCAF troops following the army troops. The army had a drum that tolled out the death march. This march was painfully slow and in the heat and dust was interminable. The barren boot hill was a long way out. Behind this assemblage straggled the grieving relatives and townspeople.

Upon arrival at the gates of the cemetery, the RCAF platoon respectfully split ranks for the wagon to pass through. The army stood fast, and when the wagon reached them there was trouble. The sweating sergeant major grabbed the bridle of one of the horses and roared, "You can drive that goddamn wagon through the goddamn air force, but by God you'll not drive it through my goddamn army." With the rudely awakened horses rearing and pitching, he made it known that protocol dictated that the pallbearers remove the coffin from the wagon and carry it through his (goddamn) army.

Nearly prostrate from the heat and Calgary Pink Ladies, they grudgingly complied. Now the army split ranks and stood at rigid and respectful present arms with their rifles reversed as the instructor pall-bearers wrestled the coffin through and got it on the slings of a newly dug grave. This left the instructors in the front rank while the minister had his say, and it was plenty. It ranged from the heavenly scene to the war, the drought, and even the price of wheat. When, at length, he was finished, the army's firing squad, immediately behind the instructors, let go with their weapons.

This startled one pallbearer to the extent that he leaped forward and in so doing stumbled on the mound of dirt. From here he fell across the coffin, which broke the sling on one end. This upended the coffin, and somehow the pallbearer wound up in the grave, with the coffin on top of him.

The ceremony was now over. The lad who had been so recently rescued from the grave sought advice from the two members of the Royal Canadian Mounted Police who had followed the parade out from town in their dusty old Ford. "Where," he asked, "could a man get a drink around here?" One of the Mounties studied him seriously and then studied the large, serious farmers.

"I would advise you chaps," he said neutrally, "to get your car and have it a fair piece down the road."

V

It was becoming apparent that life as an instructor must come to an end, and the sooner the better.

The CFI (otherwise known as the Chief of the Philistines) would never become a close pal. This, despite a natural gift of tolerance and forgiveness, made the desire to jerk his chain irresistible. A starting point was already in hand. It was the "Permanent Two" instructor's rating issued at Trenton. Every six months there would be examinations for the instructors to try to raise themselves to this exalted grade, and not just for fun. It meant that they could become eligible for the position of flight commander, and that meant that they got a little more money for such unpleasant duties as giving check rides to wash out marginal students.

I pointed out to his majesty that they had such an opening and would he please give me the assignment. Poor chap liked to have had apoplexy. The idea of promoting the Threadbare Buzzard, the only instructor who was younger than any of the students, to such responsibility was visibly abhorrent to him. He didn't know that it was equally abhorrent to the applicant, who firmly believed that it was more merciful to let a student kill himself rather than face the disgrace of washing out.

He was also seething under another unfortunate circumstance. Although most Canadians decried English snobbery, the CFI's class of people was pathetic in their groveling to anything smacking of the nobility. Therefore, when the hulking offspring of one of the world's superior beings came to the school, some idiot, or consortium of idiots, decided, due to age similarities, to give him to the young Yank for his instruction. This was a real blunder, since a friendship developed. That was not at all healthy in that circumstance, since the young bounder also had some wild ideas, and "I dare you" became a familiar phrase on the gosport speaking tube.

One "I dare you" resulted in a Tiger Moth sitting undamaged, save the green stains on its yellow hide, in the middle of a fine stand of wheat, near as high as an elephant's eye. This was due to a buzz job that didn't take into account the student's faulty depth perception. There was a certain amount of relief that the aircraft was intact and the crew undamaged. That was before the unpleasantness with the farmer who set a record-high price for wheat and the cost of the long road through his property to recover the Tiger Moth.

His nibs had relatives, of course, and one of them had a ranch up in the high Rocky Mountains to the west. This was not unusual for people of this ilk, as even the Prince of Wales had a ranch out there. Dropping in to see the distinguished old gentleman posed its own problems. The pasture chosen for the landing site was short, severely sloping, and at a high altitude. However, an "I dare you" cannot be ignored.

This genteel family had a quantity of fine blackberry wine with which they were quite hospitable. This did not make leaving easier, but it may have supplied the courage to make it possible. Galloping down the pasture with the little Gypsy engine striving gallantly, disaster appeared imminent. There was a deep canyon at the end of the field, and into this canyon the jolly rover boys and their flying machine fell. Fortunately, it was a very deep canyon, and by delicately not stalling the kite, flying speed was finally achieved in the thin air. This was a box canyon, and how the Moth got out of it is, even at this remove, unclear. Such stirring adventures are difficult to keep secret, and it would have taken an even stupider man than the CFI to not get wind of this. These escapades added fuel to a deepening adversarial relationship. However, there was a glimmer of light ahead.

A lot of prominent people from Canada and England, both in and out of the service, who would like to avoid the shooting were casting a covetous eye on the safe haven from combat and high pay of the Elementary Flight Training School instructors. That would certainly relieve the instructor shortage. Another encouraging thing was that as the United States got closer to war, the neutrality restrictions were relaxing.

There was to be one final hassle. Wherever there are wars there will be war profiteers, and these civilian-run elementary flying schools were looking to maximize profits. The high wages they were paying the instructors was getting to be somewhat of a cause célèbre. The school in its greed proposed to start a life insurance program for the instructors. The premium was going to be high but so was the risk, they said. That might have been true, but once the fine print was perused it developed that anything remotely connected with flying, including going to work or even talking about it, was an exception. Being the sole leader of the opposition to this generous plan led to an excellent nonmonetary settlement.

The CFI proudly informed his nemesis that the company had permission to release the recalcitrant instructor back to the regular air force for other duties if he so volunteered. When the deal was done, the CFI sneered that putting on the suit would reduce the pay from $200 a month as a civilian to $60 a month as a sergeant pilot. This apparently cheered him no end. He didn't realize that the freedom from instructing and the opportunities to fly an unlimited array of aircraft types were priceless.

One quick trip down to Montana was in order and was hardly noteworthy, except that it afforded a first flight on an airliner. On the return trip the airplane was a Boeing 247, the first of the low-wing transports carrying a handful of passengers. Had it not been for a rare misjudgment by the Boeing company, the 247 and not the fabled DC-3 might have become the airline standard.

The 247 was carrying a pilot, copilot, hostess, and two passengers when, on the approach to Cutbank, Montana, the pilot announced that due to weather, the flight would be remaining overnight and continuing to Lethbridge, Alberta, the next morning, God and the elements willing. Pilot, copilot, hostess, and the two passengers (the other passenger was a Flying Officer of the RCAF) adjourned to the local hotel, where the airline paid for the rooms and possibly the steaks. If memory serves, the many drinks and tales of flying were privately funded. The next morning the flight completed the short distance to Lethbridge. This elegant method of air travel surely had it all over what has developed since.

The experience so far had been great and proved to be valuable later, but now exuberance set in. The Threadbare Buzzard boarded a fine train that bore him away to the east, where new adventures awaited and hopefully there were to be no more students in the future. Ah, youth!

The conversion school at Ottawa, where student pilots transitioned from trainers to combat aircraft, would not have an opening for some time, so the interim would be spent at the Toronto Manning Depot. This was headquartered in the Toronto Exhibition grounds and housed various ranks and categories in the many handy buildings. Mostly they were new recruits.

Sergeant pilots, being sort of a class apart, were in relatively civilized quarters on the second floor of a brick building. In the RCAF only a small percentage of aircrew were officers, unlike the U.S. service, where the preponderance were commissioned. A few of those present were direct entries from the States, but mostly they were pilots being reassigned within the RCAF, and some of them were fellow escapees from elementary instructing. In some cases their escapes had required imagination and creativity.

One hardheaded youth from California had been assigned to lead a large flight of Tiger Moths in a local celebration at the frontier town of Edmonton. This large gaggle was bouncing around in the vicinity of each other in what they suspected was formation as they crossed the town. He then proceeded to amaze the bumpkins and petrify the officials by herding his unwieldy flock under the local bridge without a single fatality. He naturally became a confederate in further adventures.

There was very little to do except explore the conservative flesh-pots of the circumspect eastern Canadians. At this time and in this place, this was a fine education for a boy from Poverty Flats. In those halcyon days there was a nice romantic aura surrounding flying, and the formerly repressed young ladies of Canada were becoming increasingly liberated. The Norwegians supplied the only competition, and that was formidable. These foreigners infested an island airport out in the lake and were lousy with money. The report was that after Adolf Hitler chased them out of their own country they wound up here with their country's gold reserves. This served to finance the airplanes they trained in, not to mention their pretty uniforms and outrageous pay scales. This afforded them automobiles and the transitory affections of the most toothsome females.

Every one of them told a suspiciously similar story of escaping from Norway in an open boat under the most harrowing of circumstances. They never seemed to finish training to return to the fray. This is probably sour grapes.

If there was a flip side to this idealistic interlude it was those damn bagpipes. These belonged to what was probably a complete regiment of Scots who were billeted up the road from the sergeant pilot's quarters (probably in the former pigpens). These rugged warriors came a-marching in platoon strength, always at an ungodly early hour, with the shrill screeching of the pipes assaulting defenseless hung-over ears. This and pure fatigue made the orders to the Ottawa Conversion Training Squadron welcome.

VI

Rockcliffe aerodrome is quite close to Ottawa, which is, of course, the seat of government for Canada. It was a jolly little city in the picture post card throes of winter and the midst of war. The quarters assigned were excellent, and several sergeant pilots were given a house that used to be either married officers' or NCO quarters in the days of peace. Unfortunately, this happy housing didn't last, and it was all the fault of some unpleasant foreigners and a faraway island whose location was then obscure. The flying was becoming routine and interesting when there was a rude interruption.

"JAPANESE ATTACK U.S. FLEET AT PEARL HARBOR," screamed the newspapers, radios, and everybody with vocal cords. All of the Yanks who weren't wanted men in the States were immediately in favor of going back to the U.S. of A. to become heroes—or at least to get better pay than the parsimonious Canadians were offering.

The RCAF bellowed, "Hold your horses, you bloody savages, arrangements are being made." The clever buggers were already calculating how much they could profit from this turn of events. Meanwhile, every Yank was required to sign a statement if he intended to join some U.S. service when the details were worked out. Flying continued as if nothing had changed, but it had. The Yanks now had a cavalier attitude toward their careers in the RCAF, and the first thing was to have the mother of all celebrations in the local watering holes. This included an impressive nightclub across the river in Hull, Quebec.

One of the happy sergeant pilots (modesty forbids further identification) didn't realize that he was still enjoying a cigarette as sleep overtook him in the snug little house after the party. A good house fire can cause a lot of local interest on a subzero night, what with being barefoot in the snow and frozen fire hoses permitting the house and all possessions therein to self-destruct. Fortunately, some new barracks for NCOs were nearing completion, which mitigated most of the inconvenience.

The same chap who had flown the large gaggle under the bridge at Edmonton owned a car, and fine places in the States were available on weekends, like Syracuse, New York, with its swinging university. The natives being new to war provided a remarkable audience for a couple of unprincipled young rascals with genuine wings on their tunics. This pair of scoundrels didn't bother correcting any misconceptions these gullibles may have entertained concerning the part they had played in the Battle of Britain—especially the young ladies. It was only fair to accept their generous appreciation, since a lot of the real Battle of Britain chaps were now dead and unable to personally receive their rewards. "Waste not, want not," as the Oracle of Poverty Flats was fond of saying. (Plagiarism was not considered much of a crime in his circle.) The resentful boyfriends of the young ladies confided that they would have joined the RCAF, except their great patriotism had dictated that they save themselves for the U.S. Army Air Corps, where they were a-fixin' to go momentarily to lead lives of unequaled heroism and glory.

Conversion training wasn't bad, with the emphasis on cross-country and instrument flying. This had led to some good assignments when the students got up to speed and it had looked like the eventual path to fighters had become at least a possibility. Not anymore it wasn't, unless one agreed to stay, said the barely civil RCAF officers. The poor blighters were much to be pitied, being denied the glamour of life in the States, and they made disparaging remarks about U.S. pay scales.

Ferrying airplanes had been one of the desirable chores in any air force, and the two former instructors from the primitive school at Moose Jaw were so occupied. There was a vast store of Airspeed Oxford aircraft to be ferried clear across Canada. This plywood contraption was a staple of the RAF, and with their two little 370 horsepower Armstrong Siddeley Cheeta engines, a total of 8,751 were built. Some later versions got better engines. The drawback here was that due to Canada's minuscule airline system, ferry pilots usually had to return by train, and that could get tiresome. The other problem for ferry pilots was that the problem of getting the warplanes to England was difficult, with German submarines sinking so many ships.

First, the British had paid adventurous American civilians $1,000 a crossing (a staggering sum of money in those days) to fly aircraft over, and lost many in the cold North Atlantic. However, a sergeant pilot could make the same trip for $60 a month, with itchy blue wool uniform furnished. Usually a one-wing officer navigated. In the British service only pilots had a full set of wings. The one-wingers included wireless air gunners and air observers. The air observers were also navigators and apt to be commissioned officers. The planes were mostly Lockheed Hudsons. The route went out to Goose Bay, Labrador, to depart in blizzards and other unattractive circumstances. After a long grim night, and if lucky in all respects, a reckless young man in a Spitfire would meet the Hudson over the solid overcast and, squaring away, start a standard instrument letdown of 120 knots at 500 feet-per-minute descent. The Spit would promptly vanish in the muck, but following this course would put the Hudson over the fence at Prestwick, Scotland, in lamentable visibility. This was the plan, anyway, if the luck was running good. A frightening number vanished, and some managed to overfly and ended up in Mr. Hitler's vile clutches if the RAF failed to shoot these unfortunates down en route.

It didn't take long for the RCAF to decide that all Americans whose loyalty to His Majesty had expired would be sent to bombing and gunnery schools until transferred to the U.S. military. Here they could make themselves useful hauling the student bombardiers and gunners about on their training in the huge, ungainly Fairey Battle aircraft. The Battle was an interesting specimen with an interesting history. A prewar bird, it was painfully obsolete but had, in one of the unsolved mysteries of flight, managed to shoot down the first German pilot downed by a British plane in World War II. One can but pity Herr Schmitt, or whatever his name, when he returned to the mess to face his fellow pilots. "You were shot down by a *vhat?*"

At any rate, the bombing and gunnery school where the sentence was to be served was clear out at Mossbank, Saskatchewan. The companion from the raids on Syracuse received the same sentence, so his car was employed for transportation. During the spring mud season the Canadian highways were impassable, and a long detour was made through the States. After re-entering Canada, the car nearly reached the field at Mossbank before becoming fully mired down. A massive snow removal truck dispatched by the base also came to grief, and a farmer with a lot of horses came to the rescue.

The small base had a large supply of the Battles and many students to train. The pilots were assigned to either one of two noxious chores. The first was taking the students out over the local lake where they could practice bombing or gunnery. The other chore was to tow the target (drogue) for the gunners to fire at.

The immediate boss of the pilots was an incredibly young British aristocrat whose conversational contribution seemed to be "Tickity boo! Tickity boo!" while listening to the explanations of high crimes and misdemeanors by the pilots. The Yanks believed that this term was the British equivalent of "B.S." His air force rank was wing commander, but he was known only as "Tickity Boo."

The Fairey Battle looked sort of like an elongated Spitfire and had a wingspan of 54 feet, a length of 52 feet 1½ inches, with a height of 15 feet 6 inches. It could carry 1,000 pounds of bombs dragged aloft by a Rolls Royce engine of 1,030 horsepower and graduating to 1,440 horsepower as the model numbers progressed from Mark I to II to III to V. The Brits built 2,185 of these airplanes. Aside from downing the first German aircraft on September 20, 1939, they had a distinguished history.

With no better aircraft on hand, on May 10, 1940, Battles were used to attack a pontoon bridge at Maastricht, gaining a flying officer and a sergeant the first two Victoria Crosses awarded to the RAF in World War II. On May 14, 1940, five squadrons totaling 71 aircraft attacked a pontoon bridge at Sedan and lost 40 aircraft. With only limited operations at Dunkirk, the Battle's days of combat were at an end.

The difference in British and American aircraft was extensive. The power was measured in boost plus or minus, and the revolutions were controlled by a two-position propeller. This was referred to as thick or thin pitch. Thin pitch was used to deliver maximum power. The Battle had standard rudders without brake pedals but an interesting stick. This control stick had a spade grip in the shape of a loop with a button called the firing tit to fire the forward guns. A lever extended across the loop; when pulled, it activated the air brake on the wheel that the rudder favored in proportion to the rudder angle. With the rudder at neutral, both wheels braked equally. This was not only a coordination exercise, but the aircraft sounded like a freight truck hissing air as it taxied.

Losing air pressure introduced other perils. There has been a vexatious problem with aircraft since provisions were made to retract the landing gear in flight. The trouble lay in convincing the pilot to lower the wheels again when landing. On the Harvard, for instance, there was a strident Klaxon horn that blasted away when power was reduced. One of the British pilots landing at Trenton had continued his wheels-up approach despite the frantic radio warnings from the tower, reinforced with red flares. He explained, as he was being extracted from the wreckage, that he couldn't hear the tower's warning over that bloody horn. The Battle, being of British manufacture, had a black glass panel fitted across the top of the dashboard. When power was reduced, a brilliant red light spelling "WHEELS" hit the pilot in the eyes.

One of the worst features was the glycol that cooled the engine and had a reserve tank behind the pilot's head, with the line passing through the cockpit. One chap overheated his engine, causing this line to rupture and dowse him with coolant, and then the engine went afire. Not wishing to abandon the students in the back, he stuck it out until blinded and in pain. The Battle dove in the last thousand feet. By some miracle he survived. For the time being, anyway. Visiting this burned-to-a-crisp friend in the hospital was an unnerving experience. He was totally disfigured and would not be transferring to any U.S. service.

Towing a target was the most boring of jobs. Flying back and forth over the lake, the reel operator in the back of the Battle would let out a target sleeve. When the gunners in another aircraft would fin-ish shooting, the sleeve would be reeled in and another one streamed for the next aircraft. A couple of hours of this and the pilot would be entertaining unkind thoughts about the RCAF and hallucinating about a cold beer in the sergeants' mess. Such was the case with the friend who owned the car. Out of boredom he executed a slow roll, ignoring the fact that he was dragging about fifteen hundred feet of steel wire and a target sleeve through the friendly skies of Saskatchewan. The wire wrapped right around the airplane, which pre-sented him with a rather awkward problem, since it interfered with the operation of the rudder and elevators. He was headed right for the airfield and continued to attempt to unwind the wire by executing slow rolls in the opposite direction. To add to his concern, communication with the towing reel operator in the back of the airplane was nonex-istent, so that worthy didn't respond to urgent orders to jump. The idea of abandoning a crewman was not an option with this guy, and besides, it looked very much like extensive damage was going to be accorded the air base, judging by the projected flight path. All the ma-neuvering was only causing the Battle to get lower and lower. He did manage to give the control tower a heads up. To say it caused some degree of consternation, what with the air-raid and fire sirens reinforcing the screams of people running from buildings, would be quite accurate. By some miracle of aerodynamics the last counterslow roll unwound the wire, permitting a normal landing.

It was then discovered that the wing commander's conversation was not limited to "Tickity Boo," and he actually had quite a bit to say. Not the least of which concerned the arrival of a special train in Regina with the Joint Canadian American Military Board embarked. All the Bloody Yanks were being sold to the Americans who were painfully short of cannon fodder for their new war. "And damn good riddance!" This train had complete recruiting and medical facilities. The U.S. Army, Navy, and Marine Corps were represented. (The U.S. Air Force did not come into being until after World War II.)

The total harvest from Canada was several thousand aviators with wings. The army got thousands, the navy fewer thousands, and the marines, who refused to lower their standards, got about fifty. The Canadians got the equivalent of a new Mark II Harvard airplane per head, or so went the story. Being sold into bondage in this fashion caused me no resentment. What was important was becoming a genuine second lieutenant in the Leathernecks

This was not done out of whimsy. Being a veteran of many cold Montana winters, reinforced by a couple more of the same in Canada, always reminded me of a picture in front of the post office in Poverty Flats. This was a picture of a handsomely turned-out youth in what appeared to be a bellhop's uniform from a fine hotel standing in the sun's rays on a beautiful white beach under a coconut tree. "Join the Marines!" the poster commanded. Visions of warm tropical islands could not be denied. This was to be a promise kept. Some of those damned islands did get pretty hot.

It was the 27th of May 1942 when my commission in the United States Marines, signed and sealed, was delivered.

Not so fortunate were the American pilots serving in the Eagle squadrons in England. (A threadbare buzzard would have been included in their numbers had I succeeded in my quest for assignment to fighters while in the RCAF.) These eagles didn't get into U.S. service until the end of September when they were finally discharged from the RAF and inducted into the flying branch of the United States Army. An American RCAF acquaintance from High River had been successful in getting into fighters, resulting in his assignment to an Eagle squadron. In a letter received during the summer of 1942 he bemoaned the situation of the American fighter pilots in England; it didn't appear that they were ever going to be repatriated.

The Eagle squadrons had an interesting history. After the Battle of Britain the Brits were hard up for pilots and the United States, with its small prewar military, had a lot of civilian pilots, flyers with varying degrees of experience. Some were barely qualified; others were washouts from military flying schools.

There was an infamous committee recruiting any aviators they could find and funneling them to the RAF. Inexperience did in a certain number of the American pilots in the RAF, but the survivors were fortunate in being able to fly the British fighters, particularly the Spitfire. This airplane had very low wing loading, making it exceedingly easy to fly. It was quite short ranged, however, which was usually not a problem because the Spitfire was employed primarily as a defensive animal. On the negative side, the weather was foul and the Germans still had fine pilots. With insufferable snobbery, the RAF high command bluntly informed the Yanks that they were unwelcome as they had proven to be an unmanageable lot of savages, an opinion it turned out the RAF shared with the general commanding the United States Army's flying corps.

This American officer had never gotten over what he considered a personal insult in the First World War: he was a trained pilot but never saw combat. The outraged jealousy he and some of his fellows bore the pilots in the Lafayette Escadrille, an all-volunteer American squadron, because of the publicity they received, was still alive and well. He had no trouble voicing his opinion that the Eagle squadrons should be disbanded and sent home—in disgrace, it may be assumed. This officer always wore a fixed grin that won him the nickname Hap, but actually it was as a result of a facial characteristic and not idiocy. When later in the war a new Japanese fighter was nicknamed the Hap, he saw to it that this was changed to Hamp. Winston Churchill, who knew a propaganda weapon when he met one, overruled the RAF concerning the Eagle squadrons. He knew that even more than in World War I he must get the United States involved if Great Britain were to survive.

As the war went on, the surviving eagles, reinforced by RCAF-trained American pilots, were getting quite good at their trade. One of the RCAF-trained pilots was an outstanding leader, but this didn't prevent the uptight Brits from punishing him. When off duty, he was cementing relations with the English ladies who were ill served by their men. When two of these ladies were discovered in his quarters for this purpose, he was demoted two ranks and put to towing targets. (So, towing targets really was a disgrace.) Upon being transferred to the hard-up U.S. Army Air Corps, he became one of their best fighter-group commanders. This also got him more pay and better rations than the egg a week plus fifty pence a day the RAF made do with.

The three Eagle squadrons were in existence for two years, from September 1940 to September 1942. They shot down seventy-three of the enemy while losing eighty killed. Their hard-won combat experience, once they finally changed uniforms, was a real boon for the United States.

VII

All of the British officers of all services were considerate enough to stay off the streets of Regina until the last Yanks had made their farewell toasts and entrained for the States in the beautiful spring weather. In those days of great trains, the lounge car of the Burlington Zephyr snaking along at 120 miles an hour was not an experience to be missed. With the United States so new to war, the new recruit still attired in the Canadian uniform was provided with a lot of free medicinal libations pressed upon him by the other passengers. Most of these were businessmen attired in fine suits and of bloodthirsty outlook. Their demand for vengeance on the "damn yellow Japs and goddamn Huns" was most inspiring. Business would be splendid and the profits staggering. It has been often and truly remarked: "Patriotism is the final resort of the scoundrel." Other fine trains (The Broadway Limited comes to mind) reached eastward to New York City and as far south as Washington, D.C. They were populated by the same affluent types.

Washington, D.C., had gone absolutely ape. Great crowds of self-important politicians, civil servants, and ranking military types infested all of the watering holes, making weighty proclamations for posterity. To wit: "Damn it man, this thing is bigger than either of us." It was a relief to clear the swarming railroad station to board a ramshackle train crowded with new recruits, mostly from New Yack, headed for the marine boot camp down at Paris Island, South Carolina. This type of train seemed to typify the transportation afforded the military heroes. These chaps would be shorn of their hair, self-respect, and egotism, drilled, abused, and finally, thoroughly brainwashed. Then, with the raw product to work with, the management would turn them into the known world's most disciplined professional killers. In their own enthusiastic opinion they had already achieved this status.

It could be seen that explaining about being a marine officer and a gentleman wearing a crummy RCAF sergeant pilot's uniform to these young toughs wasn't about to come to any good end. They didn't yet realize that, very soon, when they saw an officer they would salute. If he had a dog, they would also salute the dog.

Fortunately, Quantico, the home of the Marine Corps, was not all that far down the tracks of the deplorable southern railroad. I debarked while the recruits continued on to meet their miserable fate. The impression has always been that the U.S. Marine Corps is able to cope with any emergency. That is except what the hell to do with a bunch of unwanted and unexpected palefaces claiming to be not only marines but also aviators.

Until this was straightened out, the new arrivals were placed in an old wooden barracks with some other mystery personnel. Some of these proved to be exceptional chaps. One was even the former mayor of Philadelphia, and some of the others had occupied even more exalted positions in the country. They were extremely patriotic, and some were here as a result of exerting pressure at the very highest levels to get commissions in the marines.

The other engaging thing about this barracks was its location, with its rear door only feet away from the main North-South Railroad track, which roared through the base. This came complete with the required story of the new recruit who in obedience to his general orders had stopped the main-liner one night to demand a pass. No trains were stopped during the time in residence, and the nerve-shattering roar of a through train became routine if not entirely reassuring. "War is hell, men!"

Fortunately, the princely pay was started (newly raised to $125 a month), and another sum was presented as a uniform allowance. Finding uniforms was easy. Right outside the front gate was the town of Quantico, whose major industry was selling uniforms. The nice old gentleman was very impressed to find such a perfect specimen in his hands, and additionally impressed with the specimen's distinguished career in the cold latitudes of the Canadian air force. Naturally, this would require a huge and very expensive beaver overcoat. This and the other items on the list devoured the entire allowance and most all of the victim's current savings. The nice old gentleman explained, free of charge, that his son had a government job in Washington and, despite his extreme patriotism, would be unable to attend the shooting phases of the war.

Down in the steamy islands somewhat later, the group legal officer, with a cynical smirk, noted that there was a bill for the unpaid balance that I owed for uniforms. Vehement denials widened the smirk, and he noted that of course without a receipt or canceled check this presented a dilemma. The Marines Corps, he pointed out, was not in the collection business, but such matters on the record could surely impede a career. It turned out that this was a very standard and common shakedown. Much later, after the war was over, there was a silver lining to the story. A frigid bum in Poverty Flats, Montana, was awarded a stylish, expensive, and unused heavy winter overcoat.

Now clothed and indoctrinated, it was found that the marines had determined to send their new flying officers to Corpus Christi, Texas, to do something about getting them fitted for the navy's Wings of Gold. The marines, as it turned out, depend on the navy's flight schools. Therefore, Marine Corps wings are nothing but navy wings, and the marine flyer must forever bear the onus of being a "naval aviator" and is awarded a document attesting to this sad fact.

One of the fellow officers and gentlemen had a Ford sedan, which afforded a leisurely tour of the Deep South and Gulf Coast on the road to Texas. This trip was actually a sort of lineal party with all of the enthusiastic southerners of the Red Neck Riviera who seemed to have a great affection for the marines. And why not? In all of the ports were ships with various parts blown off by German submarines, which were running amok and practically unopposed in the Gulf at this time. Historical statistics show fifty-six U.S. ships versus one German submarine sunk here between 1942 and 1945.

When Corpus Christi was finally reached, the navy was found to be running a program called transition training. Each phase of the regular training was skimmed through to get the Wings of Gold. This started with primary school, using the wonderful Stearman biplanes as well as an abortion designated the N3N, which was a biplane trainer built by the Naval Aircraft Factory. Although of respectable appearance, it flew like a flatbed truck with a flat tire, among its other unattractive characteristics.

The next phase was a real experience and was called basic training. The kite utilized here was a low-wing, fixed landing gear machine manufactured by the Vultee Aircraft Company. It was irreligiously referred to by its pilots as the Vultee Vibrator or the Vultee Vomiter, depending upon the degree of irritation. This was also used for the only instrument training the navy did at that time. This consisted of a few hours in a Link trainer on the ground and a few hours under the hood in the Vibrator. As soon as the student could do a standard instrument orientation and approach on the old Adcock range system, he was issued an instrument card stamped "Also qualified for instrument letdowns." Compared to the exhaustive RCAF instrument training, this was really hilarious. There was one incident that may have pushed all of the U.S. military to correct this with the red, white, and green card system to signify instrument flying proficiency, which occurred around this time.

A naval aviator in a navy fighter approached New York in the soup and announced without preamble, "This is navy number so and so over your field, request landing instructions." With a great number of civilian airliners (in those days the DC-3 was known as a giant airliner) stacked up in the weather awaiting their turn to initiate an instrument approach, the idea of this Bumble Bee snarling around at an unknown position and altitude was enough to give the controllers the vapors. Also, despite the emphasis on instrument flying that came later, an army airplane managed to fly into the Empire State Building.

By this time there were all kinds of direct-entry pilots in the navy undergoing this so-called "refresher flight training." They were universally decried by the aristocrats of the prewar regular navy. Of course the most unpopular of all were the chaps who had made themselves unpopular in the Royal Canadian Air Force by extolling the advantages of the United States. These same lads had more than a little criticism to offer the navy. A lot of it was not without merit but was not exactly tactful either.

The navy wasn't all bad, and the group of officers in the wing of the BOQ (bachelor officers quarters) occupied for the first phase at the main station became fast friends. One of them was a robust chap from South Dakota whose greatest ambition was to be a fighter pilot just like his distinguished fellow South Dakotan. Alas, he was assigned to the 18-Dog squadron, an activity down at the seaplane ramps where young aviators learned the art and science of the flying boat. That afforded a great opportunity to become familiar with and actually handle these legendary PBY patrol planes without becoming permanently involved. Although cumbersome and capable of only a painfully slow speed of advance, they had contributed mightily in the early phases of the war. The frustrated fighter pilot could cause them to perform maneuvers never visualized by the manufacturers.

The next crisis came when it was decided that all direct-entry types would be put to work instructing, ferrying, flying transports, or performing other middle-class acts.

The next episode proved what a superior education can accomplish. The oldest transferee from the RCAF was a unique chap indeed. With a Harvard law degree and a distinguished career in hand, he had decided to give the British an assist with Hitler. The RCAF thought that he was too old for fighters and put him through bomber training. They decided to make him an instructor because of his age. That was why he had transferred into the Marine Corps. He had no intention of being anything but a fighter pilot and explained this to management. The navy has never been a match for intelligence and logic. Very shortly he, and perhaps the youngest transferee from the RCAF (who just happened to be standing there when the conversation took place), were out at the navy fighter school at Kingsville, Texas. Before the war's end, all of the few marines from the RCAF saw combat, which was a lot more by a hellova reach than the cadet average.

The Harvard man was gentlemanly, courageous, and competent, as well as being a rugged physical specimen and the proprietor of an inflexible integrity. By the time the war was over, he was regarded with respect approaching awe throughout Marine Corps fighter aviation.

Only a few of the chaps from the RCAF failed to finish the course, and the failure was seldom from flying ability. The most noteworthy of these didn't belong there anyway. A large, exuberant graduate of McGill University in Canada, he had spent his life as a Canadian. The lure of the States prompted him to hatch a scheme to transfer with the real Americans. To this end he introduced evidence (perhaps spurious) that his parents in a moment of unrestrained passion had conceived him in the back seat of a Model T-Ford on an overnight trip to Buffalo, New York. How he left the U.S. service was equally interesting. Among the egotists of the old navy was a psychopath in the grade of lieutenant commander who was commander of one of the satellite airfields. Passed over for the rank of full commander, he was really teetering on the edge. In his station's newspaper, he charged the navy with stupidity and treasonable sedition for this oversight. One day he was over at the officers' club swimming pool on the main base attired in the only thing he owned that did not have his insignia of rank on it, his swimming suit. Here he encountered the McGill man attired only in *his* swimming suit and hairy chest.

The lieutenant commander, having nearly run him down, snarled, "Give way there, mister." Seeing only a fat old man with a narrow hairless chest and pipestem arms, the McGill man playfully tossed him into the swimming pool. The old school closed ranks, and the McGill man packed his bags.

This guy was last heard from after securing employment as a test pilot, which was easy to do in those days. Getting lost in a large brute of an experimental dive-bomber, he found himself running out of fuel. This required landing on a highway, and, ignoring the scattering of the automobiles in the vicinity, he taxied up to a filling station and directed the bemused attendant to "Fill 'er up, Mac." This made the newspapers.

The large officers' club did a roaring booze business every night with all of the newly commissioned officers coming into the navy. Gentlemen were allowed to sign chits for their drinks and received a mess bill at the end of the month. Trouble was, a very great number of chits for large drink orders had the signatures of Michael Mouse, William Shakespeare, Benedict Arnold, and John Paul Jones. The polite mess boys dared not question officers and gentlemen. Soon all officers' clubs sold books of chits in advance for drinks. This was the end of the peacetime military.

Kingsville fighter school was a lot of fun, and the last of the snarling little F2F biplane fighters were just being phased out. This left the SNJ or J-bird. This was the same North American trainer used in Canada as the Harvard and in the U.S. Army as the AT-6. The gunnery training was accomplished with a .30-caliber machine gun firing through the prop at a sleeve towed by another J-bird. The route to and from the gunnery ranges passed over the vast King Ranch, and some of the chaps were better on cows than the sleeves. The ranch did some entertaining for navy people. It was unclear whether this was a venue to barbecue the prematurely dead beef or to induce the top guns to lay off already.

Mexico was handy for liberty. Old Monterrey, Mexico, in those halcyon days was also a far remove from the present. Because of the war, Americans could take only two-dollar bills. These would buy the services of a grand carriage followed by a mariachi band and a lease on the best nightclub—not to mention the fine old hotel surrounding the grand courtyard. There were also a lot of rich American draft dodgers in attendance who were spending freely.

In all too short a time the navy decreed that the training days were over and it was time to pin on the Wings of Gold and start earning the flight pay. This was all fine except for one fly on the pie. While going through the flight and ground syllabus the officer candidate was supposed to be achieving a proficiency with Morse code and have it signed off by the instructor.

When signing off the station, a cold feeling in the pit of my stomach indicated that the neglect of this requirement was now at crisis stage. Forging the code officer's signature would have been not only unethical, it might have been downright dangerous. The simple solution was to scribble something illegible in the signature space. Experience later proved that this skill (the Morse code), for the serious fighter pilot, would have been just as worthless as learning how to salute properly.

On the train to San Diego, with a brand new set of navy wings, the words of the Oracle of Poverty Flats were recalled: "When all is said and done, more has been said than done." That certainly applied to the navy's version of flight training. It would be a great relief to no longer hear the tiresome refrain of "Deep in the Heart of Texas" at every turn, or to hear the sloppy, insipid accents of the natives. Small wonder why so many of them joined the RCAF.

The training squadrons most certainly wouldn't be missed. Many of the instructors entertained great egos concerning their flying skills. This was somewhat at variance with their frantic desire to avoid being sent to the Fleet. Being classified by some of their students as the chaps with the "Gang Plank Knees" did little to improve relationships. It was also depressing to watch the cadets humbly knuckling their forelocks, being browbeaten, and marching off demerits at the behest of these rear-rank heroes.

The soggy Texas climate had been no more attractive than the large resident population of mosquitoes. One cadet swore that he awoke one night from a deep dream of getting washed out. There on the foot of his bunk two of these mosquitoes were sitting. "Shall we eat him here or take him home?" the first one asked. Giving this matter mature consideration, the second mosquito said, "We better eat him here. We go taking him home and the big guys'll take him away from us."

"The Fleet" was always referred to with great reverence in the training squadrons and actually meant any place outside the continental limits which held the threat of combat. A young navy ensign friend later detailed his introduction to the great and shining Valhalla of the Fleet right after the spit-and-polish discipline of flight school.

Sent to report to a carrier-based fighter squadron that was ashore from a tough combat cruise, he found them headquartered on the second deck of a hangar at Ford Island Naval Air Station (NAS) in Pearl Harbor. The attack was of very recent history. The wreckage was everywhere, and martial law was in effect. Still wearing his hot stateside blue uniform and carrying his hat under his arm in the approved fashion to make a good first impression, he located the office of the squadron CO.

He found his heroic leader asleep with his head cradled in his arms on the desk. When aroused, this worthy raised bloodshot eyes in an unshaven face and rudely snarled, "Who the hell are you?" At rigid attention the ensign gave his name, only to face a further aggressive question. "Do you drink?"

"Oh no sir!" he cried. That was a damned lie.

"Well then gimme your whiskey ration card you dumb SOB." Before the night was done, he and the CO, with some others of his new squadron mates, had fallen into a muddy shell hole. They were lustily singing a song deploring the war. The bawdy verses might well have been interpreted as having a treasonable theme. They were, at that time, waving a bottle of rationed whiskey.

VIII

It was easy to tell that there was a war on. The West Coast was exploding with war plants, and the inrushing hoards were filling the mushrooming shantytowns with the newly affluent. Mr. Roosevelt had already ended the long, bitter Great Depression, but the full employment and high wages for war work were causing a new gold rush. It was also the beginning of the significant switch from an agrarian population to urban. After the war the "good ole boys" would decrease in numbers along with their rabid patriotism. For now, it was an exciting time. All of the watering holes were filled with loud talk and cigarette smoke, and the jukebox that didn't feature "Remember Pearl Harbor" just didn't exist. A marine uniform, especially one with a set of wings, offered unprecedented opportunities. In fact the currency of the cruder element was, "What will you give me for a pair of navy wings, young lady?"

San Diego was only partially recovering from the panic caused by the fear of a Japanese invasion, as silly as that may sound now. The city was going through a period when property values had plummeted and all of the hardware stores had sold out of anything resembling a defensive weapon. This foolishness was being somewhat mitigated by the reassurance of the huge military expansion in the area.

At the Naval Air Station on North Island, my first billeting was in the Bachelor Officers Quarters at the historical "Building I." In addition to a pool and bar, the officers' club was close at hand. However, it was even better over at Coronado Island with the magnificent Hotel Coronado across the causeway. The "Nickel Snatcher" was a small ferryboat that deposited the pleasure-bound man in uniform over in San Diego proper, where the action was intense.

Out at El Cajon, the parents of the Threadbare Buzzard had a small almond orchard as sort of a refuge from the worst winters in Poverty Flats, Montana. There was also a car to be had there, and since the country no longer manufactured cars, this was luxury indeed. The problem with cars was that gasoline was rationed and very expensive on the black market.

One fine morning, with everybody else gone, it seemed like a good plan to burn off some of the dry grass on the premises. This turned out to be a very unsound plan, and an uncontrollable inferno developed. Very shortly there were fire trucks all over the place, and the fire laddies fought a valiant battle to bring the conflagration under control. These sturdy chaps weren't a bit outraged and were actually downright pleased to meet a genuine U.S. Marine fighter pilot who did little to depreciate his role in the air battles now raging in the Pacific. This jolly attitude did not seem to extend to the old pirate who returned home just as the last of the hoses were being rolled up. In fact he seemed uncharacteristically quiet and, yes, even pale.

With the departure of the last fire truck this turned out to have a simple explanation. Never suffering from any inclination to acquiesce to governmental interference with human rights, and that extended to being told how much rationed gasoline he was to have, steps had been taken. These steps concerned burying a good quantity of black-market gasoline in drums throughout the orchard. Fortunately, it hadn't lit off. Pearl Harbor revisited.

This interesting diversion was soon followed by another one. It developed that the United States Marines were developing an airfield out at a place called El Centro. Back in the Imperial Valley, it was far from finished, but a handful of pilots with a few ground officers were dispatched to make their presence felt and perhaps defend it from evil. This was a sound plan, although most of the defending was done in the bar of the fine local hotel. There were some interesting personnel present in the bargain. One was a warrant officer who, although not flying now, had been a pioneer pilot for the New York City police force. Not long before that, the police department had more members than the total muster of the United States Marine Corps.

Another of this group was a large, self-assured patrician from Boston. A brand-new aviator, he had also attained a degree from Harvard. He was called the "Other Harvard Guy" to distinguish him from the "Real Harvard Man." The sobriquet "The Horse" was assigned to the "Other Harvard Guy" a few months later, and it was a perfect fit. He rather loftily observed that although he knew there was such a place as Montana, he was very surprised to learn that there was a university there.

The leader of the pack was not a pilot and held only the rank of first lieutenant. Nevertheless, with his robust exuberance and an edge in age, he was a natural leader. A husky type who always seemed to need a shave, he confessed to having been the country's youngest circuit judge. After the war, he became one of the best-known senators in all of history. Although the present company called him "The Judge," his name was actually Joe—Joe McCarthy, that is.

Somebody must have belatedly discovered that there were no airplanes at El Centro, and the war machine was stridently demanding more bodies. This brought this party to an end, and the pilots in the group got in an old Dodge Carryall and returned to North Island, where the night life was conducted behind blackout curtains.

Before transportation for the far Pacific was found, there was one more adventure to be had. There was an old Sea Train ship being loaded with bombs at the docks and the longshore work was being done by enlisted troops. These lads were under the impression that they had joined up to fight and were becoming somewhat mutinous.

The answer seemed to be to equip some young pilots with side arms and place them in the holds with these unfortunates.

Actually, it got to be rather fun, with some little competition developing between teams to see who could roll the most 500-pound bombs into position and nail them in the cribs the fastest. That was fine until a reckless winch operator upended a cargo net full of these bombs, causing them to come crashing down. Fortunately, the fuses are kept separate, but this did not minimize the panic-stricken rush for the ladders. This unfortunately required drawing weapons on fellow Americans and raised hell with the camaraderie.

There was a feeling of great relief when, in the dark of night, I boarded the first ship I ever sailed in. It slipped out to sea blacked out and alone. At this remove the name of this rust bucket can be nearly, but probably inaccurately, recalled. The *Robin Wently* is certainly close, and she sailed with an eleven-degree list. Her destination was Pearl Harbor. Her recent past had been spent rotting on a mud bank until she was resurrected for the emergency. This was while Germany was sinking ships faster than they could be built. The Kaiser shipyards were just getting up steam, and shipping was critical.

In addition to her freight, she was carrying a lot of Marine Corps line officers and a bunch of marine aviators. The ship's crew said they should probably have the list off her before they got to Hawaii. Actually, the list was much worse when she did arrive, and this may have been beyond the crew's control.

Every soul who has taken a trip to sea claims to have been in history's worst storm. That may be, but the one the *Wently* got into was bad enough. Some of the grizzled old marine line officers, men of much experience, had been speculating, none too politely, about how seasick the pink-cheeked young aviators would get if the weather acted up. What they didn't know was that it is nigh impossible to induce motion sickness in a fighter pilot. It became the norm for the young pilots to speculate on the luncheon menu. Would it be greasy pork chops? This always got those damn gravel pounders headed for the rail. The "Harvard Man" from the RCAF was also aboard, and he quizzically described the motion as "bounding over the main."

After about ten days of bounding over the main, things quieted down, and one sunny morning Diamond Head appeared on the starboard bow. Some U.S. Army P-40 fighters showed up to impress the ship with a buzz job. Impress they did. One of them attempted to execute a sloppy slow roll at minimum altitude and provided a spectacular crash. His marine pilot audience limited their expressions of regret for his short career to criticism of his flying skills and general comments about his intelligence. Youth can be cruel.

In no time at all the gangway was down and an old truck appeared to take the pilots away from the wreckage of the naval base to their new home. This was to be the Marine Corps Air Station at Ewa Plantation. It was at the end of a long, two-lane road through pineapple fields and jungle. There was also a narrow-gauge railroad mostly to haul the products of the plantation to the docks. Ewa was also somewhat wrecked from the Japanese attack. Since this was far from an impressive place to begin with, the bullet holes, although plentiful, were not particularly noticeable.

Marine Air Group 21 had been formed composed of three squadrons: VMF-213, VMF-214, and VMF-221. In navy parlance, V means heavier than air, M stands for marine, and F for fighter. The assignment was to VMF-214 along with the "Harvard Man" and the "Horse," among others. This was an all-fighter air group rather than the usual fighter, dive-bomber, and torpedo squadron composition. These squadrons were pitifully small in numbers compared to later outfits. However, there were few pilots available, and the new boys were needed for the squadrons to gain enough strength to go off to war.

The kites were Grumman F4F-4's (Wildcats). They were manufactured by an outfit sarcastically called the Grumman Iron Works, and the stubby, barrel-like, midwing construction gave them a certain raffish appearance. Actually, they were only a small extension of the old Grumman biplane fighter minus a wing. Primarily designed for aircraft carriers, they teetered high up on an incredibly narrow landing gear that could cause the unwary pilot to be lured into a vicious ground loop when landing. This landing gear had to be hand-cranked up and down with twenty-some vigorous turns. The crank was on the right-hand side of the cockpit and required changing hands on the control stick. This also left the throttle and propeller controls untended during the operation. The throttle could be locked in position, but the prop pitch was a different matter. The kite was fitted with a Curtiss electric propeller. The revolutions were controlled by a lever on the throttle quadrant. This was fine, except that the miserable contraption had a bad habit of failing at critical moments and going into high pitch, which wouldn't deliver enough power to sustain flight on take-off. The redundancy was provided by a three-position toggle switch on the left side of the instrument panel (dashboard). This switch could be pushed to manual increase or decrease. Developing the necessary dexterity to deal with this awkward setup in times of terror was stimulated by the occasional sight of a Wildcat burning merrily at the end of the runway.

There were no fripperies with this machine. The guns were charged by three T-handles on each side of the cockpit, one for each of the six .50-caliber guns. Even the cowl flaps were hand-cranked. However, the landing gear gave the most trouble. An experienced pilot learned right quick to raise the seat well up and rest his feet on top of the brakes on the rudder pedals and direct his attention straight down the runway and ignore any dropping wings. Although the wings could be folded for storage on carriers, they seemed to have a good record of not doing so in flight. However, one of the senior pilots was witnessed breaking the airplane up pulling out of a high-speed dive when the landing gear came down all by itself. He was naturally unavailable to add anything to the investigation. Most of the pilots had already been there awhile and had suffered some brutal losses mostly due to pilot error. These plank owners only grudgingly welcomed the new boys to their already established tight little society.

The islands were a new experience and incredibly beautiful, especially from the air. The pure white beaches and orderly pineapple fields and shaggy sugar cane was backstopped with verdant green jungle rising up into the abrupt mountains. There was Honolulu now boiling over with sailors on liberty. Much farther along was Waikiki beach, a far cry from today's mega-hotel scene. The modest Royal Hawaiian and Ala Moana were the principal hotels. Of course, the base had an officers' club, and although rather primitive, it was stocked with a good quantity of fine booze.

Operational training for marines was almost nonexistent at the time due to the exigency of war and few fighter pilots available. The average flying time of most of the pilots was shockingly low. The new arrivals were only able to get checked out and get in one gunnery practice at most before the operation was secured to be shipped out to a place identified as "Cactus." (It later became obvious that this was the code name for Guadalcanal.) The planes were brought up to the best possible standards and the compasses swung and the guns boresighted. This last took place in a pit at the end of the strip. The tails were jacked up and the guns fired at a target. Early in the war there were many schools of thought on proper boresighting. Later, all guns were targeted to converge at 300 yards which, with bullet jump, et cetera, gave a cone of fire of about 14 feet in diameter. The resulting bullet density in this area was awesome.

After all adjustments were made, the planes were flown over to the Naval Air Station at Ford Island to be hoisted onto a carrier. One Wildcat developed some infirmity that made it impractical to take along, although it was marginally flyable. I was recruited to fly this piece of junk back to Ewa. At this point one of the squadron's mechanics approached with a sad tale. He, it seemed, had missed the last bus back and how about a ride? That appeared to be ridiculous, but he pointed to the small access door down low aft on the fuselage. This led only to the radio and there was plenty of space. In fact, he said that they rode back there all of the time. That was news, but why not?

After warning him to keep his big feet out of any control wires, a takeoff was negotiated, and that little Wildcat was *tail heavy*. A lot of compensating was required to land, and after a few resounding bounces the kite came to a halt right at the end of the Ewa airstrip, and the engine quit. A passing jeep pulled alongside, and damn if it didn't have two colonels in it. Now these were big men in that society, and they offered to help get the kite started. No help was desired from them, and things got worse when a pounding started inside the fuselage that could not be ignored. This would have made a great comic opera scene, but it didn't appear all that amusing right then. With some disbelief, one of the colonels produced a dime to use as a tool to open the Dzus (pronounced "zeus") fasteners on the access door. Boy, were those guys surprised when a frantic (and probably deaf) member of their command fell out on the runway in a state of advanced dementia. They got back in their jeep without comment and took their departure. The Wildcat got towed to the line, the passenger staggered off, and it was time to get to the primitive officers' club.

As far as could be discovered, people never had and never did ride in the back of a Wildcat. Those enlisted men sure liked to put a gullible young officer on. Anyway, before the air group turned its back on this paradise this episode led to another valuable experience in dealing with the troops. It would be uncharitable to suspect that those two fine senior officers had anything to do with it, but there was an interesting assignment in store. This entailed loading the air group's equipment that was being placed on other ships down in Honolulu Harbor. All sorts of stuff up to and including gas trucks had to be loaded, and some of the junior pilots would supervise the groups of enlisted men who were readying them and assisting the longshoremen. A highly uncoordinated maneuver of this nature is bound to produce missteps. Some insensitive jerk sent the gas trucks down full of gas with time running out, and the ship said if they weren't emptied and filled with water they wouldn't be loaded.

How it was done was a very great mystery, but permission was given to pump the gas out into the harbor with fireboats standing by. This was high-test aviation gas and had to come from the States, where the old pirate was willing to jeopardize his almond grove for a much lower grade of motor fuel.

Accomplishing this was tough, dirty, sweaty work, and noon soon approached, as did the dirty, sweating sergeant in charge of the detail. He even saluted and informed the officer that no provision had been made for chow. A Marine Corps officer is supposed to take care of his troops, and this did pose a dilemma. "Not to worry," assured the extremely polite and respectful young man, "with the Lieutenant's permission, Sir, the lads are willing to pay for their own lunch if allowed to go into town." With great relief at this solution, permission was gladly given.

At some interval later a jeep followed by a van with a cage arrived on the docks, and a grim lieutenant commander of the United States Navy, beautifully turned out in a dazzling white uniform, inquired after the officer in charge. He gestured to the van and explained that the occupants would be in jail if he had anything to do with it, but only because of the emergency they were being released to their own outfit and they had better be severely punished and just sign all of these papers.

The sergeant in charge was indignant over this episode and offered an explanation. "Just like the lieutenant said, we went to get lunch and we wuz over at the Birdcage [a celebrated whorehouse of the period] getting a box lunch at the Y when a bunch of doggies [army] come in. We just about had 'em whupped when the damn shore patrol got inna act."

Fortunately, a salty marine major from Ewa showed up to check on the gas truck caper. He seemed entirely unimpressed by the gravity of the crisis and said, "Gimme those papers." Tearing them into several pieces he filed them in Honolulu Harbor. "We'll be out of here before that son of a bitch checks this out." A young man could certainly get an education around the Marine Corps.

While this was going on a grizzled old wreck of a longshoreman stuck his face in and sneered, "So yew young fellers is agoin' off to war, 'eh?" Immune to an icy attempt to ignore him, he removed his teeth, which he placed on a handy bollard before his now attentive audience. Then he unshipped his left leg and proceeded to beat himself over the head with it. "Got me a genuine silver plate when I wuz afightin' with Gineral Pershing inna first war."

This required no comment, and when the day was done, the young pilots went into town. Here, after many libations, they discovered a tattoo parlor. Sobering up when confronted by what appeared to be a painful process, everybody except one brave pilot from one of the other squadrons chickened out. He got a pair of navy wings engraved nipple to nipple with his squadron number above them on his chest. For the rest of his life he was known as "Wings." Mercifully, that was a rather short period, and his early demise, as will be seen, saved him from any complications that might have arisen had he been transferred to a different-numbered squadron.

VMF-214's pilots were split up, with the originals getting to stay with the airplanes on the small carrier *Nassau*. The "Harvard Man" was the exception, since he already had the rank of captain so could not be denied the honor of getting to fly off the carrier at the end of the trip. This was to be extremely fortunate for the squadron. The rest of the pilots embarked on the *President Tyler* for the journey. The well-worn old passenger ship had a staggering number of troops aboard living in appalling circumstances. Running far south without convoy to avoid submarines, she took about a month to reach "Buttons." That was the code name for Espíritu Santo island.

The officers made the trip in staterooms with so many per room that sleeping was done in shifts. The enlisted troops were berthed in the holds in stacks of cots that reached staggering heights. Their bathroom was an array of open-air facilities constructed of wood clear around the fantail. This affair resembled the nesting grounds of the great auks when fully occupied.

The officers made do with two execrable meals per day, while the enlisted types got one. Given the quality of the food, this was a debatable advantage. Anyway, for the first few days most of the food went begging, except for the fighter pilots who are always hungry anyway. The trip crossed the equator, and the initiation into the Kingdom of Neptune Rex was administered rather brutally.

After an interminable period the old ship steamed into the channel at Espíritu Santo to reunite with the contingent from the carrier. They had a camp established, and the Wildcats were being made ready to be ferried up to Guadalcanal, where the action was. Fortunately, the Harvard Man, with his superior RCAF training, had been with this group.

After a hairy catapult-launching off the carrier, the situation rapidly deteriorated. With a little weather problem, the squadron leaders got hopelessly lost. With this major disaster staring them in the face, they had little choice but to listen to the Harvard Man. He had been quietly tracking this fiasco and calmly recommended a course that brought them out where they belonged and at nearly the exact time he predicted. Being a gentleman, he made no further mention of this. There were to be similar incidents in the future, but for now he busied himself by taking over the engineering functions and making the kites combat-ready. It was a strange occupation for a lawyer, but after devouring all of the tech manuals available he gained the respect of the mechanical types and was treated as an expert and final authority.

Meanwhile, the other chaps played cards, went beach combing, and drank beer. The squadron had a nonflying adjutant who owned one of the world's great publishing houses and had been a New York playboy of legendary fame. The famous Club Buttons over on the channel was supposedly restricted to navy only after some unpleasant encounters with marine officers. The adjutant managed to circumvent this ruling, so many fine times were had over there, except that the adjutant could become somewhat unmanageable himself when in his cups.

The day came when the squadron was set to invade the legendary battleground of Guadalcanal. The new Wildcats that the Harvard Man had so meticulously prepared were seized by the navy, as is their custom, and replaced with a few cast-off wrecks. Eight of the pilots would ferry airplanes up, and the rest would get into the DC-3s (navy R4Ds) for the trip. Those flying Wildcats were again selected from the original pilots. The navigation was left to an army second lieutenant flying a DC-3 for them to follow. Again, there was a weather factor and chaos. If the Harvard Man had been leading, it would have been much better. As it was, the squadron's executive officer went missing, and one of the enlisted pilots managed to crash-land on the southern end of Guadalcanal. Five TBFs out of a squadron of these cumbersome torpedo planes known as "Turkeys," as were their pilots, vanished. When an equal number of Turkeys disappeared in the so-called Bermuda Triangle after the war ended, they entered the hall of lasting fame. Such was never the case with vast numbers of planes that went missing during the war. At least, the executive officer survived after a harrowing five-day voyage in a rubber life raft after parachuting into the angry sea. This chap was a close friend of the few fighter pilots at the battle of Wake Island. These marine pilots fought on the beaches after their last Wildcat was lost. One of his best friends died with a rifle in his hand, thereby sparing himself the hell endured by the survivors at the hands of their merciless Japanese captors.

The exec was very critical of the navy, which had lost none of its carriers in the Japanese attack at Pearl Harbor. They steamed a relief task force almost to Wake Island with plenty of power to win a significant battle and change the course of the war at an early stage. The navy, in an unforgivable act of caution, paused to unnecessarily refuel their ships while the island was overrun. The marine pilots aboard those carriers who were to reinforce their comrades on the island were very close to mutiny. As usual, the navy's attitude, which was to be repeated with sickening frequency during the war was, "What the hell. They're only marines."

IX

It had taken a long road to get into fighters and to a place where the guns were being fired in anger. It had been a jolly time, and the background of Poverty Flats was extremely useful. This squadron was filled with Ivy League college graduates whose past lives might not have been much like the marine's crude existence in the field, but they did soon adapt.

On Guadalcanal, all of the squadrons lived in the coconut grove. This vast plantation of orderly rows of towering coconut palms was ideally laid out for spreading the tents. Camping out in a tent spread-eagled between four coconut trees in the huge grove was much better than a Montana winter. Of course, there were a few inconveniences. There was the constant supply of mud guaranteed by the tropical rains, which also assured an endless supply of blood-thirsty mosquitoes. These miserable insects gave malaria to about 90 percent of the command despite the daily ingestion of the bitter Atabrine tablets.

There was also a large population of huge rats that had fattened on Japanese bodies. Rumor had it that they turned up their noses at the food that was fed to the marines. Actually, these king-sized rodents who liked to race around the top of the tents at night provided some happy diversion. The engineering creativity of the

rattrap builders was most commendable. There were long, complicated runways constructed and baited at every turning until the rats
reached a cunningly arranged morsel. Acquisition of this treat usually caused the rat to fall into a barrel of high-octane gas. When the
cry "Rat in the barrel!" was raised, the refined young savages would
pour out of the tents for the cremation ceremony.

There were four or five chaps to the tent. The squadron doctor
of one outfit was a conservative older man and had good reason to
regard his tent mates with suspicion. This was reciprocated when he
started boiling the meat off of Japanese heads and placing the skulls
around the tent. Medical research, he said. Necrophilia, said his tent
mates. In these rather uncivilized circumstances, two of the pilots
used to put candles in the skulls to make macabre jack-o-lanterns.
Unfortunately, this got in a stateside magazine, and there was some
unpleasantness over this evidence of uncivilized conduct.

The Doc had another reason for his mistrust, and that was the
fault of the mosquitoes. The two jack-o-lantern chaps devised what
they imagined was a foolproof way to drive the mosquitoes away. It
entailed a smoldering fire of coconut fronds in the tent, which, so
the plan went, would be removed after the insects took to their heels.
The coconut fronds did not cooperate, and the fire kept going out.
There was a simple solution to this problem, which entailed getting
in the jeep and going down to the airstrip for a pail of gas. One dignified squadron commander was sitting with his back to a coconut
tree reading—possibly the Bible, considering the personnel in his
command. One of the exterminators was a famous athlete and was
therefore elected to throw the gasoline (bucket included) through
the tent flap on the smoldering fronds.

The explosion was spectacular, with the CO and his book lift-
ing straight up and the tent going up in flames. Of course all of the
cots, mosquito netting, and skulls, along with other valuables and
possessions, did not survive. It was rather quiet for a few nights while
the tent was being re-established. The rats must have figured that
this was done for their benefit, and they re-invaded en masse. The

Doc really hated and feared them. One night there seemed to be an unusually large convention of them under Doc's army cot. Forgiving past offenses, he loudly called upon the bucket thrower for assistance. This obliging fellow was also a superior shot with the Colt .45, which all pilots then carried. He had this weapon in his cot inside the mosquito netting in case there was a Japanese invasion, or something.

Raising the mosquito netting, he focused his flashlight on the Doc's cot. The Doc was a heavy man, and the cot sagged nearly to the ground, leaving only enough room for a row of beady eyes. Enthusiastically shouting to the Doc to fear not, the pistoleer opened fire with gratifying results, and not a single round penetrated the medical man who lay quite still during the barrage.

The camp area was equipped with bomb shelters of ingenious construction, and were L-shaped to minimize the blast effect. They had several layers of tough coconut logs over them, and that was covered with coral. Only one guy in the area was killed in one, and that was the result of a direct hit. Their real worth was discovered right off.

Air raids were certainly worthy of an enraptured audience. When the bombers came in with the thrumming of their badly synchronized engines, the searchlights would seek them out, and the big antiaircraft guns would throw up a most impressive display of fireworks that no county fair could afford. Sometimes this fire would light off a bomber. Once in a while a fighter could get up there in the dark and shoot a plane down. This was a real show, with the flash of tracer followed by the flaming wreckage and, only much later, the sound of the guns and the sound of the explosion and the screaming engines in the death dive. The interval between the sight and the sound depended on how far away the action was. The value of the bombproof shelter was now amply demonstrated. The antiaircraft fire would explode at about the height of the incoming bombers. Then this shrapnel would fall back to earth and would shred tents, bedding, and anyone who lingered too long watching the show.

This wasn't a one-way show, and some of the bombings were quite effective. One night a well-placed stick of bombs lit off an impressive number of valuable airplanes on Henderson Field, and the fires went on all night and into the next morning. The entertainment value of these events never replaced the lack of sleep they engendered.

Another event that robbed the troops of sleep was an exploding ammunition dump in the area. The report was that some eager beaver was burning some junk in the wrong place and set off the first of a chain reaction that lasted a long time, making it hazardous to expose any body part above ground level. There were uncounted episodes of these accidental explosions during the war, and given its huge scope, had to be considered just part of it. Although the Port Chicago explosion at the naval ammunition depot on San Francisco Bay is commemorated to this day, there were many reports of larger disasters out in the islands that were not widely reported. This was both because the disasters would be bad for civilian morale, and they could be concealed or at least the reports minimized.

The fighter squadrons were here to work, and work they did. The one routine that never varied was the patrols. After being shaken out of the sack at about 3:30 and attempting an execrable breakfast, the truck carrying the pilots crashed off to the fighter strip. The Wildcats would be coughing into life, and the plane captain would help the pilot with his shoulder harness and hand him the yellow sheet to sign, accepting the machine as ready for flight. With the primitive facilities for maintenance at hand, this was somewhat of a joke, for if the magnetos checked out, it would be a pilot impervious to the scorn of his fellows who would decline to take anything that had a chance of leaving the ground. The impenetrable black of night in those islands cannot be described, only experienced.

After a Wildcat bounced out to the end of the strip, the engine was run up, magnetos, head temperatures, and trim tabs checked. The final move was to lock the tail wheel before pouring on the coal.

The strip was surfaced with Marston matting, which was made up of interlocking steel plates with round holes in it. Sometimes there were void areas where the undersurface (mostly coral) was missing, and the sensation was like bouncing on a bedspring. That was best ignored, and intense concentration focused on keeping the Wildcat headed straight down the extremely narrow and poorly lit strip in the velvety blackness. At full throttle, the main concern was that the aforementioned electric propeller could fail at any moment, sending it into high pitch and placing the young aviator over in the trees. In case a pilot lost control as he raced down the strip, there was a permanent lookout stationed in the ready tent halfway down, to monitor all takeoffs. One chap managed to escape this onerous task by a simple ruse. On his first tour of this duty he screamed, "Get out of the tent, get out of the tent!" With terrified people returning from the blackness of night to the shambles of the tent with no sign of a fighter in the wreckage, he explained that it was only a drill. He could have been murdered, but was only punished by never being allowed to stand this crucial duty again.

Aside from the narrow landing gear making the landing and takeoffs dicey, the Wildcat was pretty safe. As these veteran planes got more and more beat up, they did acquire a few of the debilities of advanced age. When their engines had been run full out in combat, they sometimes hated to quit. More than one pilot was astounded when his engine continued running after being shut down due to the overheating, causing something known as pre-ignition. Somewhat more dangerous was the tendency of the guns to start firing after a hard bounce on landing. There was some extensive damage from this, but nobody got killed. Usually, having all of the gun switches in the off position prevented this runaway gun syndrome.

Once in the air, it was necessary to switch hands and take the stick in the left hand while using the right hand to raise the landing gear. Flipping the little locking lever above the crank, the work got underway. Taking twenty-some full turns to heave the wheels home, losing the grip on the crank would allow it to violently spin down. Many Wildcat pilots had severely bruised right wrists and sometimes broken ones. The pumping motion of the right arm cranking up the wheels sometimes caused the left hand, which now held the stick, to acquire a sympathetic motion that sent the fighter porpoising through the night. If the luck was not running good, there could be further complications. The propeller pitch could pick this time to start slipping, which necessitated using the left hand to hold down a three-position toggle switch to "manual increase." To add to this acrobatic balancing act, it was necessary to fly on instruments in the black night while also trying to find the lights of the plane ahead to effect the rendezvous. By the time dawn arrived and the guns had been cleared, one by one, there was a feeling of great accomplishment.

As the sun climbed into the sky, the Solomon Islands from the air were deceptive in their beauty. The blue sea, orderly coconut plantations, and lush green foliage growing up the high mountains were every bit as attractive as the Hawaiian Islands had been. Here the similarities ended. Down there was heat, humidity, death, diseases, and limitless infections. The viciousness and extent of the fighting had filled the sea with the wreckage of ships and planes. On the land there were torn-up patches so blood-soaked that the jungle had not grown back. The only pleased inhabitants were the powerful bone-in-the-nose Melanesian natives. They had hated the Japanese and now loved the Americans and that American delicacy, Spam, the ubiquitous and universally hated canned main course of the troops worldwide. In an amazing adaptation of primitive peoples to the advantages of modern living they were soon driving jeeps lettered "NATIVE LABOR BATTALION."

But whatever else was going on, the squadron's work continued. The first patrol of the day was the "Dawn" and was the first of three during the day. The other two were the "Knucklehead" and the "Assbuster."

These ran from "The Canal" (Guadalcanal) north across the Sealark Channel to Tulagi and then west to Savo Island and Cape

Esperance, which was the western tip of Guadalcanal. Farther west were the Russell Islands, which were the next step up the island chain and were more or less included in these patrols. The patrols were all necessary due to the primitive warning system owned by "Recon," the call name of the fighter directorate. There had been some unpleasant surprises, and Recon was known as the "Opium Den" for that and other reasons.

The Coast Watchers were on some of the islands up the line. These former Australian planters and civilian authorities with their radios and loyal natives played a hair-raising and sometimes fatal game of hide-and-seek with the Japanese who infested the islands. Their early warnings of inbound enemy planes or ships were the most valuable asset of the system. Not only that, some of the rescue operations of air and sea survivors they pulled off became the stuff of legends.

The work was unremitting, and when not flying patrols, the strikes were scheduled. These included escorting dive-bombers and torpedo planes rigged to glide bomb, up "the Slot" to the Japanese airfields at Munda and Kolombangara. These strikes often called for flak suppression. This entailed diving in front of the dive-bombers to try to take out the antiaircraft fire. On other strikes the fighters would make aggressive fighter sweeps by themselves and strafe assigned targets.

Back on the ground, a lot of time was spent on duty at the ready tent a short distance back from the strip. The claim was that at approximately sunrise, the mosquitoes patrolling the premises were relieved by flies. The pilots not immediately available for scrambles or briefing for upcoming strikes were usually flaked out in the depressing heat on an assortment of canvas cots. The only attire was the sweat-soaked summer flight suit. One suit was usually considered a sufficient wardrobe for the entire combat tour. At the end of six weeks or so its occupant would leave it, as the saying went, "Just standing there." By that time, reinforced by sweat and grime, the suit could easily stand alone.

Down at the other end of the strip was the ready tent of the valiant men of the first Corsair squadron in combat. A remarkably resourceful bunch, they had scrounged, promoted, and otherwise acquired the finest creation to be imagined. The spread-eagled tent had been raised, allowing plenty of headroom, and the sides were framed with two-by-fours. These were covered by genuine wire screening whose point of origin is still shrouded in mystery. It did do a remarkable job of holding the flies and mosquitoes at bay.

However, some people just can't stand prosperity, and their roster of distinguished pilots included a jolly tech sergeant pilot. One hot morning he entered the tent that was keeping the flies at bay holding a U.S. hand grenade. "Hey, look what I found," he said, holding up this lethal bomb in one hand with the pin in his other hand. "Can't seem to be able to get this damn pin back in," he explained to his mesmerized audience. With care and caution he was talked into being very still and particularly not releasing the lever until they located the squadron's ordnance expert. With the arrival of this worthy, the chap with the hand grenade appeared visibly relieved and handed him the grenade with an overdone fumbling act that dropped it on the ground. Then began the most famous exodus in recent history. When the shaken chaps returned through the shredded screen and broken two-by-fours to inspect the "dud" grenade, an interesting discovery was made. It would never have exploded, having been professionally disarmed by the sergeant pilot who, it was discovered, had been an ordnance man in a former life in the marines. He could have gotten killed like the "Get out of the tent" chap in VMF-214, had his squadron mates not been otherwise distracted.

The Marine Corps, in its attention to the details of morale, provided the ready tents with five-gallon tins of sealed-in hardtack. These were stamped with dates from the First World War. About the size of a graham cracker and tough as reinforced concrete, they were rather superior to the regular rations when spread with peach jam. This jam came in one-gallon cans and, once opened, became a main target for the aggressive flies.

The plumbing facilities for this modified resort area were located up the slight rise toward the coconut grove. A deluxe two-hole open-air installation, it often entertained a refugee or two from the ready tent, often with tattered paperbacks that could be either read or otherwise employed. There was a tale bearing great currency that a chap was so occupied when a bunch of Japanese Zeroes came strafing. Obeying the cardinal rule to get below the ground's surface in this circumstance, he kicked over the box and dove in. This not only saved his life, it occasioned the digging of some foxholes in the vicinity. There is absolutely no evidence that any VMF-214 pilots were involved. However, there were cases of bored people around the ready tent hurling a few chunks of coral and insults at the occupants. Another amusement was the Colt .45 side arm then used by pilots. With unlimited ammunition from a nearby ammo dump, there was a lot of shooting. Some developed accuracy and speed on the draw that could have run Wild Bill Hickok out of Dodge City.

Much farther up the island chain was New Britain island, where the fearsome Japanese bastion of Rabaul was located. Here was the headquarters of the Japanese Eleventh Air Fleet commanded by Capt. Yochiro Miyano.

Admiral Isoroku Yamamoto decided to reinforce this outfit with his main assets and apply the final solution to the Solomon Island problem. Despite all of the postwar apologetics for this criminal, he had done his damnedest to beat the United States into submission first at Pearl Harbor, which went well, and next at the Battle of Midway, which didn't do so well. His statement that he intended to dictate the terms of peace in the White House may have been taken out of context, but the intent remained the same.

To this end, he brought in the planes off the aircraft carriers *Shokaku*, *Zuikaku*, *Zuiho*, *Junyo*, and *Hiyo*, along with other units of new aircraft and pilots. This was the first team. He came down to Rabaul to mastermind this venture and, after a few days of weather delays he was able to wave *Banzai!* to the departing armada.

Down at Guadalcanal it didn't take long for the Coast Watchers' reports to indicate that something big was going to go down around noon. The executive officer got to make one of those memorable statements so highly prized by military men. Airborne at the first warning, and estimating that it would be an hour or so before the brawl would open, he called Recon and requested permission to "pancake, gas up, and chow down." Granted. This show occasioned a sad experience with victory claims and personal combat. Having a much-prized day off was not a desired circumstance with this major battle shaping up. Fortunately, the wingman of another division leader was indisposed, so getting his slot posed no problem. The leader of this division was a captain and one of the squadron's entrenched old-timers. A popular personality, he was also demonstrating some discrepancies in flying skills and leadership.

After becoming airborne, the long climb to the altitude and location assigned by Recon started. The rate of climb for a Wildcat equipped with an external right wing tank for endurance was pathetic. The transition from the sweltering heat of the fighter strip to the freezing temperatures at altitude was finally completed, and the division was orbiting down by Cape Esperance. That end of the island was blanketed by towering clouds, and although Recon was reporting heavy enemy formations, nothing was seen. Then suddenly a great V of Vs of fixed-landing-gear Aichi 99 "Val" dive-bombers starting emerging from the wall of weather well below the Wildcats. With no further ado the fearless leader traded off the greatest advantage a Wildcat could have in a fight, precious altitude, by promptly descending on the bombers. This brilliant maneuver didn't include racking off the highly volatile auxiliary gas tanks. Well into that blunder a great swarm of Zero fighters emerged from the weather. They were behind and above where the action was nearly joined. The ubiquitous Recon took that time to repeat its plaintive refrain, "Has any division in the air got any bogey dope?"

"Bogies?" cried the leader of men. "Geezus, I got a million of them cornered." This remark became even more repeated than the "gas up and chow down" bon mot.

A startled look back and up revealed that he did indeed, and explained where he had gone. He had broken off his run on the Vals and gone up to destroy the Zeros. He arrived fresh out of air speed, and they promptly flamed him just after he made his historical reply to Recon. This circumstance negated any desire to go up and help him, had any such sentiment been entertained anyway.

The six .50-caliber guns in the Wildcats were lubricated with cosmoline, and experience had long since proved that it would thicken in the extreme cold at altitude and that the guns would not function unless they had been wiped clean. Now as I was closing on the last Val in the very great V of Vs, only one gun fired. Getting close and flat caused this encounter to get up close and personal. Being nearly on top of the frightened-looking gunner in the rear cockpit of the Val didn't provide the impersonal feeling of air combat. The .50-caliber machine gun chopped up the valiant rear gunner who was firing back right to the end. This sight was not pretty. Meanwhile it was obvious that all of the other rear gunners in the formation were firing but fortunately without much luck.

It used up all of the ammunition in the one firing gun to knock pieces off the Val and get it smoking. Then out of firepower and with Zeros starting their runs, it was time to head for the deck. The Wildcat was square enough to have a terminal velocity in a vertical dive. In fact, to slow up in a dive, running up the engine would furnish a braking effect. On the way down I observed a plane crashing off Lunga point about where the trajectory of the torn-up Val would have gone. The Zeros had broken off in the direction of Tulagi, where the action was intense.

A Wildcat pilot from one of the air group's squadrons shot down seven Vals. Rumor (which wasn't particularly true) had it that these kills were confirmed by the same U.S. Army antiaircraft unit that shot him down. This record was against the first team and was never broken, even later in the war when the Japanese pilots became pitiful targets.

An enlisted pilot of the same squadron underlined the Wildcat's ability to fly slow. Pursued by two Zeros sending hot rivets past his cockpit, he could see that he faced a limited future unless he could devise a defensive plan. It came to him in a brilliant revelation. He could fly slow. To this end he chopped the throttle and dropped the flaps. Immediately he found himself with a Zero on each wing with their props windmilling. One panicked and broke right. The American figured, what the hell, he might as well follow this guy and kill him, while the other chap got to shoot him. This Zero promptly flamed, and it took the American a second to realize that nobody was hitting him. Rolling back, he discovered that the other Zero had simultaneously broken left, and he was able to send him to the promised land with his buddy.

Back on Guadalcanal there was a lot happening, with a few crashes and a lot of wild talk and arm-waving going on. The air combat intelligence officer was a man of great integrity and careful in handling claims. By afternoon the troops down by the beach verified that a Japanese plane had hit the water at the appropriate time required. That was before the guy who had "a million of 'em cornered" returned after having a very busy time with his parachute and the water off Savo Island.

After a few versions of his tale, he heard about the airplane that had hit the water down by Lunga Point. This, he claimed, must have been the one that he had heroically shot at, despite any other evidence. With misplaced sympathy and suspicions of what damage one gun would do, not much of an issue was made of this. There was also a feeling of astonishment that anyone would cause such a hassle to gain title to some dead bodies.

Not only was this claim made, but after the war, his erstwhile wingman, who was on the sick list, put himself back on the guy's wing with only one gun firing. The same chap who claimed the Val that crashed at Lunga point had a lot to do with the downfall of the squadron through bad judgment and poor leadership. Later there were to be increasingly shaky claims until all claims became suspect.

That evening there were still wild rumors of more incoming. That called for participating in a flight covering Tulagi at dusk, with the Harvard Man leading. There was only some smoke rising from the remains of a U.S. tanker, destroyer, and corvette (this a very small New Zealand escort vessel). This and the American fighters shot down was the pitifully small bag for the Japanese, but it led to a major event in the war.

The Japanese pilots returning to Rabaul were worthy rivals of the Americans in the great claims department. This stimulated Admiral Yamamoto, "The Victor of Pearl Harbor," to go down to the forward airfields to personally congratulate his heroes on this sweeping victory. He never suspected that his nemesis was otherwise occupied in these, his few remaining days as a live admiral.

One of VMF-214's pilots had been on a bombing escort over on Santa Isabel island when engine failure forced him to ditch. He swam ashore very close to a Japanese outpost. This young Stanford engineering graduate was one of two sons of a distinguished pilot of the peacetime army air service and had an older brother flying P-38 fighters on the island to good account. The marine was Chuck and the army brother was Tom. The pilots from VMF-214 along with Tom got a rescue underway, first with an old Grumman Duck floatplane and, when that failed, with a PBY flying boat that Tom rode in as a passenger. With a water landing, a rubber boat paddled nearly in to the beach, and after a hair-raising sequence, with the Japanese charging in, the flying boat staggered off just in the nick of time with Chuck aboard. A few days later a great number of the P-38 fighters took off, with a lot of speculation on where they were going. There were no escorts, strikes, or strafing missions scheduled.

Before leaving Honolulu, the air group had come by a large store of tax-free booze, and although the Seabees had stolen the major part of it, there was still a fair supply. Another thing about the squadron was its fame in the musical department, with its predominately

Ivy League membership. Boy, did those representatives of the most refined and cultured members of U.S. society know the dirty versions of all of the popular songs. They also knew some really filthy songs reflecting their distinguished alma maters plus those of the distinguished finishing schools for girls. Vassar comes to mind. The harmonizing and canteen cups of old forty rod made the squadron's evening campfire a valued destination.

That evening Chuck's brother, the P-38 pilot, and some of his buddies appeared at the campfire in a state of high excitement. Canteen cup in hand, Tom divulged that he was the triggerman that had sent Japan's most famous military leader, Admiral Yamamoto, to hell, or wherever good Japanese go.

The admiral had flown down to the lower end of Bougainville on his planned tour to congratulate the troops on the recent great victories. The long-range P-38s made good the longest intercept of the war, and the "Betty" bomber he was flying was creamed. (Some accounts claim he was actually doing the flying, which he was fully qualified to do.) His chief of staff in another Betty was the only person to escape when it too was shot down. The army lost one of the covering P-38s to the escorting Zeros, but the rest got out and flew home. Pearl Harbor was avenged.

Since the Japanese code had been broken to make this strike possible, it was supposed to be of the highest secrecy, and there was hell to pay when the talk at that party blew it. All of the P-38 pilots were threatened with court-martial and sent back to the States and never returned to combat. It didn't really matter, since the arrogant Japanese refused to believe that their code could be broken by the stupid Americans anyway. After the war it became fashionable in certain circles to call this operation an assassination, since it was sanctioned at the highest levels of the U.S. government.

One evening just after dark some strangers landed at the fighter-one strip. They were a navy division of four Wildcats from a carrier out there some place, and were either reinforcements or just plain lost. The famous ground-looping characteristic of the Wildcat turned any hope of being reinforcements into a farce. Since they were used to landing on a carrier with arresting gear, and not a primitive strip, they suffered some elemental failures in technique.

The first one ground-looped to the left, and the second one ground-looped to the right. The third one was doing better until the guy behind him landed on top of him in the dark. The bloody work the prop accorded his head was most unpleasant to witness.

By now the squadron was no longer the newcomer to combat and was due for a leave in Sydney, Australia. It was also to be nearly the last Marine Corps squadron to fly the Wildcat in combat. One of the other squadrons in the air group had already transitioned into the F4U Corsair and were the second outfit to reach combat with them. The first squadron using them, although having some successes, had had many serious problems.

This airplane was certainly one of the most interesting machines in the war. It had a huge radial 2,000-horsepower engine and was the first true 400-mile-an-hour fighters. It swung a fourteen-foot propeller, and for this to clear the ground, it was constructed with a unique inverted gullwing. The cockpit was located fourteen feet back from the fourteen-foot propeller.

This cockpit had a very low canopy, and to further obstruct the pilot's forward view, the tail wheel Oleo strut was short to increase the prop clearance. The low canopy caused this model to be called the "Birdcage." Corsairs were best landed wheels-first for visibility, a good thing too, because below a certain speed and a certain angle of attack, a wingtip could stall before the wing root. This would cause the kite to initiate a snap roll at an embarrassingly low altitude, like fifty feet. This was partially cured by the mechanics taping a carved block on the leading edge of the wing just before the break in the gull portion.

The magnetos sometimes arced out at altitude, blowing out the intercooler ductwork of the blower system, which supplied the manifold pressure in the thin air. Corsairs also refused to recover from inverted spins.

There was a huge, self-sealing gas tank immediately ahead of the pilot. This was made of reclaimed rubber and was known to flame if enough of a concentration of enemy fire came to bear. It also leaked, and the fuselage in the tank area had to be taped up to prevent the escaping vapors from getting lit off. In some insanity of engineering, there was a fifty-five-gallon reserve tank in each wingtip that was not self-sealing. When approaching combat these tanks were supposed to be purged with CO_2, which was furnished by a bottle in the cockpit. Unfortunately, there was a duplicate bottle next to it, which was the emergency blow-down for the main landing gear. The main landing gear was also the dive brake. Blowing down the wheels at altitude while up in Indian country doing bomber escorts, just as losing manifold pressure did, dropped the victim out of the protective scissors. That gave the Zero pilots in the Flying Circus great opportunities to be decorated. Of course, if the tip tanks went unpurged, enemy fire would flame the Corsair.

For these and other idiosyncrasies the machine was known as the "Bent Wing Widow Maker." The Corsair was a necessary step in gaining air superiority and, in nearly every category, could outperform the Zero except in turning radius. It could also kill an unwary pilot in the flick of an eyelash. Since the navy had rejected it for carrier use because of sometimes-fatal tests, the U.S. Marines were available. By the end of the war it had been so extensively modified and redesigned that it was a real pussycat, and any little old lady in tennis shoes could fly it. It got so safe that the navy started using it again and put it back on carriers, where it gained a fine reputation. There are still a few of the old Birdcage pilots alive. They can, as a rule, be identified by their humble mien and devout manner.

The first squadron in the air group to be honored by owning this machine had, fortunately, some really outstanding pilots. Their skipper was one of the best, but one black predawn his Corsair ran amuck on takeoff and blew up over in the flight line. Two of VMF-214's pilots raced right into the inferno and tried to pull him out. He was hopelessly jammed in the cockpit, and their experience was horrifying and, despite serious burns, unsuccessful.

With these precursors of a future with the Corsair in evidence, they were, at this time, totally insignificant to VMF-214, who had suffered its own losses. What was important was to finish the combat tour and get to the promised leave in Sydney, Australia. As the next to last Wildcat squadron in the Marine Corps to fly in combat, the tour had been expanded to an unheard-of eight weeks from the normal six weeks. The extra time allowed the squadron to experience "The Flood."

The first night of the flood there was a hard rain that made it possible for me to go out in front of the tent in the altogether, rather than grope through the pitch-black night to one of the barrels hung in the trees to shower. No sooner than well-soaped-up than the rain quit. Becoming disoriented on the way to one of the primitive showers in the black night permitted a fall into a deep shell hole. The soap certainly picked up a real plaster of mud along with bruises and contusions. Not feeling well enough to pursue the elusive shower any further, the tent was relocated and the refuge of bed was sought, mud and all. A few hours passed before the main body of rain arrived. For days it continued flooding out the camp, putting out the cook fires and inundating the fighter strip.

As the squadron's time at Guadalcanal was running out, there were a few more strikes, patrols, and scrambles left, but nothing heavy went down. Unfortunately, the skipper of the first Corsair squadron whose ready tent adjoined VMF-214 on the strip was killed in action at this time. This made him the second Corsair skipper killed in a short time. This was going to have an effect on VMF-214 that was not recognized right then. There had been so many experienced squadron commanders killed since the war started that the command was getting nervous. In the near future they were going to limit these senior people to one combat tour versus the three tours required of lesser mortals.

X

Happy was the day when word came to stand down.

The last night in camp the Japanese sent a bomber over to pay their last respects. With his typically out-of-synchronized engines thrumming away, he dropped some wonderful red flares with a stick or two of bombs included and got a lot of heavy antiaircraft fire in return. This was an expensive and spectacular display of fireworks. Since neither side suffered any visible damage, all of the surviving whiskey was inhaled, the songs were sung, and official requests to reduce the size of the campfire were turned away most rudely.

All too early the next day the squadron was loaded into a couple of DC-3s (navy R4Ds) belonging to the joint Marine Corps and the U.S. Army transport organization known as SCAT. This stood for Southern Cross Air Transport, a versatile, raggedy-ass outfit used for all manner of weird and often rugged assignments. They deposited the recovering celebrants first at transit quarters at Espíritu Santo island and soon thereafter hauled them a short distance to the island of Éfaté. This was far removed from Cactus and may have deserved the sobriquet of "Island Paradise."

The camp was at an airstrip named Quoin Hill. Across the small island was Havana Harbor and the town of Vila. Needless to say, this Havana was not in Cuba and this Vila had nothing to do with the

Vila on Kolombangara island, which was still under Japanese management. After Guadalcanal the "livin' was easy" and there were no duties except relaxing. The water was crystal clear and the breeze helped with the flies and the heat. Nearly every day the natives in their outrigger canoes would come into the lagoon and run them up on the beach to trade. This supplied a lesson in economics, British style, and the value of the Australian florin (a coin about the size of a half-dollar). A supply of these coins was included in a pilot's jungle pack, allegedly for the purpose of bribing natives if shot down.

The Brits owned the coconut plantations, and the islands had a sad history of labor relations. There even had been outright kidnapping for slavery (called "blackbirding") by pirates of the "Bully Hayes" stripe. The Brits were smarter than that. Their solution for keeping the natives' wandering interest focused was to put the men to work on a plantation on an island apart from the women. They were paid in florins, and when they had saved enough they could rejoin the ladies for marriage or whatever. On one of the natives' trading visits, a really great grass skirt was displayed and offers of large U.S. bills were declined. Folding money apparently wasn't held in high esteem. However, idly jingling a handful of florins from the jungle pack brought the natives crowding round ready to deal on any terms.

It may be true that the British collected good American money for every coconut tree destroyed from battle damage or removed to make runways. It also may be true that every vehicle put on these islands was charged a license fee. If landing fees were also charged it boggles the imagination, even if Merrie Olde England was becoming impoverished by war and in desperate need of American gold.

Some memorable parties were held here, but the main course was yet to come. One day half the squadron got into one rickety DC-3 (R4D) and the other half into its sister, and after a noisy, miserable flight, arrived at Tontouta River on New Caledonia. This was the headquarters for the valiant SCAT and afforded a jolly night's entertainment before continuing to Sydney. This leg was flown with airplanes so heavily laden with gas, freight, and passengers that they could

hardly get airborne. Now it was really getting cold since it was coming on winter in the upside-down land of the Southern Hemisphere.
After a long, cold night riding on top of lumpy freight, the old bird
bounded to a stop in a cold rain at the Sydney airport.

Words could describe this liberty in Sydney as far as the drinking, eating, partying, and general joy were concerned. However, without the circumstances then present, it could never be experienced
again. The pace of wartime life, the relief of even being there at all contributed as well as being far away from anything familiar. Then there
was the certainty of returning to the dicey life of fighter combat in the
very near future. It was, literally, a short seven days of magic. One enthusiastic southern boy in the squadron described it as the most fun
he'd had since the hogs ate little brother.

The Aussies in residence loved the marines and voiced their dis-
taste for General MacArthur, who had fled the Philippines and was
now their personal "man who came to dinner." Self-appointed to the
title of supreme commander, it seemed like he had more public relations officers (seventy-seven by actual count) than combat troops.
Claiming command of everything, he issued such communiqués as
"MacArthur's troops in deadly battle in New Guinea." Trouble was
that most of the troops were Australian and his majesty gave them little credit. Instead of believing that President Roosevelt had ordered
him out of the Philippines, the Aussies preferred to believe that he was
a supreme egotist who had abandoned 110,000 troops and that upward of 10,000 had died in the infamous Bataan death march. The
other Australian troops were being the Rats of Tobruk in the terrible
fighting in North Africa at that time. In Samoa many years later, in a
conversation with the manager of Burns Phillips, the great South Seas
trading company, the war years were mentioned. After a long reflec-
tive silence this giant redheaded Aussie spoke in measured terms. He
expressed the thought that if any of the bloody rotten Yank buggers
who had been entertaining the Sheilas (meaning females in the quaint
vernacular of the Australians) while he and his cobbers (Australian
for buddies) were in Tobruk were not then burning in hell's fire, he

would be pleased to help them on the way. It would appear that this was not the time to discuss how the gallant VMF-214 had saved the grateful Aussies from the contemptible Japs.

The miserable return flight again wound up at Éfaté by way of New Caledonia, where the vacation continued. The old CO was transferred out. This was serious since he was a real leader, but the new policy of only allowing senior people one combat tour was now in force. The squadron got a new major who was a splendid fellow but short of fighter experience. The squadron was now going to enter the world of the Birdcage Corsair, but this transition would take place up on Espíritu Santo at the marine airstrip at Turtle Bay. This place had a fine new officers' club to recommend it, but only a few cast-off Corsairs to accomplish the training.

Before leaving Éfaté there was the matter of the milk punch. Some creative souls found a use for the powdered milk, powdered eggs, and powdered anything else available. In fact, the only nonpowdered ingredient was the booze. The resulting celebration rivaled an outbreak of the plague and was a fitting conclusion to the carefree life of the vacationing fighter pilots.

Back on Espiritu Santo there were some factory representatives for both the airframe and the mighty engine of the Corsair, and one of the pilots from a squadron already checked out came down from Guadalcanal to offer advice on how to fly the machine. He noted that with the virtually nonexistent visibility on three-point landings it was best to put it down on the main gear first. This made for surplus speed, so full flap was necessary to stop before the runway ended. However, he continued, full flap tended to destroy the airflow around the rudder, which could cause loss of directional control on the narrow strip that was let into the coconut grove. If control were lost, the best policy was to try to aim between a couple of the neat rows of coconut trees to tear off the wings and keep the fuselage intact for the sake of survival. Unless, of course, this caused a coconut to fall on the pilot's head. Unburdened of this sage council, he departed.

Actually, it wasn't a bad kite, and its speed and climb were breathtaking after the clumsy Wildcats. The few airplanes available were in sad condition, and the Harvard Man functioning as engineering officer performed miracles, getting most of the limited number in the air. One of the chief problems became abundantly clear in very short order. There was little or no time for familiarization, so combat practice was initiated immediately.

Doing an onshore strafing run on the Turtle Bay strip, and right over the beach, the big engine quit. Fortunately, the speed was very great so it was possible for me to chandelle out of the jungle and head for the water without generating a high-speed stall. Whatever the heavy Corsair was designed for, it wasn't graceful water landings. It hit like a ton of bricks, with the safety harness breaking and a rough encounter with the gun sight causing some disorientation. The hatch, although locked back, slammed shut. Getting it free from the rapidly sinking kite posed a vexing problem. No sooner was this problem solved, and when almost free of the cockpit, the lanyard to the seat-pack life raft tangled on the throttle quadrant. Freeing this while now far under water was equally difficult. However, the crash boat was prompt and its crew very helpful.

The "Other Harvard Man," who was now known as "The Horse" and was a fine vocalist as well as pilot, had a similar experience the same day. The elegant Horse was no ordinary human being, so he had a much more colorful adventure. Besides, he was doing high altitude gunnery when he lost the plant. He started down for the water with plenty of time to prepare. That of course was before it became apparent that he was on fire and dragging an impressive tail of flame. By now he was running out of height and had a real scramble getting out and opening his chute. That would have been enough for one day, but there was more to come.

By great good fortune he came down on dry land. By great bad fortune the dry land was on top of a very high cliff with crashing seas on the rocks below and impenetrable jungle close at his back. This dilemma was solved by some natives who had witnessed his descent and had chopped through to him. Having been to missionary school they were sure that they had witnessed the second coming and bore him away to what may have been the plantation house of later *South Pacific* fame.

The proprietors were a highly civilized French couple, and although it was only midmorning, they offered the highly civilized Horse a highly civilized drink. By lunch time the niceties of civilization had dictated a few more drinks. By this time the crash boat with one of the squadron pilots and the squadron's flight surgeon along had arrived at the plantation's dock, the hosts with the enlarged guest list determined to have a highly civilized lunch replete with the appropriate highly civilized libations. After lunch it was time for the highly civilized cocktail hour with the medicinal brandy that the foresighted flight surgeon had the foresight to bring in quantity for the comfort of the survivor.

It was coming on dark when this party returned to Turtle Bay. Here the worried squadron awaited their arrival with much concern. Concern turned to rage when this highly civilized party stumbled ashore holding each other up and roaring forth the most sophisticated versions of the bawdy ballads.

The struggle to accumulate flying time continued, and the chore of taking and recovering airplanes to and from Guadalcanal afforded at least some time in this type of aircraft. One trip up there was quite instructive. Finding it necessary to remain overnight, shelter was found with the survivors of the sister squadron that had already entered combat with the Corsair. Since the Corsair was still a product of Vought Chance Aircraft, the official navy designation was F4U-2 or, as the pilots now referred to it, a fork you too.

The huge buildup in pilot training had not yet been felt, and like VMF-214 this squadron originally could muster only twenty-one pilots. In a few weeks in combat they were down to eleven. There were plenty of empty cots available, and all of them, along with the remaining tenants, were crowded down at the end farthest from the door of the Quonset hut they occupied. These half-round galvanized iron buildings were beginning to replace the tents. Between this area and the door were several sets of trip wires connected to tin cans or anything that would sound an alarm for the zonked-out pilots. One unfortunate mess cook sent to arouse them for the coming day's battles nearly died, since he was not properly briefed and stumbled over one of the wires in the darkness. The barrage of fire from the rudely awakened pilots was intense but fortunately inaccurate.

There was a reason for all of this security on this weird, black island. The "Sighing of the Dead" was already an established fact. On some bright moonlit nights when there was no bombing it would start. First a deadly silence would fall, and all of the night cries of the birds in the jungle would be stilled. Then, from the direction of Bloody Ridge and Bloody Gulch, it would start as a nearly inaudible sigh rising in crescendo to a moan before fading only to start again. Fear and superstition would not deter a worn-out fighter pilot from his slumber, but the night strangler was something else. With evil intentions this mysterious monster would take his victims by the neck in clawlike hands on dark nights. The accepted version was that it was a mutation or mutations formed by the horrors of war in this dark place. The monster was never shot or captured, and the legend has faded with the other aberrations of the times. At that time and under those circumstances, however, nobody found this aspect of daily life amusing.

Down at Turtle Bay life was pleasant, with swimming in the lagoon and drinking warm beer with the fish fries. The fish fried were mostly barracuda from the same lagoon. Only the training, with the limited number of aircraft, was difficult.

Now the squadron had acquired several replacement pilots for the losses sustained on the first tour. Much better trained than the original pilots had been, they still lacked Corsair time. One poor chap, although a competent pilot and a fine fellow, was replaced by another lad who already had two tours of combat and several victories. Also, one other replacement pilot was a two-tour veteran. Another husky chap right out of flight school was the tough son of missionaries and was soon going to accomplish astounding things. On the other hand, Chuck, whose army brother had killed Admiral Yamamoto, was temporarily detached to be the air controller with the ground troops now engaged in the bitter invasion of New Georgia. He did not even get a chance to check out in the Corsair.

By this time, and due mostly to the enthusiasm of the "Horse," the squadron had a name and an insignia patch testifying to this spirit. The name was "The Swashbucklers," and the squadron didn't even have to get to the combat zone to get it blooded. Over by the Santa Cruz Islands, a couple of hundred miles from Espiritu Santo, a seaplane tender had been hit and was under attack by Japanese airplanes while a destroyer was trying to tow it out. The new major and his division arrived on scene as night was coming down and he flamed one enemy that was confirmed. The Marine Corps was still functioning with honor, so the tough rules of confirming kills applied. The other Japanese bombers, although hard hit, were listed as probables. With this accomplished, the chaps flew home to Turtle Bay where they were in time for the movie. The movie was open-air with coconut log seating.

A short while later the movie was stopped and an excited messenger from headquarters announced that a communication from the destroyer confirmed a clean sweep. All of the Japanese planes involved had been splashed by the Corsairs. This gained the embarrassed hit men wild applause from the other theatergoers.

There was another chance for action on this rear-area island, but it was not so successful. The Japanese occasionally sent down a long-range, four-engine seaplane to photograph the channel. Along with the flares, he dropped a few bombs, or perhaps they were empty saki bottles, which sound about the same on the way down. VMF-214 pilots in collusion with the local radar chaps attempted an intercept. No contact was made, but perhaps this group of Birdcage Corsairs blundering around in the dark of night frightened the intruder so badly that he never returned.

This island was as close to combat as a young navy officer who was being a clerk for SCAT, the transportation squadron, would ever get. Years later when running for president of the United States of America he wished to modestly refer to his extreme heroism under fire in a speech. He placed his right hand in the area where he estimated his heart might be and bowing his head emoted as follows: "As the bombs were falling all I could think of was 'the flag, the flag.'" What then, Mr. Nixon, if the falling bombs were only a few empty saki bottles?

This ended the Corsair training and, ready or not, the war couldn't wait.

XI

For some obscure reason, otherwise intelligent people seemed to think that going up the famous Slot in the Solomon Islands meant going north. Actually, "up" went west by northwest. In that direction from Guadalcanal lay the Russell Islands, consisting of two main islands, Banika, which came first, and, across Sunlight Channel, Pavuvu. MAG (Marine Air Group) 21's colonel and staff had built a wonderful fighter camp on Banika.

Banika will always be remembered as having the whitest coral airstrip in memory. This strip crossed the whole small island in a narrow cut in the stately coconut palms from Sunlight Channel to the deep blue ocean at the east end. The pilots of each four-plane division had their own Dallas hut provided with screening to keep the mosquitoes and flies at bay. The grass under the stately rows of coconut palms had the appearance of having been mowed and gave the area a parklike feeling.

This oasis of civilization had the famous hamburger hut. In a world of execrable cuisine ranging from the infamous Spam to powdered anything, this was indeed remarkable. It was made possible by the same instrument that kept the grass so neatly maintained. This was a herd of cows from the former plantation whose proprietors had fled as the Japanese approached. A certain number of these cows were said to sacrifice their lives to the falling shrapnel from the antiaircraft fire during air raids. What charges the former owners would have levied had they witnessed the deployment of the sharpshooters during these attacks is unknown.

On this island, over at Yellow Beach, there was a PT (patrol torpedo) boat base populated by the natural allies of the fighter pilots. An opportunity to go out on one of their speedy craft on a search for a downed air group pilot afforded an unexpected adventure. As the war moved up the Slot, these go-to-hell young men established a base up at Rendova, an island across from Munda airfield, the better to interdict the Japanese barges and destroyers reinforcing Vila on Kolombangara island. They were getting a lot of tough action in Blackett Strait, and MAG-21 resolved to help them. To this end the MAG-21 executive officer strapped on an SBD dive-bomber and on a black night flew up there with illumination flares to light up the scene. The plan was for the Corsairs lurking in the darkness to then strafe the lit-up barges or destroyers. Unfortunately, the first flare hung up in the tail of his aircraft and he was killed.

About this time one of the PT boats was involved in an action that years later became famous. The name of the boat was PT-109, and it was used to demonstrate the heroism of its young skipper under fire when he ran for president of the United States. This action included the boat getting cut in half by a Japanese destroyer and had nothing to do with empty saki bottles falling from the sky.

An interesting sidelight to the operations of the PT boats was the air group's endeavors to help control the barges that were reinforcing Kololambara and later evacuating it. Sometimes at dawn the barges had not reached cover, and a fighter flight could wreak havoc on a deck-load of troops. The word got around, so at any sign of aircraft the Japanese occupants would jump overboard and when the planes were gone climb back on. This circumstance was remedied by splitting a division; two planes would chase the people into the water, and after they were climbing back aboard, the other two fighters would come out of the rising sun to do their thing. When the Japanese realized this, they would stay in the water so long that all planes would have to be gone. The final solution was to go through this evolution and then, with all of those people in the water, send in a TBF to drop a depth charge or two.

The brutal invasion of New Georgia was now well underway, and the squadron got plenty of work. With the increased range afforded by the Corsair, the bomber escorts on strikes against the airfields on Bougainville island became feasible. The main base there was at Kahili, and the army B-24s now stationed at Guadalcanal would come over Banika, where the fighters would rendezvous with them for the long haul to the target area.

By the time Bougainville hove into view, the fighters would be very high in their protective scissors over the bombers. At this altitude it would be miserably cold in the thin air, and the fighter engines would be maintaining their manifold pressure with high blower while the pilots maintained life with their oxygen masks. At this time the fifty-five gallon wingtip tanks would be purged with CO_2, since these were not self-sealing and a tracer or incendiary round would flame the Corsair. The other risks concerned loss of oxygen and loss of manifold pressure, either of which could occur accidentally or from the guns of the Flying Circus.

The Flying Circus was composed of Japanese Zero fighters usually hanging off to one side and often doing slow rolls and other aerobatics. They had a habit of placing a lone Zero in a vulnerable position as bait to lure a reckless pilot out of the protective scissors, and then the other Zeros could fall on him.

This gambit put paid to the pilot who had the navy wings tattooed on his chest along with his squadron number before leaving Hawaii. He was a genuine, natural-born pilot and used to put on one-man air shows and do things with the primitive Corsair of that era that were theoretically impossible. Of course, he was known as "Wings." So far he had not shot down an airplane, and that troubled him deeply.

As his squadron scissored over the bombers at Kahili he called the squadron commander on his VHF radio. These radios were a startling improvement in clarity over the nearly inaudible low-frequency radios in the old Wildcats. "I am going down and kill that SOB," he announced, referring to the Zero who was being the bait.

"Don't do it, Wings," counseled the leader. "We can't leave the bombers, and you leave this scissors and you are dead."

"I'm going to do it," said Wings. "I'll get down there and back up before they get me."

The squadron skipper voiced his final concern. Every pilot had only one valued possession, since venerating other personal possessions under the current circumstances was pointless. This treasure was his slender secret store of booze.

"Where," his leader demanded, "did you hide your whiskey, Wings?" Unsportingly, Wings deigned not to answer as he made his first and last successful run on a Zero.

All too often the B-24s rained their bombs down in the water off the end of the enemy air base. This used to infuriate the Corsair pilots and supply the resident Japanese with a good supply of freshly stunned fish. On one escort a B-24 that had been hit over the target had lost an engine and was falling behind the formation and smoking. If the other B-24s had slowed up, the Zeros could have been beaten back. Instead the other B-24s pointed their noses down in the direction of Guadalcanal and poured on the coal, abandoning their comrade to the Flying Circus. The Harvard Man was outraged and led his division back to have it out with a vast number of Zeros. This put the four Corsairs in a rat race of unbelievable violence. It was impossible to concentrate on any one Zero, and although there were flamers going out of the brawl, no claims were sustained for kills. Any possible confirmation that could have come from the crippled B-24 vanished when it finally started burning fiercely and a wing tore off. None of the crew that gained their chutes were ever recovered, and they probably were dead when they reached the water with the Zeros strafing them. Fortunately, all four battered Corsairs landed at Banika, where the Harvard Man poured some more fuel in his kite and took off for Guadalcanal to have words with the army.

These long-range escorts before the fall of Munda had a new and very troubling aspect. Heretofore, the preponderance of air combat had been close to home. This gave a pilot in trouble a greater chance of survival than being far up a line of islands populated by unfriendlies. The only possible emergency strip was at Seghi, which was under construction on the southeastern end of New Georgia. New Georgia was the next island up the chain from VMF-214's strip on Banika in the Russells. Munda itself was on the western end of New Georgia, farther up the island. This strip was to figure in a personal adventure for me.

One escort only required twelve planes to be supplied by 214 for the large fighter cover. With the usual mechanical difficulties with the Birdcage Corsairs, only six of them arrived over target, and these had joined with divisions from other squadrons to rather haphazardly fill out the integrity of the defensive scissors. At thirty-some thousand feet in the crossing altitudes while turning back from the outer limit of the scissors, there was a jarring bang and my kite started dropping out of the formation. A quick look at the instruments showed the manifold pressure falling drastically. One thing the heavy, well-streamlined Corsair could do was outdive a Zero, so a quick split–S ending in a vertical descent for the deck was initiated to get away from the Flying Circus.

Care had to be taken in prolonged dives in the Corsair because of a dangerous characteristic. Whereas the old Wildcat fighters had a terminal velocity, the Corsair had none, and after a certain speed there would be severe buffeting and loss of control. This was later called compressibility and was caused by the thickness of the wing not allowing the air to flow smoothly as the kite approached the speed of sound.

As the altimeter unwound, the manifold pressure increased marginally, and when finally all alone at minimum altitude, it was time to contemplate salvation. The incomplete emergency strip at Seghi came to mind and soon into view. It seemed to be mostly composed of down timber and mud and was extremely modest in its proposed length. Desperation and terror are known to drastically improve fly-

ing skills, and after a few monumental bounces and much flying mud
the Corsair was stopped short of the jungle and in one piece. That was
more than could be said for the only other flying machine in evidence.
This was another Corsair that didn't have such luck and would never
fly again.

Some of the mud-spattered chaps present soon had the cowling
off and pointed out a large hole in the ductwork behind the engine.
Whoever these filthy young men were, they apparently knew something about mechanical things and soon proudly announced that they
had riveted a patch on the ductwork. It looked suspiciously like the
bottom of a tin tomato can. Upon winding up the engine the manifold pressure held, so all that remained was to see if the airplane could
be gotten out of there without a barge.

With full flap and everything firewalled, the old bird threw a lot
of mud around and scattered the tops of the trees at the end of the
run, but praise be to Icarus she was flying. The run down to Banika
was uneventful, but there was a surprise reception. The side number
on this airplane was a large fifteen. Another of the few 214 pilots who
reached the target had a number fifteen Corsair blow up right beside
him in the mixed-up escort. Fortunately, arrival put paid to the
search for the whiskey of the, until now, missing pilot. It was soon
found that there was another side number fifteen belonging to another
squadron. Rejoining the living is always such a relief.

All of MAG-21's squadrons, plus any other fighter outfits in the
area, participated in these strikes, including the superior New Zealand
outfit that was flying out of the strip on Pavuvu. Unfortunately, they
were flying the inferior American P-40s. These were the type of airplanes flown by the Flying Tigers in China. They had some successes
there, but the Japanese didn't use either their first-team pilots or best
aircraft in that theater. Fighting in this show, the limitations of this
airplane cost the splendid New Zealanders dearly, despite their determination and aggressive tactics.

These P-40s caused the replacement pilot, "The Son of Missionaries" whose real name was Bob, some confusion with his first vic-

tory. On his very first combat flight he was lagging behind the formation with a badly running engine, which would have sent a lesser
man home. One of the first Japanese "Tony" fighters, with an in-line
engine, came out of the clouds, confident that he had the last man in
the formation boresighted. His run placed him between the main body
and the trailing Bob, who was a champion college wrestler. He proved
that he was also a champion shot. At first it was believed that he had
creamed a New Zealand P-40, since the Tony was wearing markings
similar to the ones painted on the P-40s for identification. No P-40s
were missing, and subsequent intelligence further substantiated his
claim.

The road to Kahili was paved with American airplanes and high
adventure. At one time the "Opium Den" (the command) got so tired
of the army's fish-killing expeditions that they ordered everything that
would fly to attack Kahili, from SBD dive-bombers with auxiliary
tanks to the cumbersome TBF torpedo planes that employed a tactic
called glide bombing. At this precarious trade they were quite accurate. Aside from the fighter cover, other fighters were assigned to go
down on flak suppression to try to neutralize the heavy ground fire.
Nowhere was this fire more intense and accurate than on Ballale just
offshore from Kahili. If the intelligence of the day was accurate, this
hellhole played host to all of the British guns captured at Singapore.
Any pilot who ever made a flak suppression run there certainly believed it. On one run the sight of a TBF pulling out with too much
enthusiasm and having both wings peel off was most memorable. This
show continued from very high altitudes down to the deck with plenty
of action at all levels.

On one of these actions, the chap who said "I got a million of
'em cornered" at Guadalcanal, before being shot down, got his division into another regrettable situation. One of the lads with him
was a very popular second lieutenant who was newly field-commis-
sioned from tech sergeant pilot. He along with three other enlisted
pilots had already been on the first combat tour where one of their
number had been the first man killed. In an action fought from a

decided disadvantage of the leader's making, he went missing and ultimately was never heard from again.

Back at the Banika strip there was some hard talk, and the suggestion was made that the fearless leader should be banned from leading divisions. Unfortunately, due to seniority, he was now the squadron's executive officer, which translates into second in command.

In wild fights people could get separated from their formations and even wind up without another airplane in the sky. This happened to another pilot who found himself all alone and out of sight of land. That wasn't so bad but for the fact that numerous bullet holes had disabled his compass. In a well-remarked episode of the war, this resourceful young man performed the acrobatic miracle of digging out the small waterproof matchbox from his jungle pack. The head of this box had a compass about the size of a dime. Holding it between his knees to minimize the deviation, and estimating the variation, he got back to the island chain and home. Necessity is indeed a mother.

Another such case was a TBM (torpedo plane) pilot who found himself all alone and was sneaking home down the coast of Choiseul island when a Zero fighter appeared on his wing. Its grinning pilot assumed that the turret gunner was dead since he was not visible. He was making motions for the TBF pilot to turn around and go back and land at Kahili to become a prisoner.

If there was one constant terror that aircrews fighting the Japanese entertained it was becoming a prisoner. In the European theater the Germans were a civilized race and the prisoners had a good chance of survival. This was not the case with the Japanese, who beat, tortured, starved, and made slave laborers out of those who fell into their clutches. Those were just the lucky ones who were not beheaded or employed in medical experiments.

Fortunately, the turret gunner was actually quite healthy. He was down on the floor of the turret gathering the few loose rounds and link shoes scattered there after the prolonged firing during the attack. By the time he had belted up this pitiful supply the Zero pilot was becoming more vehement in his gestures and the TBM chap was doing his best to pretend ignorance. This vaudeville act distracted the enemy from observing the turret gunner as he completed his arrangements. At nearly point-blank range the gunner blew the stupid bastard into a bloody mess. The TBM crew figured that nobody would believe this tale, but here they were wrong. An Australian coast watcher verified the essential facts. This coast watcher was involved with another bizarre action soon after.

One division coming off target at Kahili had the leader hit by a lucky long-range burst from a member of the Flying Circus. This killed his engine and he was far from home, surrounded by hostiles with designs on his scalp. The other three planes in the division stayed with him. Since they had been on high cover, they had a lot of altitude to use. The chap with the dead engine elected to enter a fairly steep glide over to Choiseul to both get as far from the action as possible and maintain a high speed to make the runs of the attackers difficult. He intended to continue until he got right down on the water and could level off and ditch. Before the horrified eyes of his mates he did not pull out but crashed at high speed at a steep angle. The pilots and the Zeros whom they were holding at bay went home, and both friend and foe reported him killed.

Many days later the "Poop Sheet" (an informal little newsletter around the combat camps) reported a strange occurrence. The coast watcher on Choiseul had advised that he had a Corsair pilot who was in bad shape in his possession. It turned out to be an incredible story. When the pilot reached the water he pulled the stick back to level off, but the kite did not level off, probably due to the controls to the elevators having been hit. After uttering that final expletive that pilots in extremis employ, he knew no more for some time. Then he had a hard time figuring out who he was and where he was. He seemed to be floating in salt water with one half of his Mae West inflated, and he could tell that he was seriously and perhaps fatally hurt. After an indeterminate time drifting that could have been hours or days, he sighted a beach. How long it took to get on the beach and by what torture could not be estimated. Nor could the time spent gathering a small store of strength or what he ate.

Next he nearly walked into a Japanese camp and lay behind a tree as they practically walked over him; he could hear them talking. Retreating when dark came, he was now terrified of meeting anyone. So successful was he at hiding that the natives who had heard rumors and were looking for him had a devil of a time getting him. By then he was out of his head from his injuries and exposure. The coast watcher called for an immediate evacuation, which brought a PBY flying boat with a fighter escort to take him off the island. Encountering this chap a few years after massive rebuilding, he looked a great deal like his former handsome self, but he would never be that young again.

During the war, there were so many incredible survival stories that they went largely unreported. Some of these included people living for unreal lengths of time in the sea, mostly in their little rubber rafts, but on a few occasions with only a Mae West life preserver. At one time, all of the original pilots from MAG-21 had either bailed out or ditched, and not a few had done both and more than once.

Of course, the squadrons operating with MAG-21 were also experiencing extraordinary adventures. One of them discovered that any ideas that may have been entertained about gentlemanly conduct in aerial combat did not apply with the Japanese. This chap, having had his airplane shot out from under him, took to his parachute and was doing what was known in the vernacular of the day as a "nylon letdown." Hanging here defenseless, he was attacked by a Zero pilot who opened fire. He managed to pull himself up by his chute risers, causing the slugs to pass below him. This maneuver was repeated several times until the Zero apparently ran out of ammunition. By then the chap in the parachute was so exhausted that he could no longer pull himself out of harm's way. That's when the raging Jap made a ramming run and severed one of his legs and his other heel with his prop.

In this incredible saga of survival, the badly injured pilot hit the water, somehow got his raft inflated, and rigged a tourniquet on the leg. Fortunately, he was soon picked up. In an aftermath of this episode the top admiral of the Pacific promised the pilot that he could fly again when he recovered. He ultimately not only flew again, he flew the Corsair again.

After that, any of the few Japanese pilots to parachute seldom reached the water—perhaps never, if there were marine pilots present with any ammunition aboard. Of course, no marine pilot would ever strike a hanging body with his prop, out of deference to the mechanics who would then have to clean up the mess.

Another pilot who had an interesting experience with a parachute didn't realize that the intense fire he was taking from a Zero on his tail had totally destroyed his chute right under his posterior. Of course, his attention was distracted by the total destruction of the Corsair. Imagine his surprise when he found himself a couple of thousand feet above the blue Pacific with a nonparachute.

He reported that on the way down, with nothing else much to do, he became worried about his survival and inflated his Mae West life jacket. The surgeons said that if he hadn't done this, such was the perfect angle at which he hit, perhaps he would even have escaped the fractures in his lower back. Not only did *he* fly again, he was last encountered instructing operational training in Corsairs at El Toro. He was not the only one, but one of the very few who survived the long fall during the war. (After all, in a free fall from a plane, the terminal velocity of the human body averages a mere 128 miles an hour. Naval personnel are invited to convert this into knots.)

The Battle for Munda was moving forward. Both marine and army troops were involved, and this is where the squadron's detached pilot Chuck (brother of Yamamoto slayer Tom) was serving as the forward air controller for the air support. One day he walked into camp at Banika and announced that he was done with that duty and was rejoining the squadron. He had little good to report concerning the morale of the invading forces. The other problem was that he had never had the opportunity to check out in the Corsair airplane. Fortunately, along with almost everything else this unusual young man had attempted in life, he was an unusually competent pilot. His checkout and first familiarization flight in this demanding and problematic aircraft were condensed into one flight, and that took place on a hair-raising combat attack on Kahili. As some humorists sarcastically reported, he apparently passed that check ride. A few tough missions later he shot down a Japanese airplane in the Corsair.

XII

VMF-214 had always been a lucky squadron with high morale, but this was about to come to an end in a series of misfortunes. Some of this was attributable to the mechanical difficulties of the primitive Corsairs. These growing pains not only made combat operations more hazardous, but also any operations. On a test flight for an engine problem, one of the really great pilots, who had come to 214 after his squadron went home, suffered violent engine stoppage at high altitude. He dove down to get in heavy enough air to make bailing out more practical, and then decided that he could dead-stick into the strip. Coming in short, he did a perilous ditching procedure just offshore, but due to his ability and experience he escaped, despite being somewhat banged up.

Next came the squadron commander who volunteered to test-fly another Corsair with similar problems. When his engine blew up he also set off for the strip and would probably have made it if a SCAT transport (DC-3) hadn't taxied out on the strip in front of him. Although a splendid leader, he was hampered by a lack of experience. He tried to jump at about a hundred feet. This left 214 with the now thoroughly unpopular "man who had a million of 'em cornered" as the Squadron CO. About the only thing now holding the outfit together was the strength of the Harvard Man, Henry (Hank) Miller, who was now the executive officer.

The pilots from another squadron were kind enough to take one of VMF-214's strikes so they could bury their major. In those days very few fighter pilots got buried by their mates, since just not returning was the more normal procedure. Not much later in the day, 214 took off on another strike.

The bitter and prolonged battle for Munda on New Georgia was beginning to bear fruit. The airstrip fell, and a few days later fighters started landing in the most hellish conditions since Guadalcanal. VMF-214 was later given credit for being first, but that was not true, although they landed on the same day as the first airplanes.

Despite the loss of the airstrip, the Japanese were making a major issue out of Munda, sending in a lot of air strikes. Many of these, due to the still prevalent radar problems and general mismanagement, were getting in and out scot-free. The heavy bombardment strikes to Bougainville were killing more fish than they were intimidating Japanese. This wasn't doing much for the morale of the fighter pilots whose attrition rates were running high on this chore.

This gave the Harvard Man an opportunity to distinguish himself. As usual, he was the same self-effacing, courteous, and efficient leader who often managed to provide some exciting times for the pilots flying with him. The four pilots in his division along with four from another division were enjoying that rarest of occasions, a day off from the meat grinder.

The genteel hobby being pursued over at a makeshift machine shop was sharpening a butcher knife for the jungle survival pack. It was believed that these would be quite handy for disemboweling a Japanese if capture were imminent when shot down. Into this peaceful and worthy pursuit a recklessly driven jeep intruded, and the driver said "Cummon, you're wanted over in the Opium Den." That is where a lot of otherwise intelligent people hatched plots to win the war.

The air combat intelligence officer, Peter Folger, who did this only out of patriotism (his day job was scion of one of the country's

leading social and cultural families as well as the president of one of
the world's largest coffee companies) seemed to be presiding. There
were also some other grim-looking pilots and the radiant Harvard
Man. Although only a captain, he had clout far beyond his rank. Never
known to take credit for anything or even to claim to have shot down
an airplane, he routinely pulled the fat out of the fire.

What Hank Miller had done with his day off was fly down to the
supreme Opium Den at Guadalcanal and, over precious little opposition, sell them on his "Plan of the Day." Since the only real way to
deal with the enemy was up close and personal, his plan was a dandy
for anybody sitting in an operations room and making comments on
the progress of the clock and speculating on the fate of the warriors.

It was now midafternoon, and with two divisions of pilots (eight)
and with enough spare and/or marginal Corsairs available, the time
had come. About dusk a large Japanese strike force was going to be
returning to Kahili aerodrome from the furious attacks on the Munda
landings. Leaving right now and making the entire dogleg transit at
wavetop height, he figured that with his meticulous navigation the
eight jolly marines could afford the Japanese a warm and surprise wel-
come-home party. With no further ado, the two divisions cranked up,
and joined by two other volunteers who would act as spares, took off
to accomplish a running rendezvous at not more than 100 feet altitude in order to preserve secrecy. This was going to be a long jaunt,
so the formation loosened up to ease the strain of formation flying at
this altitude. The course led northwest by north between Santa Isabel
and Choiseul Islands, both with Japanese occupancy. Once out of the
Slot, the course bent to the left parallel to Choiseul, which was kept
just below the horizon. By now one of the Corsairs was in failing
health, and its disgusted pilot was forced to turn for home and was
replaced by one of the spares. Not long after, the Harvard Man wag-
gled his wings as a signal to the other spare to leave, since he did not
want an extra airplane to complicate his exact plan. As the late afternoon wore on, the loose gaggle made a substantial left turn and came
on to the final heading for the attack. Still out of sight of land, the

leader bounced his airplane up and down as a signal to close up the formation and get into a compact line abreast.

After a considerable time in this configuration, the coast of Bougainville grew out of the sea, and all the forty-eight .50-caliber machine guns were charged. Normally, on strafing attacks only four of the six guns per plane would be used. This would reserve two in case it was necessary for the strafers to shoot their way out. With dark coming down, this would not be necessary, nor would be firing in bursts to preserve the gun barrels.

Now the marines were roaring over the jungle at treetop height and up and over the ridge, exposing Kahili aerodrome. It was later discovered that after hundreds of miles and several course changes, the Harvard Man was off on his estimated time of arrival by something over one minute. This was rather astounding, considering that he navigated with the aid of a dollar watch hanging from his gun sight and had a few wind changes en route.

Also astounding was the view of the field. In the evening light there were people all over the place, with gas trucks, taxiing airplanes, and, best of all, some Japanese pilots on their final landing approaches. After their exertions killing Americans down at Munda they were no doubt looking forward to a drink of saki and some wild bragging. With the guns already hammering, it took only a minor course deviation to send one such hopeful to join his ancestors, which reportedly was extremely pleasing to a Japanese. Some of the other chaps were also able to provide this service, but the main chore remained the same, and the volume of .50-caliber was quite effective. In fact, this caper was described by Admiral Samuel Morison in the *History of United States Naval Operations in World War II*. He said that many a sailor on the Love-Sugar-Tares at Munda owed his life to this surprise raid. In the phonetic alphabet of the day, that stood for LSTs, which were landing ships tank. (An LSD, on the other hand, was a large steel desk manned by many a self-admitted naval hero.)

Morison's account, although naming some of the pilots, ignored the Harvard Man in accordance with the policy of not giving any more credit than necessary to anyone who had been in the RCAF. This was most notable in the case of Donald Aldrich, who shot down twenty airplanes. All other marines who reached this level got the Medal of Honor.

By now the tropical dark was upon the warriors, who were somewhat disorganized due to concentration on individual targets, and several close calls with the terrain were encountered on the way out. At any rate, the formation was soon well tucked in and flying without lights and keeping station by exhaust flames.

Down in the darkness were the wakes of a task force, which may well have been commanded by the redoubtable Thirty-One Knot Burke (or however many knots he was). Although the Harvard Man flashed the recognition code with the lights in the belly of his Corsair, the surface ships responded with a heavy and remarkably accurate antiaircraft fire, which required strenuous evasive action. Also remarkable were the recognition lights and code, which were probably known only to the ever-meticulous Harvard Man.

After a long flight through the impenetrable Solomon Islands night, while nervously inspecting declining gas gauges, the Russell Islands were sighted. This was easy since they were hosting a Japanese air raid with searchlights and bursting antiaircraft (AA) fire. Some fine and responsible leader had the landing lights on the strip lighted anyway, and a long day was coming to a close. The chaps were almost, but not completely, too tired to preclude arm waving and bragging, or the nightcap that at least some of the Japanese were denied. Again the Harvard Man's navigation was within minutes of ETA.

Long before dawn, the same pilots were rousted out and assembled for briefing. The Harvard Man, flushed with success, figured that an exact repeat could be accomplished at dawn. Since everybody else was speechless, I, as the only other veteran of the RCAF present, suggested that every gun at Kahili was no doubt now sighted in on that ridge. This slightly puzzled the Harvard Man, who somewhat embarrassedly pointed out that perhaps, with the war and all, personal safety should take a back seat.

Not much later a message came in that an army airplane on a weather search up the Slot reported heavy weather was blanking out the target. God bless the army.

With the airstrip, and not much other real estate at Munda in allied hands, things got even more frantic. The squadron started inserting some of its strength on the strip into certain operations, like combat air patrols and protecting the small invasion of Vella Lavella, an island between New Georgia and Bougainville. The call name of Vella Lavella was "Serious Base." Often when the squadron arrived too late, there would be bomb smoke coming up from the beachhead, which put paid to Serious Base's transmissions. These would start with Serious Base vectoring fighters off on wild goose chases. Next, growing more earnest, they would start hollering, "Serious Base under attack," and conclude with, "Serious Base going off the air." One could visualize the radio operator chucking his microphone and diving for a hole. Often, but not always, the fighters would get there in time to observe the rising smoke but no attackers.

Munda had practically no maintenance facilities, and what little food could be found was at an improvised chow line crawling with flies down by the beach. When not flying, in order to escape the shelling on the airstrip, this was a favored spot. One day down, I was down there with a young friend from another squadron, watching the Japanese dive-bombers withdrawing from a nearby attack. The inevitable topic arose: "Just how the hell did you get into this mess?"

This young fellow was of such economical stature that he used a pillow in the generously proportioned cockpit of the Corsair in order to reach the rudder pedals. His demeanor was equally modest and innocuous. Aside from that, he was a stone killer with a growing reputation. He explained that to go to school he had had to work in a service station.

"Have you ever," he asked bleakly, "had to clean out a women's toilet?" Apparently that even made flying fighters for the United States Marine Corps look pretty good. Then the conversation wandered to "Flaps."

Flaps had been a squadron mascot, and a very cosmopolitan dog he was. He started out as a small, friendly cocker spaniel that had fallen in with evil company—to wit, a fighter squadron. He was brought along when the squadron deployed to the Pacific. He was the first in the foxholes during attacks and had been on a leave to Sydney, Australia, with the other members of his squadron, where it was believed that he had taken part in all the pleasures available to the others. When he and his friends returned to combat, it was noted that he had ridden in cars, trains, ships, buses, and airplanes, and it was believed that at some time in his past he had ridden on the subway.

The only lapse in Flaps' record was that he had never flown in combat. This was rectified when he shared a cockpit with a small pilot on a scramble. As luck would have it, they got in the fighting, so Flaps was a genuine combat veteran. After that, and as a result of a lot of finagling, he got back to the States and was sent to a farm belonging to the parents of one of his squadron mates. This was supposed to be a rest cure but turned out badly. His conduct deteriorated until he was attacking children and had to be destroyed.

In the light of more recent history, Flaps did better than the professional war dogs of Vietnam. These were well trained and accompanied the troops on dangerous patrols. Their heroic and loyal actions were credited with saving at least ten thousand American lives in that sorry conflict. Always seeking a solution to the "veteran problem," the leaders of democracy (and the free world) did not bring these dogs home, but destroyed them in-country. It must be admitted that this prevented them from begging on the streets of San Francisco like the two-legged veterans or urinating on the fireplugs of Pacific Heights.

It was decided right then that war isn't good for man nor beast. This certainly applied to my small friend. When his squadron went home, he had an impressive score. He was killed when a Corsair he was testing at a stateside base augered straight in before the horrified eyes of most of the squadron and their dependents, who were getting ready to go on a picnic after he landed. At least he never had to return to the women's bathrooms.

Eventually, the Japanese artillery found the range of the chow line at Munda, with fatal results for some hungry marines. The smell of death from rotting Japanese bodies was overpowering, and the flies dispensed dysentery with a generous hand.

About this time there was an interesting episode during a scramble. The Corsair assigned to me was in an abandoned Japanese revetment on what was called "the back taxi loop." After I jumped off the speeding truck in full gear and set a record for scrambling up and into the lofty cockpit, things started to go to hell in a hand basket.

Some of these early Corsairs had a shotgun starter like the old Wildcats. This was reached by opening a flap just aft of the engine and inserting a shotgun shell in a breach. The plane captain standing on the wing performed this chore, and then the pilot fired it from the cockpit. This spun the propeller and the engine caught, but not always. Down at Guadalcanal, on the old Wildcats they had had an interesting device in case the shotgun shells didn't do the trick during scrambles. Then the shout would go out, "Get the boot." The boot was a sleeve that would fit over a prop blade and was fitted with a very long bungee cord of impressive diameter. The prop would be rotated to compression, and every available man in the vicinity would lay to on the bungee and run with it. When the tension was sufficient, the engine spun with enough vigor to usually start it. This, of course, suddenly released the tension on the bungee. The sight of strong men falling on their asses in formation would have been quite amusing under other circumstances. Here on Munda such high-tech options were not available.

Just before the breech was closed, the Japanese started laying artillery rounds all about, and the plane captain fled. Around the revetment the exploding shells looked like a scene from a cheap John Wayne movie, and there were a number of people running for their lives. One of these, who turned out to be an army chap, ran right into the revetment seeking solace. This he was denied, and he ran right up on the wing when screamed at. With some frantic exchanges of ideas, it was established that he was a southern "good ole boy" and understood shotgun breeches perfectly. What he didn't understand was that he could have told a frightened marine officer to go to hell. As this angel in ragged fatigues got the breech loaded, the artillery really got the range. One round exploded with a blinding flash on top of the stone revetment to the right just as the engine fired. With the bloodcurdling scream of the shrapnel, the Corsair rocked. The southern gentleman was rewarded for his good deed by being blown off the wing by the prop blast as the old kite accelerated like a jackrabbit bound for the end of the strip. Fortunately, and for obvious reasons, this gentleman was never encountered again.

Formal engine warm-ups and magneto checks, under the circumstances, were for the lace panty set. With everything firewalled, the Corsair leaped into the air, but this was not a good idea. It shook almost uncontrollably, and getting it around and back on the ground provided a few gut-clenching minutes. The shrapnel had dug some deep scars in the prop, and why this didn't shake the engine right out of the airframe was almost inexplicable.

A lad in another squadron had a very interesting experience with this artillery. Somehow nobody thinks of the high trajectory of this fire. When just entering the traffic pattern he had a wing blown off by an artillery shell. His actions had to be of the highest quality in getting out of a Birdcage Corsair with so little advance notice and at such a low altitude. Landing in the jungle close to the strip, he wound up with his chute tangled in a tree. When he hollered for help, some of his fellow Americans emerged below him with automatic weapons and advised him to shut up before they killed him. They were well behind Japanese lines and were reluctant to draw attention to themselves. Once that formality was taken care of, they got him down and back to his own kind.

Now being without an airplane, it appeared that my only way out of this hell would be to get a ride on a SCAT Transport. This "Go to Hell" airline was not only already doing evacuations, they were dropping supplies at practically zero altitude to the beleaguered troops. These guys all wanted to be fighter pilots anyway. Before the day was over, however, there was the opportunity to ferry a crippled but fly-able Corsair back to the Russells. With some others in the same boat, the plan was to leave at dusk to avoid any unfriendlies.

When night comes abruptly to the tropics, it is literally like the lights going out. That was all right, except that the worthless airplane got only a few miles toward home and the engine started seriously cutting out. It was either get out or go back. Getting out at such a low altitude in the inky blackness was quite unappetizing. After a nervous trip back to Munda, I noted with joy that a flare path was down one side of the strip. Having once practiced on a simulated RAF operational flare path in the RCAF, it was reassuring to know which side of this string of flares to land on. On the ground there was some news to give pause. This flare path had been on both sides of the strip until a bomber in distress had wiped out one side of it a very short time before. Thank God he hadn't wiped out the wrong side. What passed for operations said that they didn't know anything about single-lane flare paths.

That miserable night was spent in a muddy dugout with another stray member of the squadron and a navy man who was in an advanced state of hysteria, as the shelling came in all night. The next day a ride was secured with a friend flying for SCAT Transport, who obligingly did an unscheduled stop on Banika in the Russells on his way out to the rear area.

That brief life at Munda left its own scars. A few days after getting back to Banika, the Sea Bees were doing a little blasting in the vicinity of the ready tent. The first explosion resulted in violent personal contact with the ground, as the chaps who hadn't been shelled as yet laughed uproariously. They wouldn't be laughing too much longer.

It looked at that time like the leadership problem fo   IF-214 was going to be solved and a fine major with the unlikel nickname of "Peggy" would be joining. Unfortunately, it was determined that he had little if any fighter experience, so he was sent to a TBF squadron, where he was very popular, but only for a very brief time.

The TBF was the large, cumbersome torpedo plane that was being used by the marines mostly for glide bombing, which was just short of dive-bombing. On occasion it was used to sow mines or drop clusters of 100-pound fragmentation bombs. Soon after joining his new squadron, "Peggy" came into Munda, with his bombs aboard after a "frag" run. What he didn't know was that the fragmentation bombs had released all right, but the bomb bay doors had not opened, and the bombs were lying down there armed. He shut down the engine and was nearly out of the cockpit when the crew chief hollered up to him, "How about opening the doors, Peggy?" He obligingly reached back into the cockpit. Better he should have been in fighters.

After not much rest I went back to Munda, but that didn't last long. Malaria was the curse of the Solomon Islands and had been held at bay with Atabrine tablets. These quinine substitutes made the skinny, unhealthy fighter pilots' sallow complexions turn a yellowish tinge. At Munda the "Bug," the vernacular for malaria, got through the defenses, producing a condition of fever and chills that cannot be described, only experienced. This time the ride out was on a hospital plane.

A memorable fellow traveler turned out to be a navy lieutenant who, with some other wild-looking specimens, had been sunk on the cruiser *Helena* in the Kulu Gulf a few days before and then survived on the Japanese-infested island of Kolombangara until rescued. He adamantly refused to give up some Japanese heads that he had apparently separated from their rightful owners. The great navy nurses on those evacuation flights would never make it in the movies but would easily qualify in the angel business. One of those SCAT nurses was the originator of the "Mile High Club," which maintains to this day. With their kind consent, the lieutenant was last seen in possession of the unshrunken heads.

Now the view of Banika was from the primitive sick bay until large doses of quinine got the patient back on his shaky legs. The other patient from the squadron was the amiable "Ledge," whose father had been a fighter pilot in the First World War and possessed impeccable

Ivy League credentials. A little time was allowed for recuperation before returning to operations.

Of the many weird schemes of the war, one was a real humdinger. The nation's popular picture magazine, caught up in the glamour of it all, came to the conclusion that primitive people were suckers for junk jewelry. Therefore, any pilot who found himself out of luck and in the vicinity of natives should have in his possession some junk jewelry. This was based on the premise that if the early Dutch could purchase Manhattan Island from the gullible natives, so too could America's young men do business with the natives in the islands.

A large pasteboard box of this glittering ten-cent-store finery had been duly delivered to the squadron. The two recovering patients had made friends with, of all things, some U.S. Coast Guard sailors who had some landing craft in the Russell Islands. With fishing gear and packed lunches, this afforded an adventure not accorded many warriors of the South Seas. Some of the picturesque native villages around the islands, although allegedly off-limits, were visited with the happy Coast Guardsmen, who indicated that the officers could take the responsibility for these transgressions.

It must be reported that the Russell Island natives were apparently more sophisticated than the ones in New York. Nary a pig nor virgin was to be had for the jewelry. Finally, in disgust, the whole lot was bestowed on the puzzled population of one village. Then with some of the reliable Australian florins, a matched set of cat's-eyes and some mother-of-pearl inlaid clubs were purchased at probably inflated prices.

XIII

While still somewhat shaky from the malaria, the failed jewelry salesmen, Ledge Hazelwood and I, were given a couple of Corsairs to join the rest of the squadron, which was doing hard time at Munda. Malingering was not considered cricket at that stage of World War II.

The master plan was to ultimately take a location for an airstrip on Bougainville in order to mount attacks on Rabaul. The stepping stone for this operation was to be the strip at the newly invaded island of Vella Lavella between Munda and Kahili. Already this strip was taking shape at the beachhead on that island. Needless to say, the Japanese disapproved of this plan and were vigorously opposing it. The action was getting even hotter up at Kahili and its immediate vicinity. Fighter sweeps and escorts were seeing a lot of excitement.

Some interesting speculation on tactics often arose during the evening cocktail hour after some of these actions. The most recurring one concerned evasive action and went something like this: When a fighter is on your tail and starts firing, it is, of course, considered quite prudent to skid your airplane to cause him to miss. Now comes the dilemma. When he becomes aware of this, will he correct his fire to compensate for this, or will he assume that you will now skid the other way, or will you, assuming that he will do this, continue the skid in

the same direction or will he . . . ? Since this could never be satisfactorily resolved, it was best to refresh the aluminum canteen cup with
more raw whiskey and the local limes, which grew wild and were free.

The U.S. Army pilots in Europe were claiming aircraft destroyed
on the ground for kills in their scores, as had the Flying Tigers in
China. The marines did not permit this, since they reasoned that the
only sporting thing to do was to shoot them on the wing. Had this not
been in effect, one of VMF-214's former enlisted pilots would have
been number one at that time. He got into this situation through an
unusual series of events.

There were now more squadrons coming out, and although better trained in the States, their local knowledge was sometimes lacking. One predawn strafing mission to Kahili was to be led by a
division from one of these squadrons and included a couple of VMF-
214's divisions. The predawn launch got screwed up, and as they were
getting ready to take off, a Japanese bombing attack laying a lot of high
explosives nearly in their laps didn't help. All mixed up and disorganized, they proceeded anyway. Before dawn they were getting close to
the target when the leader flew into what developed into a serious
weather front. Now they were really screwed up. The former sergeant
pilot came out of the weather some miles from the target and thought
he heard the missing leader order the attack.

He located the airfield some distance away and charged in just
at dawn all by his lonesome. He opened up on a bunch of bombers
parked at one end of the field as the ground fire started and kept right
on going. Doing a wingover in the ever-lightening day, he looked back
to see some satisfying fires coming from where he had just been. Not
only that, but he saw some fighters parked at the other end of the strip.
He charged back in and lit off a number of these before going home
for breakfast. His cool report of the action corroborated by photo recon gave him a conservative fifteen planes destroyed. Not only that,
but the photo recon showed that a total of twenty-four planes were
destroyed. Other planes in the vicinity during the attack reported some
fires on the runway that he denied responsibility for. This led to a lot

of speculation and a scenario that was highly likely and was most certainly accepted by the squadron.

Another VMF-214 pilot on this strike was Chuck, the brother of the army pilot Tom who killed Admiral Yamamoto. As was nearly everyone on this mixed-up mess of an attack, he was separated from the other planes. He did not return from this flight, and being the only one missing, he would have been the only one able to inflict the rest of the damage without reporting it.

Chuck was not dead yet. A call to his mother in Detroit after the war revealed a horrifying story. Chuck was captured on Bougainville at that time and taken to the Kempei Tai prison at Rabaul. Here he was savagely beaten, starved, and mistreated until a miserable death overtook him many months later. The army pilot who related this was one of the *eight* survivors out of *one hundred and twenty-six* who were verified to have been held there. There may have been more. This was the standard treatment for prisoners of the Japanese. What worse they might have done to him had they known who his brother was can only be imagined.

The days at Munda were withering down, and several strikes and scrambles later, which were impaired by an extensive sick list due to rampaging dysentery and malaria, about did for this. The new and unpopular CO flew fewer flying hours than any other pilot in the squadron. This had to be noted up at air group.

All pilots owed the company store three combat tours, if they survived, and this was number two. The squadron straggled down to Guadalcanal as the pilots came out of Munda and out of sick bay. Here there was a chance to ferry a used-up Corsair down to the Turtle Bay strip at Espíritu Santo and avoid the long journey on a SCAT Transport R4D.

It took a little while at Turtle Bay before the squadron could continue on to its leave in Sydney, Australia. During this period there were some disturbing rumors about the squadron being broken up. After the "Harvard Man" went over to headquarters and got some reassurances, these rumors were discounted.

Sydney was just as good and probably more intense than the first trip. Possibly the intensity of these "rest cures" was so exhausting that they added greatly to the fatalistic attitude most of the youthful participants were acquiring.

Not expecting much of anything by that time, everyone was nevertheless absolutely shocked by the contemptible duplicity of the United States Marines. In the judgment of the squadron as stated by the famous O.K. Williams, they had been awarded the Royal Order of the Purple Shaft with the Cross-Limbs Cluster when they returned to Turtle Bay. VMF-214 no longer existed as the Swashbucklers and the weirdest chapter in the history of Marine Corps aviation got under way and maintains to this day. This is a good time to examine this aberration and then let it lay decomposing in the light of day. As the Oracle of Poverty Flats would have it: "It is time to take the bull by the tail and look the facts in the face."

Before the war, marine aviation was a very small but very active participant in the development of the airplane as an instrument of war. Naturally, everybody knew everybody, and it was unavoidably a tight little society. One member of this clique was a talented fighter pilot named Gregory Boyington, with a notable affinity for fermented goods. This was hardly a liability and probably even an asset for a real working fighter pilot. Unfortunately, he was running up debts pursuing this hobby, and that gave the Marine Corps bad publicity—a very big no-no in the barely tolerated military of the period. Just as this situation was reaching critical mass, he got a tremendous break.

The disorganized nation of China possessed quite a few warlords. One of these was named Chiang Kai-shek, who excelled in suppressing democracy and social reform and whose real strength was his American-educated wife Madame Chiang. The chief enterprise of this assortment was taking the American suckers for their treasure. Fortunately, the Japanese were involved, so this worked very well. The Chinese air force was a ragtag mob recruited by an American outfit. This bunch was no match for the Japanese, so a plan was hatched to recruit active-duty American military aviators to resign their com-

missions and form a highly paid mercenary group. The Marine Corps
was happy to contribute the debt-ridden fighter pilot.

This Chinese fire drill was conducted by an aging army aviator
named Claire Chennault, who was retired with only the rank of captain but was the self-appointed colonel of this lot. They were actually
the American Volunteer Group but were called The Flying Tigers due
to a shark's mouth painted on the air scoop of their P-40 fighters.
Even this design had been stolen from the British. The pay was very
high and re-enforced by large bonuses for any Japanese airplanes destroyed. This "destroyed clause" applied equally to those on the
ground as well as in the air. Since this money was supplied by the
United States and gave the Madame and her husband a nice profit
anyway, the claims allowed during this outfit's short tenure were liberal, to say the least. Just how shockingly liberal was brought to light
after the war, but by then who's counting? As liberal as these al-
lowances were, Madame Chiang was shocked enough to prevent the
now "colonel" of this assortment from claiming a personal score of
seventy. His actual score was zero and this would have provided very
bad PR if uncovered.

A couple of other things were that the Japanese never did deploy
their first team to China, and the other was that the AVG didn't even
score a kill in the air or on the ground until well after Pearl Harbor.
The propaganda was impressive, and of course the media was always
ready to follow the Hollywood pattern of romance.

When this organization came to an end, it was already coming
apart from internal dissension, and some were inducted into the U.S.
Army—but not the former marine. Boyington was unemployed for a
considerable time, and although there was a war on, he even parked
cars in Seattle to live. He finally got back in the marines and of course
resumed his friendly relationship with some of his old drinking buddies. Some of these were now generals.

He claimed to have shot down six airplanes in the AVG, which
was by the most conservative evidence at least twice what he could
possibly have accounted for. The really unbelievable part of this was

that the Marine Corps, which had been, until then, meticulous about claims, accepted this figure.

When he reached the South Pacific he wasn't doing much and suffered a combat injury that sent him to the hospital in New Zealand. He was not awarded the Purple Heart for this injury, since this combat took place in a tent in a rear area when he challenged the wrong guy.

When he got out of the hospital, he occupied his time administrating a group of pilots who were being stockpiled at Turtle Bay. Amongst them were several who had completed two of their three combat tours with other squadrons that had gone home. Some of these had more airplanes to their credit legitimately than their new leader. Others were new to the area, but all of them had a great deal more flying time and experience than the Swashbucklers did when they entered combat. There was a number who had been in the small group of well-trained RCAF veterans. Not a single one had any disciplinary action against them and, as far as is known, ever would have. All told, this was an average, or possibly a slightly above average, bunch. One pilot from the RCAF was even older than their leader, the former AVG pilot who was well publicized as an elder statesman.

Boyington observed the fact that VMF-214 was out on rest cure and now lacked strong leadership. He went to see some of his thirsty general friends. He not only got himself appointed the CO of VMF-214 but somehow managed to switch the pilots to the ones in the reserve pool at Turtle Bay.

The pilots may have been average, but one new member of VMF-214 exceeded any possible description, and he couldn't even fly an airplane. His chief claim to fame was his background as a Los Angeles cop who had managed to get a commission in the marines as an air combat intelligence (ACI) officer. Up until then, these chaps had been mostly distinguished Americans, usually of above average age, and some of them had used their high-level positions in American life to get into the marines at all. This was a unique position, since it did not require personal combat with the enemy, as was supposedly the case with all other marines, but did require a high level of integrity. Anyway, it had up until then.

This chap had been around Hollywood and knew a movie plot when he saw it. In the materiel he had to work with was a genuine "bad boy," who was also a veteran of the Flying Tigers, whose publicity exceeded reality, and a group of pilots who were far from happy being stuck in a replacement pool.

In this rear-area base, as far from the fighting as possible, he had the chaps suit up and run for the airplanes just like a fighter scramble during the Battle of Britain. He also had the leader demonstrating, with waving arms, his version of tactics. Since this ACI had never been any closer to combat than the future president who had heard the empty saki bottles falling, this was really creative work, and he got these pictures published in stateside newspapers. Not only that, he informed the pilots that up until now a lot of Japanese airplanes had been claimed only as probables but had, no doubt, never made it home. He was going to remedy this situation, since the ACI officer made the determination of credit after considering the debriefing reports.

The manufactured history of this new squadron had the pilots all being poorly trained discipline cases who were probably going to be shot anyway. Now their brilliant leader would rescue them, teach them how to fly, and make them the all-time heroes of fighter aviation. Not only that, they adopted the name of the Black Sheep. Any Buzzard from Poverty Flats, Montana, recognized that a sheep (whatever its color) is an exceedingly stupid herd animal with vacuous eyes, and stinks to high heaven in the bargain.

When the gallant leader came back from prison camp (where he was the only prisoner of the Japanese to gain weight) after the war, the ACI pulled off the coup de grâce. Even with the liberal scoring he had been assigning his PR creation, this man was still short of being the highest scoring marine.

This was solved by the ACI by simply going into Marine Corps Headquarters in Washington and modifying the combat report to

claim a couple of more scores in the last battle. Then he had the re-
cipient sign it off as the commanding officer! Historical assessments,
including Japanese records after the war, showed these claims to be
preposterous.

The claim that this man was responsible for the new tactic of the
fighter sweep is equally fictitious. These had been taking place regularly during the Kahili battle long before there was a sheep within sight
or smell. It was also used by the RAF and U.S. Army in Europe long
before that. To the everlasting shame of the once estimable Marine
Corps, they have never, so far as is known, denied or corrected this
fairy tale.

The former L.A. cop placed right up there with the German
Joseph Goebbels and America's own General Douglas MacArthur in
the propaganda field. The TV version of this monumental fabrication
has indeed made VMF-214 the most famous squadron of all fighter
aviation. The myth endures to this day. Some of its pilots were at first
outraged as being portrayed as a bunch of frightened and/or criminal
losers, but with the passage of time have even become somewhat
proud of it.

Why not? They were competent at their trade and took their
losses and made their contribution while some of the last critical air
battles were being fought. The total ranking of VMF-214, including
the records of both the Swashbucklers and the Black Sheep, was a
modest seventh overall. While the truth may be the first casualty of
war, the propagation of historical fiction after hostilities end cannot
be denied. And who cares. Anyway, as the Oracle of Poverty Flats
would have further expounded: "It takes more than one monkey to
make a circus."

The depression of being at Turtle Bay without a squadron was
promptly mitigated by a distraction that I could have most easily done
without. The footwear for all hands was the Marine Corps field boots,
which were extremely durable and surprisingly comfortable high-top
shoes much like what a farmer would wear. After months of these, the
transition to low quarter oxfords to be presentable in Sydney was of-

ten painful. In this case the low quarter shoes retrieved from the rear-area storage with the rest of the Sunday-go-to-meeting clothes wore a blister on the arch of the left foot. Soon after returning to the tropics this became infected and was soon ulcerated, becoming tough to walk on.

The young flight surgeon panicked and took the victim over to the "base hospital." This was a large circus tent with a lot of human wreckage enjoying the advantages of an atmosphere more appropriate to the Napoleonic wars than the early 1940s. Here was a *god* without wings. An overworked gray-haired surgeon with a perpetually worried look caused the now repulsive foot to be elevated in a frame with a large light bulb in it and covered with a blanket. After several days the foot started getting back to normal.

On the way out, the harassed old doctor was sought out to be thanked. He looked sad and said, "You are a very lucky young man. Your flight surgeon brought you here to see about removing the foot to arrest the infection." He added that it had happened all too often, since they had little knowledge of some of the virulent tropical diseases and infections. He happened to be the right guy at the right place at the right time. The new world outside that accursed hospital tent looked like a fine, bright place and somewhat mitigated the loss of the squadron.

That had already been remedied. With all of the frantic training of pilots in the States, the squadron musters were being raised to a standard forty pilots. This certainly destroyed, once and for all, the family feeling of the pitifully small outfits that had taken the brunt of the first desperate phases of the war.

The posting was to VMF-215, who already had one combat tour and were going up for their second one. Quite a few of the former VMF-214 pilots went along, including the missionary's son (Bob Hanson), the fellow jewelry salesman, the former enlisted pilot who had single-handedly shot up Kahili, and the famous O.K. Williams.

XIV

The association with VMF-215 began with a meeting at which their air combat intelligence officer stated his views. He left the former VMF-214 pilots looking at each other in amazement. What he said was similar to the views of the new ACI of the reconstituted VMF-214: no doubt, many of the probable kills weren't getting home anyway, and that would be corrected by his more liberal determination of enemy losses. It was a whole new ball game for the once uptight and upright United States Marines who would, from now on, be indistinguishable from the aviators of the army and navy.

Close examination of claims after the war with the benefit of enemy records showed how faulty this reasoning was. At any rate, this philosophy allowed the United States, alone, to shoot down every enemy airplane ever produced at least five times. This is not including the number claimed by the other allies. The most inflated claim may have been made following a U.S. Army B-17 raid on Lille, France, on October 9, 1941, when the returning crews claimed to have shot down 102 German planes. The actual figure turned out to have been 1!

In a few days the squadron deployed to the new strip at Vella Lavella. This lay between Munda on New Georgia and Kahili on Bouganville. This narrow strip was carved out between the base of the mountain and the ocean. The living area was on the side of the hill and required going up a long lateral road. One end of the strip was approached from the open ocean, but the other was not so pleasant. It led to a very small cove fronting more high ground, where the island made an L shape. With the squadron down on the ocean end of the strip, a lot of takeoffs were made in this direction. This was bad enough under normal circumstances but could be disastrous on black nights or in bad weather. Soon after takeoff it was necessary to initiate a steep right-hand turn to avoid the high ground past the small cove.

Immediately after arriving at this new home, this limitation became painfully apparent. Due to the crowded parking at the squadron's end of the strip, the order of takeoffs was dictated by whatever plane was closest to the end of the runway, and the airborne organization would be sorted out later. That pitch-black morning with another airplane taking off in the lead position, it looked like a piece of cake, with that pilot doing all of the work.

In those precomputer days and the fly-by-wire concept far in the future, airplanes were wrestled by hand and aided by trim tabs to overcome control pressures. The Corsairs were beyond question more reliant on those trim tabs than any machine built. With the powerful engine and huge prop, the trim changes were very great on takeoff as the kite got off the ground, rapidly accelerated, the landing gear retracted, and the prop pitch changed. This required that the aileron, rudder, and elevator tabs be continually manipulated. Added to this, the utterly impenetrable blackness and the necessity to go on instruments, while starting a substantial right turn, offered a recipe for disaster. There was no light for a reference point, and it was much easier simply to position on the leader's lights than to do all of this sweating personally. That is, if the leader was as skilled as he was expected to be.

In the brilliant flash of flame immediately ahead I saw that the Corsair, now rambling along at well over one hundred and fifty knots, was nearly on its back at an altitude of approximately ten feet. This was a brutal reminder that not all aviators had the advantages of RCAF instrument training. After that, predawn takeoffs, as much as possible, were initiated in the direction of the open sea, and the beam from a searchlight was laid across the water.

The main chore from this base was to support and protect the landings that were starting halfway up Bougainville island at Empress Augusta Bay. This operation was code-named Cherry Blossom. This name hardly required any leap of the imagination to supply its Japanese connotation. There were still a number of Japanese airdromes on this island reinforced by the base at Rabaul, and again the Japanese decided to be disagreeable. The landings were of course vigorously opposed and allowed a member of an allegedly noncombatant naval construction battalion to distinguish himself.

An area where they were going to put some heavy construction equipment ashore from landing craft came under fire from a machine gun nest. A bulldozer operator started his great, hulking machine and, placing the blade at half-mast, had the chaps lower the ramp. Snorting vengeance with slugs ricocheting from this portable armor, he and his machine soon had the problem not only neutralized but buried. These exciting events were covered by VMF-215 and other squadrons in the Cherry Blossom combat air patrols.

Getting the first patrol of the day up there from Vella Lavella just before dawn every day required the pitch-black takeoffs with their attendant risks. An off-duty pilot could be sleeping peacefully despite the repetitive snarl of the planes of this patrol launching. One thing that would bring him rudely awake was when the increasing roar of an engine would suddenly end. Then peering down at the strip usually revealed a fireball going aloft to mark the point where control was lost on takeoff.

In one of the first actions of Cherry Blossom, the navy put on a spectacular show. They had a formation of ships in line astern some distance offshore and at right angles to it. As the attack developed, they opened up with their heavy guns and actually erected a wall of water. This, it was found later, was a tactic to discourage low-flying torpedo planes from getting into position to launch their torpedoes.

Being seriously occupied with other matters, no Japanese torpedo planes were seen down there. However, Bob Hanson, the son of missionaries, scored three clean kills up in the cover. A tough competitor and a great shot, he was not given to B.S.; his kills were all con-

firmed and never the product of imagination or public relations. He
never cultivated ACI officers or anybody else, and couldn't have cared
less about their evaluations. He never knew when to quit, and that allowed some Japanese ace from Rabaul to shoot him down. When he
was rescued he was just mad as hell and not at all impressed by his
close call or Japanese firepower.

This rather quiet guy was really tough. On a scramble he met another Corsair that was scrambling from the other end of the strip. In
the ensuing head-on collision he suffered severe damage to some fingers, of all things. Memory seems to indicate that he continued life
without them. That didn't dissuade him from crawling into another
Corsair to continue the war.

According to some of the people with whom he attended flight
school, he did not suffer fools gladly. By then the flight schools were
adding all sorts of claptrap. One of the stupidest was the emergence
of the "Jocks" (short for jockstrap admirals, who weren't admirals at
all, but former athletic coaches), who were convinced that all aviators
should be some kind of hand-to-hand combat killers. When one of
these Jocks spied Bob apparently asleep during one of his demonstrations, he ordered him front and center to be humiliated. The Jock
then ordered Bob to assault him. The delighted report was that Bob
followed orders in an exemplary fashion and returned to his seat and
nap, leaving the wreckage of the Jock where he lay.

During the time when Bob was a hutmate, the talk sometimes
turned to his adventures in the far-flung world of the missionaries. His
hobby was studying the dirty fighting techniques of all persuasions.
He later became a college wrestling champion. The Jock could be
pitied if he and his ilk weren't such a pain in the tukus.

Another interesting chore during the invasion was protecting the
PT boats at dawn as they came down below the demarcation line from
their night actions farther up the island. This arbitrary line extended
out from the invasion site, and anything that moved above the line
come dawn was allegedly fair game.

One morning an army B-25 attacked one of two PT boats in this
vicinity. In the ensuing battle the PT boat was sunk, but not before

they shot down the B-25. The survivors of both crews were rescued by the remaining PT boat. The story was that the PT crew rescued their fellow sailors with alacrity but the B-25 chaps were rather ungraciously hauled aboard and only after much argument, during which several alternatives were discussed. Rather than learn from vehement warnings about this possibility, the army persisted. A very short time later while flying an escort for some Pistol Packin' Mommas bound for Buka passage, it nearly happened again.

A Pistol Packin' Momma was an army B-25 fitted with a 75mm cannon. This monumental field piece fired though the nose of this medium bomber (the same type in which Doolittle bombed Tokyo). The weapon extended back into the airplane's waist, where a brave lad fed the rounds into the breach and was narrowly missed by the recoil. As if this treat was not enough for the Japanese who infested Buka Passage on the far end of Bougainville, some other B-25s were carrying conventional bombs.

The fighter escort was assembled from representatives of several squadrons and was led by the tough skipper of one of the original Marine Air Group 21 squadrons. Just above the demarcation line, shortly after dawn, another pair of PT boats were hightailing it for safety. Ignoring the cries on the radio of "Leave 'em alone they are ours," one B-25 peeled off and dropped a 500-pound bomb, which narrowly missed one of the boats.

The outraged fighter leader informed the bombers, in barracks room language, that if they didn't maintain tight formation until he told them they were at Buka Passage and had his personal permission to attack anything, the fighter cover would shoot them all down. The marine pilots were very fond of the PT boats, which on occasion had rescued their members. Despite this, some pilots of the reconstituted VMF-214 also pulled this trick and got one pilot and some PT boat crewmen killed.

Not long after that, while proceeding at water level after a dawn shipping search, we discovered a landing craft full of people down between Bougainville and Choiseul. This was fair game, since nobody but Japanese were supposed to be in that area. Something about the configuration of the boat raised doubts and stayed an itchy trigger finger. The other members of the flight were advised to do likewise. Not long afterward a thank-you from a marine outfit making a surreptitious reconnaissance admitted that they had not advised the air command of their intentions and were damn happy to be alive.

During operations with this squadron any losses of people from the original VMF-214 were sorely felt. The first casualty was when the weather closed in and one of the originals was unable to find the strip and was running out of fuel. After the sound of his engine closing in, there was silence, and he no doubt hit back in the jungle. A personable chap, he had been an uncanny poker player, and the inventory of his effects sent a respectable sum of money the many thousands of miles to his grieving parents.

Probably the saddest loss was Ledge, the other failed jewelry salesman from the Russell Islands. He was one of those very fortunate and rare people who was, with no apparent effort, just popular wherever he went. A good-looking lad with a great family and educational background, his enduringly optimistic outlook under any dire circumstance was, trite as it may sound, inspirational. The Numa Numa Trail and Kieta harbor were his nemeses.

This trail led inland behind the scene of the landings at Cherry Blossom. It led clear across the island over the mountains to the vicinity of Kieta Harbor, and was used by the Japanese to bring up supplies and reinforcements. It was a habit of divisions on the Cherry Blossom patrols, who still had fuel and ammunition when relieved, to take this detour on speculation. Sometimes, but not always, there would be good things to shoot at. This day the trail failed to yield anything interesting. However, over in the harbor there was a wrecked ship that sometimes the Japanese would board, to fire at approaching airplanes.

Ledge made a pass on this vessel and apparently got return fire. Going back to silence this fire, he suffered a direct hit and went straight in. With all of the witnesses there was no nonsense about "missing in action," but considerable grief among his many friends.

XV

This was probably the end of innocence for the original members of VMF-214. Now they lacked any feeling of family support and realized that they were just common expendables in a strange environment. Never again would close friendships develop with other pilots, and the whole picture would become objective. There would be no more pride and attendant high morale in squadron membership. This maturity was just as well, in the impersonal brutality of war.

VMF-214 had been one of the last small, understrength squadrons. Probably due to its high concentration of graduates of Ivy League schools, it was something special. Some of these chaps, like the "Horse," were real fans of combat aviation from the intense glamour surrounding World War I fighter aviation. They subscribed to the traditions and supplied the leadership for the evening songfests for which that incarnation of VMF-214 had been famous.

This had been real in the early, desperate days of the war, when the Japanese held all of the cards, but this was all beginning to change. More materiel was coming on line, and the flight schools were in mass production. No longer would flying attract the top tier of American youth. In fact, the U.S. Army was combing the ranks of their service for aircrew to supply the fodder for the bloody air battle underway in

Europe. At least, flying about in an airplane sounded better than dying in the mud.

As for the navy Wings of Gold, the requirements were greatly lowered, but the number of hours of training had been increased greatly. The marines, basing their projected needs on early casualties, really overshot the mark. Before the war was over they had ten thousand qualified pilots—hardly an exclusive club. The character of the pilots was changing too, and such emphasis was placed on drill and discipline that it elicited a salty comment from the salty Admiral Halsey (the Marine Corps' favorite admiral). He said that the fleet was receiving young aviators who had shined shoes, neat haircuts, and fine, subservient military manners. "But," he asked, "could they fight?"

This all worked out anyway, and after the Japanese first team was finally shot out of the war, Japanese aviation crumbled under the weight of U.S. production. Accounting for this demise was the Solomon Islands campaign, starting with the desperate and outnumbered marine pilots flying badly outdated Wildcats at Guadalcanal, and continuing up the chain of islands, where they became equipped with the rapidly improving Corsairs. With increased marine air superiority, the outnumbered and outgunned Japanese were taking a beating. By the time the assault reached Rabaul, they were in poor shape, and here, almost the last of their best were expended. There was a long road ahead after that, but really tough competition from Japanese air was negligible from that time forward.

Perhaps the single deciding factor was the rapid refinement of the Corsair aircraft. American engineering made so many rapid modifications to the aircraft that it was a different machine by the end of the campaign. This aircraft had entered combat as an almost experimental machine foisted off on the marines. The first models were dangerous and took some real flying skill. Actually, in a matter of months, many of its more lethal characteristics were modified.

Desperation has often been the motivating factor for the Marine Corps' spectacular successes in combat. Beginning with the Battle of

Wake Island, and through Midway and Guadalcanal, a handful of marine pilots had taken on the best the Japanese had to offer and denied the Japanese an overwhelming victory in the skies. This was accomplished with the terminally obsolete Grumman Wildcat fighter and pure guts and ability.

When the navy was unable to master the first Corsairs, the marines got the airplane, which, although a widow maker, could outperform the Japanese Zero. Had it not been for this, the army and the navy with their superior political clout would have soon monopolized any glory to be wrung from aerial combat. The Americans had now turned the tide with a vast training program and aircraft production that the Japanese had no hope of matching. As this took place, the Japanese first team was being decimated, and the marines were getting most of the credit. This led to an amusing ploy by the navy. The strip at Vella Lavella was the farthest forward strip at that time and was a busy place. Munda was practically rear area now. To Munda came a navy squadron that was to be based ashore for a perfidious but undisclosed mission. The navy was getting a little green-eyed over all of the publicity the marines were garnering and had decided to cut themselves in.

This squadron came equipped with the latest model Corsairs, which were still unavailable to the marines. These machines, due to many engineering changes, were entering the period where they could be flown by any little old lady in tennis shoes. With a fine, dark blue paint job, a raised tail-wheel oleo, and bubble canopy, they were things of beauty. This was in such contrast to the old Birdcage Corsairs the marines were flying, with dripping grease and badly patched bullet holes in their faded paint, that it was ridiculous. Further rage ensued when it was reported that this bunch of tea-sipping, cookie-pushing aristocrats had ice cream. One of the RCAF veterans, who was making quite a name for himself, managed to get down to Munda, where he stole one of the marvelous new machines and brought it home. Perhaps from embarrassment, nothing came of this, and the squadron kept the airplane.

This navy squadron was also equipped with one of the new-fangled air combat intelligence officers who believed that too many Japanese claimed only as probables were not getting home, and belonged in his squadron's score. In this the squadron became very successful. At this time there was a fine piece of humor pinned on the bulletin board. It was a full-color recruiting advertisement from America's premier picture magazine clipped by a disgruntled marine fighter pilot. It showed a handsome youth in an expensive sports jacket and showing a lot of white teeth standing in front of a beautiful new Corsair shaking hands with an equally beautiful navy lieutenant commander in immaculate whites. The caption exclaimed, "IT'S ALL YOURS WHEN YOU GET YOUR NAVY WINGS OF GOLD."

Beneath this was the locally supplied caption: "You'll get yours when you get your navy Wings of Gold." The lean youths in their filthy, sweat-stained summer flight suits were backed up with the aforementioned collection of beat-up old Birdcage Corsairs listing, dripping grease, and with patches over the bullet holes in their faded hides.

Surprisingly, the occasional predawn scramble alert was one chore that I didn't mind a bit. This alert was stood down at the far end of the strip by the little inlet, allowing takeoffs to be made in the direction of the open sea. To stand this alert, the pilot could be out of the airplane, and his heavy parachute paraphernalia, which included the jungle pack and the seat-type life raft, could be draped on the wing. The theory was that there would be sufficient time to take care of all of these details before the hostiles arrived. Sometimes there would be some U.S. Army P-39 fighters down there for the same purpose. Since their in-line engines didn't require the warming up of the big radials, they were ideal scramble aircraft. The only trouble was that their relatively low operating ceiling limited their effectiveness.

One of these jolly army chaps had a fine story to tell to the marines, who firmly believed that rapid promotions were to be had as an army flyer. He said that two army pilots met after not seeing each other since flight school a few years before. One of them was a

lieutenant colonel and the other was still a second lieutenant. The lieutenant colonel exclaimed, "My God, what happened to you? You were
at the head of our class."

"What happened," snarled the lieutenant, "was that I got sent to
a pursuit outfit at Clark Air Base in the Philippines just before the war
broke out."

"What's that got to do with not getting promoted? You were always the smartest guy around."

"Well, that was the trouble. We had to be ready to scramble all
of the time, and what we had to do was stay with the airplanes, waiting for the air raid siren. When it went off we had to wake up, put on
our chutes, and get in the damn airplane and start it up. Then they'd
blow the all clear. Boy, did that get tiresome. That's when I noticed
those monkeys peering out of the jungle. So I made friends with one
of them and trained him. When that damn siren went off, he would
put on my chute, get in the airplane and fire it up, and when the all
clear went he'd shut it down and I'd go on sleeping."

"That seems pretty clever, then what happened?" asked the lieutenant colonel. "I'll tell you what happened," said the lieutenant sadly.
"One morning the all clear didn't sound and the Japs came in."

"Mother of God," said the lieutenant colonel. "And then what?"

"Ha!" said the lieutenant. "That damn monkey took off and shot
down three of them. Not only that, he is a lieutenant colonel today."

The real discovery down at this end of the strip was a Naval Construction Battalion camp back in the jungle. These Seabees were a remarkable outfit and, some said, remarkable thieves. They had food that
looked like the Waldorf Astoria's compared to the sparse and revolting fare offered by the marines. They were hospitable, however, and
took to giving the starving fighter pilot a fine breakfast. There surely
was no point in sharing this bonanza with the army pilots, despite their
instructive stories, or with other members of the new squadron for that
matter, to whom little loyalty was owed. Fortunately, there were no
scrambles during these repasts, since there were no monkeys available
for Corsair training in the vicinity.

Now time was running out, and it seemed probable that the end of this tour would be reached and a trip home was possible. That would not occur, however, before one more adventure, and that happened on the ground. The camp area was on the side of a hill above the airstrip and contained the sleeping tents, mess tent, hospital (in a tent), and other primitive evidence of the marines in the field. A long lateral road led down to the strip. One day while proceeding down this road on foot, attention was drawn to a TBF parked about halfway down the strip. What was unusual was the large crowd of loafers gathered around what was obviously a large bomb lying to one side of this torpedo bomber.

What had happened was that the TBF had been planting delayed bombs up at Kahili, and this 1,000-pounder had hung up, but the delayed fuse was activated. The pilot didn't elect to abandon the airplane but notified the tower on the way in to stand clear. He and his crew parked the TBF where it quit rolling and walked away. They warned everybody they met to keep clear.

Soon a couple of self-elected bomb disposal chaps went to the airplane and, dropping the bomb on the ground, rolled it out from under the airplane. It seemed every person on the strip without other business gathered round as though it were a dogfight. Of the two experts, one was down on his knees removing the fuse and the other, while sitting astride the bomb like a cowboy, was entertaining the crowd.

At this point, the world apparently came to an end. There was a blinding flash and a blast that caused violent contact with the roadway. Parts of the formerly airworthy TBM seemed to be raining down, with some spare human body parts included. The damage was considerable, and the sight of truckloads of shattered humans being brought up the hill to the makeshift hospital would not soon be forgotten. One doctor was standing where the trucks were dumping the human wreckage. He would point to one and say, "Him." This one would be carried in. For others he just shook his head. No use wasting the time.

The squadron's flight clerk had been walking with the flight surgeon at the other end of the strip and had the lower half of one of his
hands disappear as a random piece of shrapnel passed between them,
the luck of the draw. After this depressing finale to violence, there was
only one more strike to be flown, and that was aborted. A short time
later the squadron was on the way back down to Turtle Bay.

There was one last disagreeable episode before the South Pacific
could be abandoned. Just as everything was arranged to return stateside with a homeward-bound squadron, the dormant malaria struck
and the screaming fever and chills called for me taking up residence
in another of the infamous base hospitals. They were making noises
about not releasing the shaky body in time to go with a departing
squadron. Some of the bureaucratic confusion these rear-area heroes
were capable of could have left homeless waifs out there in limbo for
eternity.

Into this void galloped an extremely fine ground officer who had
not been seen since the great party at the then unfinished air base at
El Centro, California. It was none other than "The Judge," the leader
of that pack. He was the air combat intelligence officer of a newly arrived dive-bomber squadron. He was looking up old acquaintances,
and after listening to the tale of woe, he disappeared in the direction
of headquarters. Very shortly he was back with a jeep, a driver, and
some all-important papers. Over the monumental disapproval of the
navy doctors, the Threadbare Buzzard, who was quite frankly about
out of it, was put on a SCAT R4D bound for Havana Harbor at Vila
on the island of Éfaté.

This angel of mercy, as has been previously noted, became a very
famous U.S. senator after the war and really caused a lot of people a
lot of grief. They probably had it coming. Although his friends and
admirers from the El Centro caper called him "The Judge," his real
name was Joe McCarthy.

The sick bay of the Dutch motor ship *Sommelsdijk* of the Holland American Line was in a converted hold well forward in the
bucket, and the pitching added its own torture to the malaria. But,

like everything else in life, this too did pass. The ship ran without convoy and went nearly to the coast of South America on the way to San Francisco to avoid submarines. By then, with returning health, cooling weather, and excellent chow, this lengthy sea voyage became intensely enjoyable.

Under these circumstances, who could be concerned with the invasion of Tarawa then about to take place? Probably my two highschool classmates from Poverty Flats who died like dogs in the surf as a result of disastrous naval planning by the round bottoms who do not accompany the troops but do issue macho dispatches.

Don't count your losses.

XVI

Knowing nothing of the secrets of the ship's navigation, the ocean all looked the same, but the weather certainly did not. Having been out of it with malaria for most of the long transit eastward, the first favorable impression was after the course was shaped to the north.

With the fine Dutch food and the exhilarating knowledge that home lay ahead, it became a real pleasure cruise. The nights were spectacular at first with brilliant stars and pleasant temperatures. Then the temperature started dropping until the contrast with the recent tropical experience was really felt.

One dark night, the engines slowed and there were strange noises on deck. A ship's officer explained that a bar pilot was being embarked and the ship would be entering San Francisco Bay at night, which was considered unusual. It was later found that the lads from the Tiburon Net Depot closed the Golden Gate at night with a submarine net.

With seagoing knowledge gained much later, I was to marvel at the mariners of that day. Practically no merchant ships had radar with which to see in the dark, and many did not even have gyrocompasses to give a steady true heading to match the charts. The skill and self-reliance of those guys were more than impressive but appreciated by only the few concerned with ships and the sea. Without the seamen there could have been no way for the war to have been won or, for that matter, to even have a war.

In the United States, where these men were not taken into the navy because it would have interfered with the vast profits of the steamship companies, the seamen paid a high personal price. If considered as a service, which it surely was, the merchant marine's casualties were either higher than or close to equal to those of the U.S. Marines. In probably the greatest injustice of World War II, these men were not even given veterans' status, nor did their survivors receive benefits, until the 1980s. They were even reviled as draft dodgers, and some of the garbage-mouth commentators and columnists of the day accused them of being communists. At least one of these self-made stateside heroes was successfully sued for this libel. After the war they fought a decades-long battle to realize the veterans' status promised by President Franklin D. Roosevelt.

As sick as it may sound, their chief opponent was the United States Air Force, a service that did not exist in World War II. The U. S. Air Force was formed in 1947. A good case can be made that it was formed in some substantial part by the congressional lobbying efforts of women who were disappointed by the demise of the short-lived Women's Flying Corps during the war. For an extremely brief time, these ladies ferried aircraft so the men could shoulder a rifle in the mud, *where they belonged*. Then, in a nice political gesture, these women who participated in this questionable program were awarded veterans' status in the air force many years before the seamen were so honored. They achieved all this without suffering any casualties or seeing an enemy.

At that time and in that place, that disgrace to the nation was far in the future. Now was the time to enjoy the marvelous world of a country whose citizens, with the exceptions of Pearl Harbor or the desolate Aleutian Islands, had never faced attacks or really any serious inconvenience in the war and still were able to enjoy all of the advantages of wartime hysteria.

Already, being a man of the world, I discovered that San Francisco was something else. Having visited major cities in the United States and Canada, and even Sydney, Australia, it was thought that Poverty Flats, Montana, was far in the past. Actually, these places were only extensions of Poverty Flats. San Francisco was in a class apart. The ladies wore hats and gloves. The civilian men wore three-piece suits and neckties, and a feeling of sophistication prevailed. The fact that the girls were even more beautiful than those in Sydney may have been enhanced by their proximity. They were certainly just as friendly.

The city was fully mobilized, and the number of large military installations and roaring shipyards seemed to be endless. The nightlife, despite the blackouts and wartime restrictions, was at least as intense as a Sydney leave. After singing raunchy songs around a campfire with a canteen cup of whiskey in the miserable Solomon Islands, the first night on the town from the "Top of the Mark" to Chinatown and all points between was most impressive. It would be for later generations to hear the matchless Tony Bennett sing "I Left My Heart in San Francisco," but that sentiment, including the cable cars and stars, was inescapable.

After a few days of familiarization with civilization, the large Fleet Marine Force installation at 100 Harrison Street issued the veterans train tickets. The next stop was the marine base at Miramar near San Diego. A few days of red tape produced the freedom of a thirty-day leave and a pocketful of U.S. currency. At a time when airplanes were still a rather exclusive way to travel, it was no small victory to score air travel, via a circuitous route, all the way from San Diego to Poverty Flats, Montana, aboard "giant airliners," seventeen-passenger DC-3s.

In this oncoming winter season, Poverty Flats had not gained much of the great times infecting the rest of the country. The military presence was limited to a prisoner of war camp at the old army fort for Italians of peaceful outlook, and some sketchy preflight indoctrination for some grubby-looking army flying cadets. One thing that put Poverty Flats on the main line was the mounting number of casualties from the war. For a small town these were far above the norm, but this seemed to be common for all of the small places where patriotism had run amok. Most contemporaries were away in the various services, and a shocking number were already dead or injured.

Amongst all nations involved in World War II, the U.S. casualties were by far the fewest of any major nation. However, even one is too many, especially for those whose generation was of the most desirable age to supply cannon fodder. The remarks of the doleful old wing commander in the RCAF were recalled. He had counseled that the war would last long enough for all of the eager children to get "bloody well pranged." Amen. There were a few resentful youths trapped by the Essential Farmers program and who were not only still wet-nursing the livestock but destined never to enjoy the glory of getting seriously shot at. They had also been demoted in title from Rancher to Farmer and stuck in position.

The first excitement and interest in the war was subsiding, and I almost missed a minor story in the local paper. It announced that Bob Hanson, the son of missionaries, had gotten himself killed after shooting down twenty-five Japanese and getting the Medal of Honor. Just like Ledge, the former fellow jewelry salesman, he was hit doing a low-level strafing pass on an unimportant target. This did guarantee him the real position as the Marine Corps' number two ace. He had shot down more Japanese in a Corsair than any other marine, a record never approached. All of his kills were made far from home base and against the Japanese first team. This was at least twice as dangerous as fighting over home plate. The Marine Corps' number one ace sure as hell wasn't the chubby chap from the Flying Tigers who pre-empted VMF-214 when it was the Swashbucklers. Eventually a statue of Hanson was erected in an eastern city. Without a doubt, he would have thought the idea of a pigeon desecrating his helmet and goggles amusing. This loss was surely the final cure for ever forming friendships with the other troops during a war.

This leave in Poverty Flats brought home a previously ignored tragedy of war. That was, the terrible grief of the relatives who had lost their nearest and dearest in the careless slaughter. In all too many cases, this grief would maintain through the remainder of their lives. In addition to the bereaved, the mothers and wives who had sons and husbands in the fighting were carrying a terrible load of apprehension. They, more than any others, were the true heroes (heroines) of the war. Wartime small towns were not cheerful places to be. It was scarcely with a heavy heart when departure was taken to return to sunny, bustling California to get on with the more pleasant aspects of the war.

Back at Miramar there was a good deal of slack time awaiting reassignment. Encountering old friends from the Solomon Islands led to a rather abundant social life. In those fine days, before overcrowding, southern California was incomparable. Some of these friends were addicted to tallyho parties. These outings required renting horses and a chuck wagon to transport the dashing marine fighter pilots and many nubile young ladies on moonlight trail rides in the hills of Escondido. Naturally, the Threadbare Buzzard, being from Montana, rode in the chuck wagon. This of course was only one of the many amusements available. In fact, if memory serves, there was even a brief occupancy of the city fountain on Broadway in greater downtown San Diego. However, that was at the witching hour on New Year's Eve, when all things are possible.

An adventure in flight occurred at this time that arose from an accidental encounter with the navy friend from Corpus Christi. At that time he had been instructing students at the 18-Dog squadron, which used PBY flying boats down at the seaplane ramps while concocting plots for getting reassigned to fighters. He was reassigned all right, but unfortunately to something bigger even than the PBYs. These were the PB4Ys and were nothing but the Consolidated B-24 of army fame. With four engines and a large capacity for fuel, they were considered ideal for long-range searches. At that time he was working up his crew to deploy to the Pacific. As unreal as it may sound in this day and age, they didn't just jump in the airplane and set off for the Hawaiian Islands. First they would do a "simulated trans-Pac," which required flying out to just short of the "point of no return" and coming back to the mainland. My going along for an unauthorized ride led to a very interesting evening.

Takeoff was in the dark of night on a northerly heading out of the relatively short North Island Naval Air Station. The copilot apparently started bleeding off the flaps instead of raising the landing gear right after becoming airborne. With an overload of fuel, the big bird was settling rapidly as the would-be fighter pilot rammed the throttles through the stops and accomplished some other chores that must have been the correct ones. The real fighter pilot sitting in the jump seat between the pilots was mesmerized by the blacked-out but easily recognizable houses on Point Loma flashing by at approximately eye height.

It was all in vain anyway, since after getting some distance offshore the drill was aborted. The PB4Ys always had fuel problems, according to the crew, and by now the smoking lamp was out and it was forbidden even to key a microphone. Any spark could ignite the gas fumes now choking the fuselage.

Much later in the war, when inquiring after this friend, a not totally unexpected tale emerged. Some contemporary navy pilots said that he, being an aggressive type, had developed a tactic to speed the downfall of the Japanese Empire. When on extended patrols, he would find a Japanese airfield just at the last light of dusk and feigning distress drop the gear and initiate a landing approach. The greedy Japanese, hoping to capture the airplane, would hold their fire until it was too late. Just before touchdown he would pull up the gear and open up with all guns. Apparently the word got around with the Japanese, and another admired warrior never got to split a bottle after the war was won.

The returned heroes, who had all been promoted to captain, could be sent to a variety of stateside duties in a variety of locations. The posting issued was considered very desirable. This assignment was to the relatively new and unfinished marine air base at El Toro, to instruct operational training on Corsairs. This base was located in the then beautiful orange grove country south of Los Angeles in the benign southern California climate—all gone now with tract housing, freeways, Disneyland, smog, and too damn many people.

Despite an aversion to instructing gained in the RCAF, the Threadbare Buzzard saw that this promised to be different. First and foremost, the students were already graduates of flight training, and not only that, with single-seat fighters, it was unnecessary to ride around in the same airplane with these insufferable young folk, many of whom would be seniors in age to their instructor. The organization was titled Fighter Training Unit, shortened to FTU, and was supposed to supply unified training to graduates of the flight schools to ready them for duty in fighter squadrons. Although all were naval aviators, many had not been trained as fighter pilots. By now fighters were supposed to be the first team. The marines were also placing greater emphasis on the Corsair, which was being refined at a dizzying pace. Its capabilities were being broadened to carry a respectable bomb load and even rockets, in addition to the guns.

The only problem was that although some of the students came from fighter training squadrons, others came from such diverse backgrounds as torpedo training and even flying boats. In addition, it was the first introduction to the Corsair for all of them. The Corsair's fearsome reputation, despite the improvements, still intimidated many of them. These circumstances all contributed to a high casualty rate. What with the unaccustomed speed and the high-test gasoline, the casualties were mostly of the permanent persuasion.

The squadron had a CO who was seldom to be found and an executive officer whose family dairy farm was out in the country at that time between the base and Los Angeles. Judging by his derogatory remarks about milking cows, it was hard to determine why he spent more time there than pursuing his duties in the squadron. The third ranking officer was "Spook" Richards, who had been a leading member of the legendary Wolf Pack at Guadalcanal.

Here the squadron was fortunate, since Richards was the operations officer and was holding the whole shooting match together. By now it had been discovered that there were a lot of people who, although capable and responsible in combat, did not have any abiding love of flying and certainly no great love for the military. Becoming the operations officer's most willing assistant was indeed good luck, since he also still really enjoyed flying and took the supervision of the instructors and scheduling to heart. This allowed unlimited access to airplanes, to go almost anywhere fancy dictated, and fancy dictated a lot of fine places within the continental limits of the U.S.A. Although the machine did gulp a lot of the taxpayers' high-test fuel, these destinations could be easily reached with the high speed of a Corsair. Perhaps the happiest circumstance of all was the living arrangement. The Hotel Laguna was taken over for officer housing for the instructors and was becoming famous as the headquarters for possibly the longest running revel of World War II.

This noteworthy establishment was right on the beach in the center of town. It was separated from El Toro air base by a considerable distance, and part of the route ran down the narrow Laguna Canyon Road. There was a suspicion that this road accounted for some of the highest casualties suffered by marine aviators. It was the habit, after securing from flight operations, for all hands to adjourn to the primitive officers' club to have a heave ahead, brag, relax, and prepare for the journey to the hotel. Civilian autos and especially rationed gasoline were in short supply at the time, but hardly a consideration for the marines. At the pilot's disposal was a vast assortment of jeeps, gas trucks, bomb trucks, carryalls, and even some cumbersome crash trucks. All of them were full of unrationed government gas. In the general rush to get to the hotel, there were some unfortunate episodes suffered by these vehicles on the Laguna Canyon Road. However, there was a war on, and it is the credo of marines at risk to "never count your losses." Besides that, the flight schools were turning out plenty of aviators, and the patriotic war workers were manufacturing plenty of jeeps, gas trucks, carryalls, and even the aptly named crash trucks.

The hotel rooms were fitted with two beds and an interconnecting bath with the next room. In effect there were four roommates.

One of these chaps had a red Buick convertible and would loan it out if anyone was willing to fill 'er up with black-market gasoline. Since no passenger cars were manufactured during the war and this was the last model built, it would be hard to appreciate the significance of this in today's world. In the declining depression immediately before the war, the red Buick convertible was a luxury and a status symbol that cannot be equated with anything now available. In fact, there was one navy pilot whose hatred of the enemy was legendary because of this. Right out of flight school and posted to Hawaii, he had his brand-new Buick convertible shipped out to join him in the islands. It was sitting on the dock and would be unavailable to him until longshore work resumed Monday morning, the eighth of December. On the seventh of December a daring aviator of the Japanese persuasion placed a bomb in the front seat, although this Buick happened to be canary yellow, not red.

The hotel had several outstanding features, and one of the most famous was an enlarged photo on one of the ceiling pillars right inside the lobby. It was of an army aviator in heavy winter flying gear standing on the wing of a training aircraft (actually, a Vultee Vomiter). His thousand-yard stare was fixed somewhere off in space above his determined Benito Mussolini-like chin and meaty face. Below it was the title "Fighter Pilot." Before this icon, it was the habit of the marines' finest fighter pilots to respectfully genuflect. This was most apt to happen when they were returning from the Los Andus (or something like that). This was the snake pit that was at the end of the alley beside the hotel and also on the beach. This joint had the advantage of great drinks and low lighting. It was here that the ritual of the lick of salt on the back of the hand, a lime squeezed between two fingers, and a straight shot of tequila became fashionable. It also attracted many females in search of genuine marine heroes.

Another and more questionable feature was the strict adherence to the federal regulation that forbade serving alcohol to people in uniform after midnight. To enforce this edict, the management would destroy the romantic gloom of the premises at the witching hour by turning on the merciless bright lights. This sometimes caused the dashing aviators to flee in horror from the object of their romancing in the lower light. All of this led to great consumption of oxygen in the airplanes in the morning as a sure neutralizer for an overdose of tequila.

Laguna Beach had been a playground for the movie industry, and this was extended to the El Toro air base to the extent that less privileged jarheads sourly referred to it as the Home of the Hollywood Marines. The town offered several fine resorts, but one that was created by the marines was certainly remarkable. It was in a large old mansion north of town and became known as the Castle. It was rented by a group of students and was passed to new proprietors as the students matriculated. The kitchen was taken over with great stores of drinkables, unrestrained by any foolish federal closing time regulations, and a little food. A few of the upstairs bedrooms were reserved strictly for sleeping, and the party continued without pause for the years of the war. There was one threat to the establishment, which was handily resolved by a tough captain who was in charge of security at the base. He fortunately liked hanging out with fighter pilots.

It was later found that this guy was a former FBI man who had been brought in to cure some outright theft at the marine facility at Santa Barbara, where some of the navy supply officers were supplying the local hotels with government beef, among other things. He distinguished himself at El Toro by dealing with a socialite who was also the owner of a major league baseball team and married to a Hollywood star. This chap was patriotically serving as a captain in the marines and, being otherwise useless, was in charge of recreation. His mistake was getting tough with the FTU squadron over some beer and baseball equipment that went adrift.

The security captain resolved to avenge this slight to his friends the fighter pilots. He noted that his nibs was in possession of a C-ration card, which gave the holder a great quantity of gasoline, as opposed to the four gallons a week allowed the holder of an A-card. This advantage allowed the recreation officer to take weekend excursions to Hollywood in a private automobile. The security captain, being in charge of gas rationing for the base, removed this card and stared down the colonel commanding the base when he vehemently defended the recreation officer. It then came to the security captain's attention that the chaps at the Castle had carted most of the bedding, linens, eating utensils, and crockery in use up there from the base. Being a man of direct action, he called in the second lieutenants concerned and laid out a hypothetical scenario in which junior officers were responsible for pillaging government property and would now be unable to return it without the risk of detection.

Their later actions with a borrowed rowboat loaded to the gunnels one moonless night did not go unnoticed, due to unidentifiable linens washing up on the beach for some time. As a logical sequence, the hotel went through a period of replacing a lot of linens, utensils, crockery, and silverware. Under their liberal contract, billing the government for these missing items was no problem—a lesson is here somewhere. At any rate, the Castle continued its career and on occasion even played host to some surprisingly high-ranking military and political persons.

XVII

The war was continuing, however, and there was work to be done. The main chore was to get the students up to speed with the Corsair airplane. Once they were reassured that the airplane was actually flyable and they had flown it around enough to build up their confidence, it was time to get serious. Nothing was more serious for the marine than accuracy with his weapons. In the fighter pilot's case, his primary weapons were the six .50-caliber machine guns in his wings. For practice purposes, only one gun in each wing was utilized, and these were bore-sighted to converge at 300 yards.

A banner instead of a sleeve was towed to fire at, since it was not as prone to destruction as a sleeve. Since it was towed by another fighter, there was no storage space to stream other banners. This required hooking the towing wire to the airplane at the end of the runway and then leading the banner as far up the field as the length of the tow wire permitted. Then, with full power and full flap, the tow plane would thunder down the runway and, when passing the banner, the airplane would be horsed off the ground abruptly to an altitude of a hundred feet or so and then pushed over sharply to give the wire a whiplash effect. This served to get the banner in the air and avoid shredding it. Care had to be taken not to stall the aircraft, which could result in an undignified (and sometimes fatal) return to mother earth.

The El Toro gunnery ranges ran seaward from San Nicolas Island, one of the Channel Islands chain, which includes Catalina among others. San Nicolas had an airstrip for emergencies and other uses. The sailors stationed here could see the continental United States on a clear day but served a regular tour of duty. Some complained of the isolation, while others blessed their good fortune.

When the tow plane and the firing flight had effected a rendezvous, the tow would head out over the blue Pacific, with the formation flying parallel and climbing to a position higher and ahead of the tow. The idea of deflection gunnery with an airplane employed the same technique as shooting ducks. Lead, course tracking, and smoothness were everything. To acquire competence, various types of runs were made on the target. The primary one was also the most fun and was correctly called the overhead run.

The Corsairs, being ahead of and higher than the tow, would do a flat peel off, individually, and start rolling on their back as they did a 180-degree turn to come on to an opposite course to the tow. As the target came under them, they would fall into a vertical dive to come down on it at right angles. The fine, newly refined gun sight projected a reflection on the windshield that replaced the old iron sights. It presented two rings with a dot in the center. The outer ring was a 100-mil ring and the inner one a 50-mil ring. The dot in the center was called the "pipper" and served the same function as the front sight on a gun. The magic of this device was that it provided a constant sight base. In other words, at whatever angle the pilot viewed it, a true view was presented to him. The theory was that if the pipper was on the flight path of the banner, which was presumed to have a target speed of 200 knots and was positioned on the outer edge of the 100-mil ring, or any adaptation of this formula, it was time to open fire.

Various types of runs from different angles used the same principle, modified to fit the angle of approach and target speed. Perhaps the most important component of all was smooth flying. The ball in the turn-and-bank indicator had to be dead center, or the slugs from a skidding airplane would be thrown to one side.

In actual combat a fighter carried three types of ammunition. Their order of loading was a matter of choice and was suited to the type of target to be engaged. There was AP (armor piercing) for general destruction, incendiaries to ignite what they hit, and tracers that looked like an illuminated ball or left a smoke trail so the shooter could correct his aim. The tracers also were, to some degree, incendiary.

As the immortal e.e. cummings might have it "Lo the mighty hunter. With pluck and luck, he shot a duck." No doubt the Oracle of Poverty Flats wished that he had said that. Just as with duck hunters, some fighter pilots were more talented marksmen than others, and every once in a while some young rapscallion would get good enough to hit the buckle where the towing wire joined the banner. Then the banner would flutter down to the water, making any assessment of hits impossible since it was now irrecoverable. The tips of the .50-caliber rounds in each airplane were dipped in different-colored paints, which made scoring the hits on the banner possible. Usually one banner was enough, after his fellow pilots in the formation offered to use the marksman's plane for a target. After all, a no-deflection shot close behind another airplane was mighty effective and required little or no talent.

The Marine Corps' greatest ace never saw the Flying Tigers. He was a farm boy from South Dakota, Joe Foss, who ran up his score of twenty-six kills in the rather primitive Wildcat fighters over Guadalcanal without a reflector sight. Rumor had it that he had even thrown out the iron sights as useless weight and used a couple of rivets on the cowling for reference. Such was his status that any such tales, spurious or not, automatically acquired the patina of truth.

With its expanded role, the Corsair started carrying bombs and rockets. The dive brake on a Corsair, to limit the speed and therefore increase the accuracy of the run, was furnished by lowering the landing gear. The main gear had fixed cover plates that became part of the fairing when retracted. When used as a dive brake, only the main gear and not the tail wheel were deployed. By now the murderous fifty-five gallon reserve tanks in each wingtip had been removed, and extra gas could be carried in a releasable belly tank which actually was mounted on a pylon at the break of the gull wing. On the side opposite, a py-lon could carry a 1000-pound bomb.

Bombing practice was carried out against ground targets and a towed sled at sea with eleven-pound smoke bombs. Rather gratifying accuracy could be achieved, but that shrank to the ridiculous, com-pared to the real dive-bomber pilot's accomplishments. These chaps routinely engaged in what has been described as the nearest thing to hand-to-hand combat seen in an airplane. The war in the Pacific most definitely could not have been won without them. They were decisive in all fleet actions throughout the war. The Battle of Midway provides the most graphic illustration of their prowess.

There was a dive-bomber training squadron at El Toro, and they were flying the ubiquitous and unassuming SBD. This no-frills prod-uct of the Douglas Aircraft Company was known as the "Speedy Dee" and boasted perforated flaps that served as dive brakes. With these ex-tended, the aircraft descended on their targets at a relative speed that gave them incredible accuracy in the hands of a skilled and fearless pilot. This airplane served for a major part of the war virtually un-changed until replaced by bigger and fancier dive-bombers whose per-formance never rivaled these legendary machines.

One of my roommates at the hotel was a quiet young man whose combat accomplishments in this airplane were legendary. He had also participated in the marine dive-bomber mutiny, which is never dis-cussed with outsiders. He was also a senior man in the SBD training squadron. In line with the Threadbare Buzzard's ambition to fly ev-ery type of aircraft available, these airplanes were soon being borrowed for cross-country trips.

The Corsairs were great for flying all over the United States on any excuse because of their speed while they consumed vast quanti-ties of the taxpayers' 100-octane gasoline. However, the Speedy Dees had an incomparable advantage for taking trips. That was the rear cockpit, where many a brave rear gunner had fought his desperate bat-tles against the enemy. There were no enemies in the warm skies of southern California.

The ideal fighter pilot is supposed to possess resourcefulness, cunning, and the nerve of a bandit. These characteristics were pushed to the limit when getting a young lady of the civilian persuasion into a flight suit and helmet, past operations, and buckled into the rear cockpit of the SBD. Until the crate was over the fence and on its way to whatever romantic destination was contemplated, there was good cause to be nervous. Some misguided schmuck had decided that the relatively small engine of the Speedy Dee could run on only 80-octane gasoline, to save the aforementioned taxpayers money. This caused a lot of engine failures in unhappy places, like at the end of the takeoff runway. Fortunately, it was never discovered what sort of flap might result if a civilian lady were found in the wreckage. This fuel edict was ultimately withdrawn, but not before the lads at the field had discovered that, although pretty powerful, the government 80-octane did run better in personal automobiles than the all-too powerful 100-octane gasoline which had been tried. The rationing of civilian gasoline was one of the great hair shirts of the war.

The society of the field and Laguna Beach was diverse and interesting. One chap from the U.S. Army casually integrated with the marines. He was a captain, and in addition to his army wings on the left breast of his uniform he had RAF wings on the right breast. On his shoulder was a Flying Tigers patch. Among the many decorations on his manly chest was the Medal of Honor. He was usually with older women with large automobiles and was accepted by the noncritical veterans of the marines' air battles of the Pacific. There was actually quite a bit of sympathy expressed when the FBI led him away. The poor chap was actually a corporal who had escaped from the miserable army training out in the desert. What freedom-loving aviator could fail to have compassion for this unfortunate lad?

Another visitor was the real goods, whose appearance shocked the pilots of FTU into silence. He was an unimpressive chap in a plain blue suit representing an aircraft company. He was to get Corsair pilots up to speed on engine operation to extend their range by practicing fuel conservation. His name was Charles A. Lindbergh. That might not mean much in this day and age, but at that time it was the equivalent of Jesus Christ walking into the squadron ready room. The operations officer managed to take Lindbergh out to dinner at Victor Hugo's by the simple expedient of asking him. He became the envy of his fellows and reported that only one person, an army enlisted man, recognized the great man. When he came over and somewhat timidly asked for an autograph, the Lone Eagle graciously signed his menu.

Despite the intense social ramble, the workload at the squadron was considerable. There were some distractions that had to be dealt with, since the instructors were all veterans of the shooting war. This entitled them to some liberties, and keeping enough of them available to fly all of the students was sometimes a problem for squadron operations. One reason for this was soon revealed.

The hotel and beach had become the object of frequent buzzing by the newest version of the army's P-51 fighter. This machine had been around for a while, but didn't amount to much until it was re-engined with the British Rolls Royce Merlin engine, which powered the Spitfire. With the good, stable North American airframe it was simple to fly and, when manufactured in quantity, was to change the character of the air war in Europe due to its ability to do long-range bomber escorts flown with less skillful pilots. Some chance gossip uncovered an astounding story. These airplanes required a certain amount of airtime before being delivered to the army, and that required pilots. A respectable stipend per hour was paid to available aviators. Damned if some of the instructors weren't reaping this benefit while neglecting their responsibilities to the United States Marines. That matter was soon made right with loud, profane threats, and the instructor ratio to students improved.

The Corsair, although being rapidly improved from its primitive days as "The Birdcage," was still intimidating many of the students. During the war, life was not held to be as precious as it is now. Flying machines were inherently dangerous, anyway, and losses had to be expected. Losses in fighters were substantial. After all, you can't

Author with his dog True on eve of joining RCAF in early 1940.

Sergeant Pilot Tomlinson in His Majesty's Service, Calgary, Alberta, in 1941.

A coyote can get under a split-rail fence, a Tiger Moth cannot. Coyote-chasing was a popular boredom-breaking pastime for the pilots training at Moose Jaw, Saskatchewan.

Downtown High River, Alberta, site of an RCAF training base.

Author flying a Mark II Harvard outside Ottawa, Ontario (Rockcliffe Aerodrome), on February 10, 1942.

Fairey Battles on Trenton flight line, April 27, 1941.

F4F-4 Wildcats were flown by VMF-214, the Swashbucklers, during the squadron's first combat tour, when it was based on Guadalcanal.

VMF-214 on Guadalcanal during first combat tour. Author is standing fourth in from right side of photo.

Author in cockpit of Corsair prior to taking off from Russell Islands during VMF-214's second combat tour, July 1943.

Portrait of the Thread-bare Buzzard during a quiet moment on "that hellhole Munda" during second combat tour.

Author in Corsair escorting USMC PB4Y (B-24) photo plane on reconnaissance mission.

The Swashbucklers on Russell Islands during second combat tour. Note F4U Corsair in background. VMF-214 transitioned from Wildcats to Corsairs between their first and second combat tours.

VMF-215 awards ceremony on Vella Lavella. Bob Hanson, the war's top Corsair ace (25 total victories) is in middle with bandaged hand. Threadbare Buzzard is on Hanson's left with O. K. Williams on Tomlinson's left. Note Williams' fashionable "six-week flight suit"—not washed for six weeks.

Threadbare Buzzard and squadron mate O. K. Williams together again at Seattle's Museum of Flight during a summer 2002 event honoring Marine Fighting Squadron 214. (courtesy: heathmoffattphoto.com)

Threadbare Buzzard headed home with a hold full of Newfoundland lobsters.

Unloading the cargo at Rockland, Maine. Each case holds 125 pounds of lobster.

make an omelet without breaking some eggs. Even the major who had commanded the famed "Wolf Pack" squadron from Guadalcanal later fell victim, although not in a Corsair. He was filling some job in San Diego and flying an obsolete fighter up the coast after the war and had just completed speech correction school when it happened. He had quite a record in combat, but on the ground he stuttered. However, in the air he possessed crystal-clear diction. This was usually exhibited when he would employ his radio to issue such orders as "Let's go get the [censored]" just before leading his lads into some brawl against impossible odds.

However, his most reported conversation took place on the ground. It concerned the hapless New Zealand chaps in their obsolete P-40s that they flew heroically but were occasionally mistaken for Japanese by the marines. Landing after one action, the general demanded, "Did you guys shoot up those P-40s?"

"D-d-d-d-did you s-s-s-say sh-sh-sh-shot up or sh-sh-sh-shot down?" demanded the major.

The general, who may have thought he was being trifled with, said, with some heat and possibly some profanity, "I said shot up."

With equal heat and possibly some added profanity, the major replied, "W-w-w-well th-th-th-th-then, th-th-th-th-they w-w-w-weren't m-m-m-m-my boys. M-m-m-m' b-b-b-boys only sh-sh-sh-shoot 'em d-d-d-d-down."

The loss of men like the major affirmed a sentiment that was later formally expressed after the war with a stroke of pure genius in the book *Catch 22*. However expressed, the thought is that the enemy is anybody who is trying to kill you. This often caused the ever-present representatives of the airframe and engine manufacturers to receive suspicious looks from the combat pilots. Some of the training crashes were spectacular, and sometimes even amusing, if one were a fan of graveyard humor. One young man had walked away from the wreckage of two Corsairs, and the operations officer and his loyal assistant determined to wash him out before they ran out of airplanes. Some colonel up the line objected, saying that with that experience the youngster was more valuable than ever. The next Corsair killed him, but one does not go over to the administration building to sneer at any bird colonels.

One instructor had a four-plane division about twenty thousand feet over the Saddle Back when entering a prolonged dive. He got the formation into a little-understood circumstance called compressibility. Actually, it was due to getting up toward what was known in those days of innocence as the sound barrier. At this speed the airplane would become uncontrollable due to the air pressure building up ahead of the wings and then escaping with such turbulence as to destroy the effect of the control surfaces. The instructor, being an old hand, started rolling his elevator trim tabs back and managed to recover, although the box-beam that stiffened the wing was badly warped. The three students augered in, still in formation, leaving little but pulverized engine parts to give weight to their coffins.

Night flying was required and was a special hurdle for many students. The operations officer and his loyal assistant had a rather pleasant routine established for this training. They would take a portable radio to talk to the students in their airplanes, and a light truck to supplement the runway lights out to the approach end of the duty runway. A crash truck and an ambulance were also taken along. There was another addition to these arrangements, and that makes it necessary to understand the circumstances of the times and the glamour of war.

Los Angeles had the most beautiful girls in all of the land, since they came in droves to become movie stars and settled for being carhops at drive-ins, and other things. There were also many pretty young things attending UCLA. There was a college song at the time that stated: "You gotta be a football hero to get along with the pretty girls." These young ladies had modified this to command: "You gotta be a Corsair pilot to get along with the pretty girls." Some of these delectable dishes also had convertible automobiles filled with black-market gasoline supplied by their rich daddies. A lot of these convertibles could be found parked around the light truck with highball glasses on their hoods.

One moonless night while some revelers were so occupied, a Corsair crashed just outside the fence on the approach and went up in flames. Galvanized into action, the crash truck and ambulance were driven right through the fence. There was a surprise in store. In addition to the burning wreckage, there was another wrecked Corsair, unburned and with nobody in it. An intense search revealed its pilot quite dead where he had attempted to crawl to the fence. He had a separated spinal column. This put a damper on the evening. Flying was secured, and the operations officer and his loyal assistant made their way back to the hotel. Driving back to the field a little later than usual the next morning produced another unwelcome development. Coming over the Orange Street overpass with the El Toro field in full view, we saw a pillar of flame going up on the field. That turned out to be another former FTU student, who had dived in from a great height.

Things were not that pleasant around the squadron, what with all of the accident reports to write up, and it was a distinct relief when lunch time came. After a good lunch, coming out of the officers' mess, which was down by the front gate, the day looked a lot better. Briefly. In the traffic pattern overhead, many Corsairs were thundering around, and two of them picked this time to lock horns. One guy promptly bailed out, but the other did not. As the doomed pilot was coming down right in front of the gate, the fed-up operations officer said with some sarcasm, "Geez, look at that poor bastard trying to get out." There was a scream right to the rear and it turned out to be one of the new marine lady officers who fainted and later tried to get the operations officer in trouble for his unsympathetic assessment of the situation. There was some friction with these lady marines, since all marines are supposed to be combat troops. The ball-bearing marines impolitely referred to them as Bams, which stood for broad-assed marines. The ladies delicately responded by referring to the gentlemen as Hams, which stood for hairy-assed marines.

There were a lot of fatal incidents, and a well-known colonel who had been a fighter pilot and was now on some high-powered staff down at North Island flew up to look around. He grabbed the operations officer of FTU and his loyal assistant, who passed for the only senior officers around, and commandeered a jeep. He took them over to the officers' club for the announced purpose of lunch and some talk of airplanes, crashes, and other matters of current interest. In the bar at the club was a group of second-lieutenant students drinking beer.

The colonel, a fearsome spectacle under the most favorable circumstances, stalked over and demanded to know just what the hell they were doing and why weren't they at work. "Oh, we have the day off, colonel, 'cause we got night flying tonight," one of these finks piped up. The colonel expressed himself profanely, and after leveling a frosty stare at the operations officer and his loyal assistant, stomped out of the club and took off in the jeep. Upon returning to the squadron, the operations officer and his assistant discovered that the colonel and the airplane he flew in on were gone. Nothing more was heard from him.

Instructing was beginning to become tiresome, and the war seemed to be dragging on. I made several requests to transfer into a fighter squadron to get back to the real war. It was with surprise and horror that orders came to proceed to Jacksonville, Florida, to take up instructing in Corsairs at the navy's operational training command. There was even an explanation of how important and absolutely essential this work was to supply the war machine with more cannon fodder. Nothing to do but go to Jacksonville to explore other avenues of escape. The trip east afforded a jolly interlude. It was accomplished in the car of a veteran dive-bomber pilot who was a friend that had been sentenced to leave sunny California to fly at Cherry Point, North Carolina. At least he was going to a Marine Corps base. He came from what could be described as fortunate circumstances in, of all places, New Orleans, which had supplied the marines with a number of fine aviators. After a very long drive, especially across the vast nowhere land of Texas, this oasis of civilization was reached with great relief.

The dive-bomber pilot's family was in Washington, D.C., helping to direct the war, and left an opulent apartment in the historic Pontalba. With the friendly folk and fine watering holes available, this place would certainly impress anyone from Poverty Flats, Montana. It must also be emphasized that before World War II the population of the United States was not widely traveled.

With no particular desire to get to Jacksonville, it was a splendid opportunity to go native. A typical day started with breakfast at Pat O'Brien's, lunch and jazz at the Court of Two Sisters, and dinner at Antoine's. Evenings leaned heavily toward the French Quarter and Sazeracs. If there was an upside to World War II, it was the metamorphosis of the hick from the sticks to cosmopolitan sophisticate, or what he took to be one. The mixing-bowl effect of the war, with Mr. Truman's G.I Bill afterward, was what really standardized the widely scattered United States and made it what it is today—for better or worse.

Pure fatigue put paid to this interlude, and it was time to continue with real life. I bid the ever-loving "Big Easy" a sad farewell and boarded a "giant" airliner (a seventeen-passenger DC-3) for the remnant of the journey to Naval Air Station, Jacksonville, Florida. Here there would be rest and recuperation. The fact that it was well past the reporting date on the orders was no cause for concern. Experience showed that the mushrooming military, with its many pompous newly commissioned officers, was easily confused and uncertain as to what action to take. Any threats were usually meaningless anyway. Combat troops in a war take the casualties while the administrators proliferate like maggots.

JAX main side, as the vernacular had it, was a place of great consequence in the scheme of naval aviation. It sprawled in a bend of the Saint John river on reconstituted swampland. Its location had the usual gossip and rumor attached. World War II was not free from corruption, and these large military installations were often placed on otherwise worthless real estate owned by some astute and politically oriented local businessmen.

It was just such corruption that was the main factor in the final ascendancy of the absolutely incorruptible Harry Truman to the presidency of the United States. Then a senator, he headed the Truman Committee to investigate graft, which is always prevalent when a nation is fighting for its life. He apparently enjoyed detective work and gleefully recounted an experience in Texas, where a big contractor was building an air base on the usual cost-plus basis. The contractor was charging for a huge number of carpenters building a barracks, and Mr. Truman staked out the place and discovered there were damn few carpenters. He struck terror to those not pure of heart.

Mr. Truman had fired one of the last artillery shells in World War I, where he had served as the elected captain of his outfit (not an unknown procedure in that war), and this saved him from being impressed by the military. When he became president after Mr. Roosevelt's death, he had no trouble with the tough decisions it took to finish the war. He was also the only president in the twentieth century who did not have a college degree. This, no doubt, allowed his uncluttered mind to exercise its uncomplicated ability to cut directly to the chase and describe horse manure by its unpolitically-correct name.

XVIII

Upon checking in, it was apparent that JAX enjoyed the luxury with which navy officers invariably surround themselves. This always provided a cultural shock when compared to the austerity of the United States Marines, Army, or RCAF during this second Great War.

Reporting as an instructor merited living quarters in the senior bachelor officer's quarters (BOQ). Seniority is what it is all about for the U.S. Navy officer, and his seniority number is his most sacred possession. However, one chap encountered here was a graduate of the navy trade school for officers at Annapolis, and he informed lesser mortals (of equal rank) that *his* most sacred possession was his naval commission. He also informed the peasants that this background made him much too valuable to risk in combat. This stance was taken by some of his contemporaries, but the unwashed marines generally ignored them, and most of these unwashed wished to return to where the action was.

The senior BOQ was thoughtfully located beyond the officers' club and swimming pool in lush surroundings. It was far enough removed from the field to minimize the risk of falling Corsairs and students. Except for the usual utility aircraft, the Corsair was the main type of kite operated here, and it was stocked in large numbers. The airfields for the lesser types of aircraft, such as the navy's Hellcats and torpedo and dive-bombers, were located in other parts of the swampy peninsula.

After getting comfortably situated, there remained the necessity of reporting to the commander of training. He turned out to be in the rank of commander. He had a large office on the second floor of the administration building with a fine view of the field. This field had runways surrounding a huge paved area called "the Mat," with the hangars and flight line on one side. Despite a few misgivings, the commander of training offered no discussion about the seriously tardy date of reporting. He did, however, launch on a one-sided discussion concerning the differences in Marine Corps fighter training at faraway FTU in El Toro, California, and the navy version at Operational (OTU) here in Jacksonville. It was the commander's contention that they were much superior here in the swamps and that the marines out in sunny California were running nothing but a (expletive deleted) bloodbath.

With impeccable timing the crash siren started up the scale to its bone-chilling heights. It must be admitted that the Jacksonville model was very superior. In fact, even the air raid sirens of London would be hard-pressed to compete with it. Out there on the mat arose an impressive column of smoke and flame.

The commander didn't seem to have any more to add to his presentation. He wandered over to the window and stared morosely out at the evidence of a student bound for the promised land. The now endorsed orders were retrieved from his yeoman on the way over to the field. This proved to be the opening event in what became locally famous as "Bloody Easter Week."

All that was needed at that time and place was an episode that occurred later. That was when a navy lieutenant commander leaped out of a Corsair that he believed was imperiling his life. He did this in the vicinity of the field, and the kite, finding itself free, decided to go back home. It made several low passes over the many airplanes on the flight line at speed before landing. Unfortunately for the taxpayers, it lit right on the flight line with spectacular results.

Actually, this was a very exciting place. There has never been anything to rival the larger air training bases of World War II and there probably never will be again. A great host of aircraft emitting the satisfying thunder of big reciprocating engines made their presence felt day and night. There were training schools for many specialties besides flying, with their multitudes of staff and students. The maintenance shops and facilities would have been impressive all by themselves. Even the control tower could add to the excitement along with the meteorologist, whose office was located in a presumably windowless office below the tower.

Great thunderstorms could be generated over the vast, swampy peninsula that is Florida. Towering cumulonimbus clouds could build up on occasion on the side of the control tower that did not face the field. With many airplanes scattered all over the skies in the vicinity, some worried instructor would call the tower questioning the weather. Since the direction the tower personnel were facing would present a scene both fair and sunny, they would sometimes give sarcastic answers. They would apparently be unaware of the Great Roiling Black Monster looming behind them.

More than once there were incredible numbers of airplanes landed in equally incredible and widespread places, as the storm moved through, closing the field. It was heartily recommended by the instructors that the tower personnel be required to look back occasionally to see what was about to overtake them. It was further recommended that a window be cut in the south wall of the meteorologist's office and that he be required to occasionally look in that direction and bring the field's official status into conformance with these observations.

Another thing about those storms that brought down torrential rains is that occasionally it actually rained frogs. Once, while I was driving on a highway during a violent downpour, a patch of very small frogs were hopping all over the place. A young lady who was present and native to this place explained that this was not unusual. Such experiences were certainly instructive for a Buzzard from Poverty Flats, where such a thing would never happen.

There were two training squadrons, VF-4 and VF-5. VF-5 was for the navy chaps, since the much improved Corsairs had now been deemed safe enough for them. Some Royal Navy Fleet Air Arm pilots were included with this lot.

VF-4 was a blessed relief. Outside of navy people used for mechanics and certain administrative duties, it was commanded by a marine lieutenant colonel, and all of the instructors were marines returning from combat. In effect it was all-marine despite the lack of the *M* in its VF designation. The lieutenant colonel owned a distinguished combat record and a fine sense of humor.

Each instructor was issued seven students and a line of ten Corsairs to go with them. This allowed two full divisions (eight airplanes) to participate in the various evolutions of training with, and including, the instructor. These students were newly commissioned and already had much more flying experience than most of the earlier crop had entered combat with. They came mostly from training squadrons using the SNJ aircraft. This was the same trainer as the army's AT-6 and the British Mark II Harvard. It was a very stable little bird of only about six hundred horsepower and a product of the reliable North American Aircraft Company. There was a group of these kites assigned to each OTU squadron to use for instrument training, which required two seats so a student "under the hood" could be checked by an instructor. Navy instrument training had been sharply upgraded, and a card system had been installed to rate proficiency in instrument flying. The red card signified restricted, white was standard, and green was the top of the line, which allowed the holder to sign his own clearances.

Maintenance for the SNJ (or J-Bird) line was assigned to female sailors. The WAVES (Women Accepted for Volunteer Emergency Service) along with the "Bams" and their army counterparts were a burgeoning population in the services. Not surprisingly, VF-4's maintenance WAVES entertained various grievances, real as well as imagined. The leader of these WAVES was fearsome, enough so that the Oracle of Poverty Flats would have described this lady as being able to fight a grizzly bear with a switch. Although she was an enlisted woman, the rather gentlemanly officer commanding VF-4 related a hilarious encounter with her, of which he seemed rather proud.

Before the Corsairs were started in the mornings, the 2,000-horsepower engines had to be pulled through. This was done by having the brawniest lads on the Corsair lines pull the huge propellers through a certain number of blades, against tremendous engine compression. The lady charged into the colonel's office and, claiming discrimination, demanded that her WAVES be accorded the right to work on the Corsairs. The colonel, in relating this encounter to his troops, said that he diplomatically tried to explain that he considered the chore of pulling the Corsair engines through to be a bit much for the "ladies."

Upon hearing this the amazon placed her knuckles on the desk and, engaging our CO up close and eyeball to eyeball, demanded in a very menacing manner, as he cowered behind his desk, "Just what the hell makes you think us 'ladies' can't pull those (expletive deleted) Corsair engines through?"

How he handled this matter would, I'm sure, have made good reading in a book on leadership. Unfortunately, the story ended there. At any rate the "ladies" remained on the SNJ line, albeit they were a bit surly.

The training syllabus required a great deal of familiarization to get the students over their reservations about the Corsair. Some of the instructors maintained that the accident rate could be lowered if they would only close the student officers' club or at least the bar. That is where those who had checked out in the Corsair would instill terror in the hearts of those who had not yet checked out. They recounted hairy tales of misadventure and great dangers that only a person as fearless and talented as themselves could possibly survive.

After successfully checking out, the routine of formation flying, cross-country navigation, and instrument flying were pursued. By the time this phase was well along, the student was becoming more confident and usually quite good at handling the machine, as he was eased into the real world. The very soul of the Marine Corps, as explained before, concerns accuracy with any weapon available to them. Therefore, live firing was the top priority and real object of all of the training. The capabilities of the Corsair had been expanded to include dive-bombing and would shortly include carrying rockets and the first primitive napalm tanks.

The dive-bombing was practiced, just as it was at El Toro, using eleven-pound smoke bombs against an armored cabin cruiser painted international orange and operating off the beach in the Atlantic Ocean. Eleven pounds does not sound very frightening unless one is in an unarmored civilian cabin cruiser (not painted international orange), where the arrival of one of the smoky little eleven-pound horrors can wreak havoc with a carelessly held martini.

It is nice to believe that it was a navy flight that attacked this inoffensive target, since it wasn't even in the area designated for bombing. This belief was substantiated by the fact that, although there were some near misses, the unwilling target survived.

The air-to-air gunnery ranges ran seaward from a distance off Fernandina Beach above the mouth of the Saint John River. A facility was established at Mayport, south of the river and near the ocean. Many years later it became a large base in its own right. Such was not the case at that time, and it was merely a place to gas up, load ammunition, and get a hamburger without going clear back to Main Side between gunnery hops. Then it was discovered that shrimp boats put in at a small dock practically on the base. After that it became customary to get a large platter of iced shrimp and a few bottles of beer over on the dock while the kites were being rearmed and fueled.

Out over the Atlantic, no matter how fine the day, there always seemed to be haze and this always posed a problem. Actually, the ocean would often be obscured and a student could get lost at the bottom of his dive. Local legend had some of them getting into progressive stalls and going right in. After the war, this restricted visibility was made famous by Flight Nineteen with their cumbersome TBMs and tales of the Bermuda Triangle.

On these air-to-air gunnery operations, a twin-engine medium bomber made legendary by the U.S. Army was used. It had many advantages, the chief one being the ability to stream and recover the banners that were used as targets. It had a reel and an operator within the fuselage for the cable, which could be recovered, allowing the aircraft to service several flights without returning to base. This was also an asset if some hot rock shot the banner loose from the cable.

This airplane was the army's original B-26 or Martin Marauder manufactured by the Martin Aircraft Company in Baltimore, Maryland. Having awesome power and very little wing, it had become known as "The Flying Prostitute" or the "Baltimore Whore" (no visible means of support). It had a distinguished combat record in the hands of some especially talented army pilots. For the less talented it provided sure passage to the big officers' club in the sky.

The ones the navy was operating had several feet added to their wings, but they were still a handful. The brave navy lieutenant that towed for VF-4 lost an engine right after takeoff at JAX Main Side and found himself flying through the tops of the loblolly pine trees in desperate circumstances. Any course adjustments or attempts to gain altitude were obviously going to result in what was sarcastically known as losing one's officers' club privileges. Bellowing for help on the radio gained invaluable assistance in prolonging the lives of the lieutenant and his crew. The number of military airfields constructed in Florida during World War II boggles the imagination, and many of them in the vicinity of the struggling "prostitute" were cleared until the pilot reached one that had a runway closely aligned with the one he had left at JAX. It would be a fine thing to report that this incident started him on a new career as a born again Christian, but that would be wholly untrue.

The aforementioned visibility problem on the gunnery ranges, especially while doing overhead runs, often had a debilitating influence on the tempers of some of the instructors. This run required the fighter (as reported before and will now be repeated) to be approaching the target quite a bit higher on an opposite course and inverted as it started down on the 100-mil-deflection firing pass. As the students recovered from this now high-speed dive after firing, some of them become disoriented in the muck and were unable to locate their flight to join up. This tended to drive the instructors bananas.

At this time, the control towers were becoming increasingly manned by women (WAVES). The navy, which believes in leadership by coercion, had a large campaign complete with vigorous penalties to protect the delicate ears of the ladies from the usual profanity on the radios. One unidentified instructor, becoming increasingly frustrated trying to get his flight back under control, snarled, "This is the most effed-up [effed isn't exactly what he said but will be close enough] flight I have ever been on."

The next voice was obviously feminine and demanded, "Will the officer using profane language on the air please identify himself? Repeat, this is Jacksonville tower, please identify yourself." The instructor promptly replied, "Lady, this flight may be effed-up, but by God its not that effed-up."

There were also references to the deity, and the one most remarked on concerned an exasperated instructor trying to communicate with a student. After receiving no answer to several requests he raged, "Jesus Christ, answer!" A very gentle and conciliatory voice came on the radio and said, "This is Jesus Christ, go ahead."

Unfortunately, the concept of women in the service was not, at that time, completely popular with the menfolk. Some of the enlisted women were cute little cupcakes, but due to the bluenosed navy with its nonfraternization regulations, they were not available to officers. Generally, lady officers were just as unavailable due to the law of natural selection; any of them possessing the required assets to be selected were already being pursued by more senior officers.

There was another factor that was hardly fair to the many fine young civilian girls who were just mad about aviation. Although JAX didn't have the great two-seat SBD dive-bombers found at El Toro, JAX did have the SNJ, which also had two seats and could have provided these confections with a severely "off-limits" reward for their aeronautical enthusiasm. Sneaking them past the lady sailors on the J-Bird line, however, was unrealistic. Unthinkingly, the navy had significantly deflected this assault on good order and discipline.

There were often crashes in remote areas, and a flight surgeon convinced the brass that a light airplane in the hands of a skillful pilot might just get a doctor on scene in time to save a life. To this end they acquired a few of the really fine Stearman biplanes used in primary training, and later they were even provided with a basic little Taylor Cub. These were a lot of fun to fly, and of course the volunteer lifesaver should have considerable practice to develop his technique. That, of course, would require landing and taking off on random remote roads rather than formal airports. More than one young female aviation enthusiast from the state of Florida enjoyed her first flight from these "random roads." Although they had to settle for less horsepower than was provided by the J-Birds, they found that light aircraft, especially an open-cockpit biplane, provides the ultimate in the exuberant freedom of flight.

One lesson learned was to exercise extreme caution and close attention to the time when returning to JAX Main Side with the Taylor Cub. At certain times, the number of Corsairs taking off on the great mat at the same time had to be witnessed to be believed. Approaching the field one morning, it was takeoff time for many flights. Sitting right in the path of a swarm of Corsairs with their fourteen-foot props driven by the 2,000-horsepower engines and in the partial control of a bunch of half-baked students would be bad enough, but in a cute little Taylor Cub, ye Gad!!! The kite didn't seem as if it could get out of the way, even in the painfully slow vertical dive it was in.

The population of lady officers led to a rather amusing episode concerning two extremely heroic marine officers. Quite a few ground officers were trying their hand at aviation and, whatever their rank, were classified as students while in training. As such, they lived in the junior officers' quarters, which were about halfway between senior officers' quarters and the field. Being in possession of two of these "students"

was a mixed blessing. Both were majors and one of these had already
been selected for lieutenant colonel. Both had great records in combat,
and the soon-to-be lieutenant colonel had performed such prodigious
feats at Tulagi during the invasion of Guadalcanal that he had become
a legend. The U.S. press had accorded him a great deal of national attention, making him a superhero. He also looked the part, which was
not really mandatory for those guys. He was a giant in stature and had
the coldest impersonal gray eyes ever encountered.

One morning I agreed to meet these two "students" down at the
junior officers' mess on the way to the squadron. This agreement had
been reached late in the evening at the officers' club, where strategy
and tactics had been discussed at length. It was early in the day after
a very short night, and a time for peace and quiet.

In fact, time had slipped away, and arrival at the junior officers'
mess allowed a limited time for breakfast before the mess closed. The
three badly hung-over, morose marine officers were addressing their
eggs when a lady navy lieutenant scurried in, much to the distress of
the waiter who needed to get closed up to prepare for lunch. She recognized the soon-to-be lieutenant colonel and, apparently to arouse
some response, started preening.

Officers could get short orders and specify how they hoped their
eggs would turn out. The lady, feeling some frustration for not pene-
trating the hangovers of the marines, extended her operation to attract attention by giving the waiter a bad time over the state of the
eggs and peremptorily ordered him to take them back for repair or
replacement. If there is one principle of the marine line officer (not
to be confused with an aviator), it is to respect the rights of the troops.
In the field the enlisted eat first and officers are supposed to lead the
charge when in combat. In return they are supposed to get unques-
tioned loyalty and obedience. They would never consider abusing the
troops under any circumstances.

The lady officer now had the undivided attention of the soon-
to-be-lieutenant colonel. He leaned across the table and placed a fore-
finger, approximately the size of a fence post, right over the subject's

eggs. His cold, impersonal, although slightly bloodshot, eyes seemed to hypnotize his subject. "Lady," he said in measured tones, "you eat them goddamn eggs." Breakfast was finished in a blessed silence, and the lady did a very commendable job with the eggs as they were.

Marine pilots of much experience were usually skeptical of newly trained pilots in senior grades. This chap, who did in fact before graduation become a lieutenant colonel, accomplished something unheard of. He engendered such respect that all of the combat-experienced marine instructors were hopeful that the marines would give him the command of a combat squadron and petitioned to go with him if this materialized. Leadership comes in many packages, some better wrapped than others.

Two other students in the other squadron were navy lieutenants (senior grade) with a fascinating tale to tell. They had transferred into aviation from the surface navy, where they were on destroyers or destroyer escorts. They had been onboard one of these in the Aleutian Islands, where a ragtag U.S. naval force was to engage a Japanese diversionary force deployed before the Battle of Midway. Their skipper was an officer of the regular establishment who was apparently falling victim to stress and/or fatigue.

He had taken to drinking "Sneaky Pete," an intoxicant extracted from torpedo juice. This led to some bizarre conduct, like mustering all hands aft to denounce a hapless ensign who was not only a reservist but, to go with his other sins, from New York. When in port the skipper would go ashore to consort in drunken revel with the native women. When the admiral messaged all ships to join up for the impending action, that is where he was. His officers claimed they couldn't find him (a lie) and were ordered to get the ship underway regardless and without delay. This was long before the famous book *The Caine Mutiny* was written, but it is to wonder at the similarities. With the navy theory that the captain is God, this was probably not an isolated incident, given the vast scope of the war.

The next class of students produced near disaster. On checkout, one student lost control and smashed into a concrete light standard at the end of a runway far from the intended takeoff path. This left the engine completely submerged in the mud of the riverbank and the student hanging in the cockpit with one eye hanging from its socket. Fortunately, this eye was reinstalled and returned to complete vision.

The next casualty was an enlisted pilot. These chaps went through flight training in the ranks, but by that time in the war they had to be commissioned before entering combat. This righted a wrong done to some of the Marine Corps' finest pilots in the early days of the war.

It was this lad's misfortune to draw a Corsair with a faulty engine. By this time in its development, the mighty Pratt & Whitney was becoming almost totally reliable. However, there was the occasional anomaly. He was tooling along enjoying the view from a few thousand feet up and a short distance inland from Ponte Vedra Beach when his engine froze. He exhibited excellent judgment, considering that his machine was gliding like a streamlined brick and would never reach the ocean to ditch. He elected to pursue a "nylon letdown procedure," although the combat chutes used in fighters afforded a rapid descent.

He wound up in the jungle just back of the Intracoastal Waterway with his chute tangled in the trees. After loudly hollering for help that never came, he started jerking vigorously on the shroud lines of his chute that were holding him in suspension rather far above the earth's surface, which was all swamp anyway. The shaking resulted in a shower of snakes raining down upon him. Coming from some civilized region like Oklahoma, he found the idea of snakes in trees so startling that he promptly released his harness buckles, the hell with the height. His fall was somewhat cushioned by the swamp, which also either cushioned the fall for the snakes with him or disturbed others already resident.

Acting with commendable speed and ignoring a fractured leg, he adopted a course that fortunately brought him out of the jungle into a clearing. In the clearing he found some Florida crackers observing him with interest. They readily admitted to seeing him coming down in his chute. And just why in the name of the deity didn't they come to his rescue?

"Wall, ole Beauregard he went in thar last week an the snakes got im. Funeral wuz only yes'tiday."

Then two students in the flight came up with medical problems and the flight was broken up. The survivors got some time off before starting again.

This also applied to me, their instructor, who fired up his fire-engine red Harley-Davidson 45. It must be confessed that a lot of this bike had been chrome-plated over in the A&R shops, which were run by a friend in the navy. There was time for a very jolly run clear down to the end of the Overseas Highway. Black-market gasoline in defiance of strict rationing posed no problem in Florida. After some time lying on a beach at Key West contemplating the vagaries of life and fate, it was time to return to the realities of instructing and to try to find some way out of that onerous chore. This was almost taken care of permanently on the way back to JAX.

On a black night up in central Florida a game of tag developed with some youngsters in a hot rod. After lying back and then accelerating to high speed and leaning out to pass them on the two-lane pavement, a very unfortunate circumstance developed. Around a curve, and out of the jungle, two bright, well-spaced headlights announced the arrival of a large freight truck on an opposite course. Without maneuvering room, the only course of action was to keep on leaning and let go of the bike.

The god of aviators provided a swamp for this emergency. The catapult shot provided when the bike hit the ditch ended in a landing in the absorbing muck. The once splendid little Harley was upside down, roaring its life away with an apparently stuck suicide throttle. The engine finally just exploded. Both the hot rod and the freight truck had come to a halt, and, back on the road, the occupants were busy exploring with flashlights. The silence after the demise of the motorcycle's engine was penetrated by a shout, "Has anybody found the body?" A sobering thought.

"Right here," said the creature from Black Lagoon emerging into the light, dripping slime, and somewhat startling these concerned chaps. The fine young hoodlums in the hot rod managed to scrape up some ill-fitting clothes and then insisted on providing transportation clear back to JAX Main Side. For this kindness they were rewarded with the motorcycle, which wasn't worth a whole lot by that time. Now, it was back to work, with a lifetime aversion to motorcycles.

XIX

The navy never gave up on its fascination with its own merits. One day they had a big lecture for the instructors by one of their great heroes. He turned out to be the commander of the navy squadron that had shown up at Munda with their advanced model Corsairs and even ice cream. They had come with their liberal scoring system to share in the glory or at least the publicity the marines were getting at that time. The marine instructors arose and silently walked out. So much for motivational speakers.

The marines at JAX had learned to treat the navy with suspicion. They had one hail fellow well met who had been the big hero, with his air group, in the early fighting. He liked to do the father figure bit in the "O" club bar and place his hand on the knee of handsome young pilots. Since he was in the rank of commander, the naive youngsters, until enlightened, found this flattering. He later departed the service under less-than-honorable circumstances. It was discovered that he was the leader of a whole ring of chaps of similar outlook in the area.

In senior BOQ, two rooms shared a common bath. The naval officer across the bath had an interesting hobby. He collected vast quantities of drinking whiskey. This at first glance appeared passing strange. However, it developed that he had been deck officer on a cruiser that had been sent to the bottom of Iron Bottom Sound at Guadalcanal in a bloody night action. Interestingly enough, he didn't drink a lot of this booze, but it probably represented a measure of security in this uncertain world.

He had returned and completed flight training as an observation pilot. These people flew a low-horsepowered, low-winged crate designated an OS2U and fitted with pontoons. In the fleet they flew off of cruisers. They had a catapult overlooking the river to practice their only exciting maneuver. Here he had been detained as an instructor, which he hated. He also hated a group of arrogant Annapolis cadets who were getting some aviation familiarization during the summer session. It fell to his lot to give these youngsters a familiarization flight. He confided with joy just how he was able to afford a great number of them this flight in record time.

He would have them strapped firmly in the rear cockpit and establish voice communication on the intercom. Instructing them to put their heads down and brace themselves, he would signal the launching officer. As the little plane hurtled down the catapult he would allow the throttle to come back to idle and land right off the end of the catapult. Many of the cadets didn't even realize that anything had happened and were surprised as the crane hooked up to reposition the OS2U.

There were still some limited adventures to be had in the area, and one concerned the Okefenokee Swamp that lay to the west of JAX. It reached its greatest dimensions across the border up in Georgia. There was a great population of alligators residing there, and young folks in fighter-type aircraft liked to drift up there and, if they happened to have any ammunition on board, open fire. There was no confirmation of kills, since evidence would be hard to come by. However, when a navy pilot managed to crash in this swamp, the taxpayers footed a staggering expense in a futile attempt to recover the body for his politically oriented relatives. After that, due to new and stringent navy regulations concerning the air space above and about this natural wonder, it was left mostly to Pogo and his friends.

Another welcome interruption of the routine was the hurricane fly-aways. When one of these dreaded occurrences was forecast, it was time to batten down the hatches. Since all of the aircraft wouldn't fit into the available hangars, many were flown away out of the projected path of the natural disaster. The first time a flight was led north, some of the navy's planning wound up landing the flight at a U.S. Army basic training field.

This was a grass field with only a single paved runway. Landing the eight-plane flight posed no problem. Having pulled off the runway and gotten out of the aircraft, the navy flyers met a couple of army pilots who came over to chat. As the conversation had just turned to mutual complaints about instructing, a distant rumbling was heard. This increased in volume at a rapid rate. Fearing that the hurricane had somehow magically spanned a great distance, all eyes turned south. Over the horizon roared an impressive sight.

There were great clouds of navy aircraft of every description, and they were all headed for this minuscule field—some planning. They all exhibited a determined ambition to land first by attempting to cut inside the traffic pattern that grew around the field. There was soon an ever-tightening, snarling vortex extending straight up above the shocked observers. Looking up this funnel as the ground shook from the thunder of many engines, one saw it had the shape and fury of a real hurricane. By some small miracle there were no fatalities, and soon the small facility was awash with aircraft. Not waiting to see what the sleeping or messing arrangements might be for this gigantic invasion force, the first arrivals slipped away unnoticed and made off at treetop level for Atlanta.

My second visit to Atlanta on a fly-away resembled the first, except that this time the original destination was an army operational training field. Its commanding officer was a rather typical army colonel, and he soon revealed that he had very little use for marine aviators since he had nearly been shot down in the South Pacific by these unskilled bastards. It didn't take long to assume the guilt for this military slight. It was added that the Marine Corps never equated a big mouth with a big man anyway. This time the flight was practically ordered to Atlanta—or at least off his field.

After once again leaving the kites at the navy's Atlanta Instrument Flying School, it was off to the fine hotel on Peachtree Street. One morning in the wreckage-strewn suite, one of the members of the flight called room service for breakfast. He was not alone in being one of professional baseball's brightest stars then serving in aviation, but he was the only one on that flight. At that time an intensive advertising campaign had ingrained the idea that the "Breakfast of Champions" was a well-known breakfast cereal for championship athletes.

"Send me up the Breakfast of Champions," the baseball star advised room service, who, with the rest of the hotel staff, were tiptoeing around this hero like he was God or somebody. When they asked for verification that he truly wanted the advertised cereal, his visage darkened and he bellowed, "No, goddamn it! I mean ham and eggs and a bottle of beer!"

That rather typified the whole vacation, and it was about a week later when the worn-out warriors found their way back to the airplanes at the instrument school. With the hurricane long past, there was trouble in the Confederacy. JAX was apparently distraught about the airplanes, to say nothing of the pilots. The god of aviators usually provides in these situations, and what he provided here was the operations officer. This chap was none other than the tough marine major who had commanded the most outstanding TBF squadron to fly in the Solomon Islands. As he explained it, although he had damn little use for fighter pilots, there was some residual appreciation of the lengths they had often gone to in the interests of his squadron's survival. Whatever messages he sent were not discovered, but the flap was over.

There was another interesting thing to experience at least once at JAX. That was to take a Corsair to Daytona Beach. During the depression years immediately before the war, there was intense interest in land speed records. The most publicized of all of the drivers was a

British chap, Sir Malcolm Campbell, who would do his act with the beautifully built speed machine *The Bluebird*. With incredible publicity the entourage would descend on the wide, white beaches of Daytona, Florida. Headlines would scream of blinding speeds in the vicinity of three hundred miles an hour. A well-handled Corsair, following a steep dive and proceeding at approximately the same altitude as *The Bluebird* had been driven, could accomplish the same course at around five hundred miles an hour. Take that, Sir Malcolm. This did annoy the natives.

Living close to this beach was a retired navy admiral. Retired admirals never forget that they were admirals and always believe that they still are. The way the navy observes their clout would tend to verify this belief. This retired admiral became outraged by the scream of Corsairs blowing the sand up from the beach and started keeping a list of the prominent side numbers of the aircraft. His reports caused some of the pilots some very difficult times and called for vengeance.

It was noted that the lower wings of the Corsairs did not have numbers. This caused some hard losers to locate the exact location of his highness' house and, screaming in from seaward, initiate a chandelle turn approximately in his front yard. This maneuver revealed no aircraft numbers to the observer, but it did rattle the windows. Management's next major project on the flight line was painting large numbers on the bottom of all of the Corsair wings.

Along with several other young marine instructors, the main topic of conversation around the swimming pool was how to escape from this hedonistic refuge of the faint of heart. One of these chaps, named Joe Lynch, came from Boston, which had furnished more than one outstanding Marine Corps fighter pilot to the war. His accent was colorful and authentic. He had distinguished himself at Guadalcanal, as much by a comment he had delivered as by his actions, which were also very distinguished.

He was in a flight that had spent a very interesting day covering some dive-bombers attacking Japanese ships at Kolombangara. Few of the aircraft had gotten up there, which was at extreme range for the

Wildcats. They were seriously engaged in fighting off a large assortment of Japanese fighters trying to prevent the dive-bombers from performing their duty. The Wildcat leader was among those shot down, and the lad from Boston continued to make runs on the aggressors even after he ran out of ammunition. This saved a few lives, especially for those in parachutes, and it was only a miracle that his remaining fuel got him back to Guadalcanal. His arrival was after dark, and the airstrip was under attack.

The local antiaircraft chaps, suspecting the worst and being in a state of high excitement, opened fire on his battered Wildcat as it skidded down the strip. Extracting himself from the wreckage, he sprinted for the command dugout, where he arrived out of breath. He ran right into the general in charge of aviation in those parts, who was a considerate man always concerned with the well-being of his troops.

Taking note of the gasping Bostonian he inquired in a kindly fashion, "What is it, son? What's the matter?"

"Jeez, general," panted the lieutenant, "a guy can get to be a veteran around here just like that." He snapped his fingers to demonstrate his point. This graphic illustration confirmed his fame as much as his continued and commendable actions on behalf of the United States of America.

He entertained many thoughts on how to leave JAX behind, and one would seem to be foolproof. When one staff-type navy officer was boasting that he played handball with the admiral, the Boston chap wanted to know what would happen if he ever beat the old boy. The naval hero looked shocked and said it would probably mean being sent straightaway to the fleet—not a popular destination in this circle. The Boston boy demanded to know just when he could arrange a match with his majesty. Unfortunately for his plot, very few navy admirals fraternize with any grubby marine types.

There were legions of these staff officers because it is the navy's belief that enlisted men are not capable of coherent thought, and an officer must supervise even the most picayune of undertakings. Sometimes it appeared that their main employment was to criticize pilots.

One night in the game room of the senior officers' quarters, with the Boston lad present, it was possible to discuss this with the senior chaplain, who also came from Boston and had supplied spiritual guidance there before the war. Also present, and assisting in relieving some young fighter pilots of their flight pay, was the base psychiatrist. His was a relatively new specialty that was endeavoring to discover what made a good fighter pilot tick. With the military's wish to standardize all of its parts, this had led to some hilarious interviews when some very personal and often embarrassing questions were asked of the irritated, and usually individualistic, pilots. The psychiatrist interceded when the Boston lad asked the chaplain how you were supposed to love your brother if the SOB was a staff officer. The brain warper explained that they were more to be pitied than censured.

It was a matter of simple jealousy arising from the frustration these staff officer chaps felt, and also their resentment of the glamorous fighter pilots. That psychiatrist didn't seem to appreciate the fact that no fighter pilot felt very glamorous after finishing a tour of combat. Anyway, he continued, the root cause of most of mankind's problems was traceable to sex. Fighter pilots for some reason had been assigned an enviable and wholly undeserved, he said, reputation of knights in shiny armor, which was catnip to the young ladies. Therefore, it was the dedicated duty of the losers to attempt to cut them down whenever possible.

It is hard to believe at this remove, but these chaps *were* more to be pitied than censured. The times were completely different then, with the war following hard on the heels of the Great Depression. Mr. Franklin D. Roosevelt's programs to cure the social and monetary inequities were introducing a new and respectable middle class. College graduation was also a much rarer and more difficult task in those days. After the struggle for education, most were still really nothing more than Bob Cratchets. The commissions the staff officers gleaned because of their educations often was their first encounter with an elevated social status, and then they encountered the pilots. Now, even with the wrinkles out of their bellies and newfound status, they were upstaged by the aviators, whose difficulties with the young ladies were few.

One night the night-flying duty was shared with the Boston pilot, and that produced another of his memorable remarks. This duty required one instructor to be in the control tower at JAX more or less supervising air operations. The other instructor was actually out flying with the students. This was supposed to exercise some control over the students, who in some cases were creative souls. In fact the lieutenant colonel commanding VF-4 claimed that one night he was out at the dog races when out of the dark a Corsair appeared and proceeded to chase the greyhounds around this very small track. Possibly he exaggerated.

On this night of night-flying duty with the Bostonian, a lot of attention was attracted to a great explosion and raging fire at a place where several roads converged between the base and the city of Jacksonville. A general recall was issued for all of JAX's airplanes, and a fire truck and ambulance were dispatched on speculation. It was an airplane all right, but fortunately for us it was an army P-51 from an army field up in Georgia that was also doing night flying. The pilot was actually giving the home of his mother, who lived in the neighborhood, a buzz job that included a serious misjudgment of distance. The local fire chief and the Boston man, who by default was representing the base, were more or less sharing the on-scene responsibility. They were also being harassed by an excited elderly woman who was greatly impressed by her exposure to fame.

She kept grabbing at the Bostonian and pointing out the place where she had been standing only a week ago, which was now a sea of flame, "And if . . . ." After many "and ifs," he became thoroughly irritated, and right in front of an eager newspaper reporter, snapped in his rich Irish accent, "Madam, if dogs ate Wheaties they would defecate [he used a less delicate synonym here] square bricks." This made the papers as an example of crude Yankee insensitivity for the delicate feelings of southern ladies.

About this time a surprise visitor appeared in the senior officer's barroom one evening. It was none other than the officer who had "a million of 'em cornered" and had certainly contributed to the demise of the Swashbucklers' version of VMF-214. He was on some staff touring from Marine Corps Headquarters and proudly announced that he had played a large part in the decision to not expose combat pilots to further action for the time being. In this he had to be in the minority of marines, who more than anyone else wanted to finish the war.

It was now apparent that getting back to an operational squadron was going to take as much effort as it had taken to get in one originally. There was one encouraging sign, however. The fine lieutenant colonel commanding VF-4 finished his tour, and this occasioned a round of parties by his friends and admirers that may have set a record in military circles. The good news was that his replacement was the squadron skipper who had revealed his intentions of shooting down a complete flight of army B-25s if any more bombs came down on the PT boats at Bougainville. He was noted as an aggressive leader and sympathized with any ambitions to return to operational flying. To this end he put on some pressure to secure a transfer for his unhappy instructor. Unfortunately, no attention had been paid to what the guy who was now flying a desk in Washington had boasted of.

This action fully demonstrated the law of the unintended result. My orders came through all right, but they were for a position in a command just across town at the Jacksonville municipal airport. The navy had commandeered a portion of it for operational training for their patrol training. In order to carry out long-range, land-based searches, they were operating the Consolidated B-24 Liberators under the navy designation of PB4Y.

This assignment came with a glowing recommendation that it would really be a promotion to department head and almost be like commanding a squadron. The "squadron" was a group of Wildcat fighters soon to be replaced with a newer version designated as the FM-2. This new model's chief claim to fame was its ability to climb like a homesick angel. With the airplanes came a group of fighter pilots whose chief employment was to make gun camera attacks on the lumbering Liberators. The Liberators' gunners would fire back with their cameras. It was almost immediately apparent that those awkward beasts needed a lot of improvement in the gunnery department.

The PB4Y was the same type of aircraft flown by the navy friend who had afforded the ride on his simulated Trans-Pac out of North Island. For a short time, the chance to learn how to fly this four-engine dog engaged my interest. However, it reaffirmed the fact that the bigger the airplanes, the more stable they were, and with their painfully slow speeds they were suited to more phlegmatic types. Physical strength didn't hurt either, since they flew like a truck and even with constant trimming required heavy wrestling. It was whispered that the ideal B-24 pilot required a small, well-muscled head and broad shoulders. He certainly needed patience if he were to gain any altitude or progress over the vast distances the B-24's fuel endurance allowed them. In addition to that, they were noisy and cramped and vibrated continually. Both for these navy crews and the thousands of army chaps who used vast numbers of these cumbersome contraptions in the bloody air battles of Europe, only the highest and sincerest respect must be entertained. Perhaps even more respect should be extended to the army pilots who wrestled them over the "High Hump" of the Himalayas hauling freight. According to some sources, there were more B-24s made than any other combat type manufactured during the war, and they certainly made a substantial contribution to the outcome.

All navy installations must have a bar, and the small facility at the municipal airport sported one in the modest living quarters. Alcohol has been forbidden on the navy's ships ever since a rash regulation was promulgated by a bluenosed secretary of the navy. His name was Josephus Daniels (no relation to Jack), and his decree lives in infamy to this day. Anyway, this stricture does not apply to navy shore installations nor cause them to obey the laws of the individual states.

This offered an interesting dilemma for the navy base where the basic training in B-24s took place. It was in a dry state in the Midwest, and it had an officers' club, of course, also with booze, of course. The JAX B-24s, being the operational training segment, wandered far afield. Hoisting good Scotch whiskey into the aircraft's wheel wells while on the ground at Hamilton, Bermuda, during navigation flights was not at all unusual. This allowed this heady treat to complete its untaxed journey into the U.S. of A.

Sometimes a JAX Liberator would take a navigation hop out to the basic field in the barren and parched Midwest with a load of this vital commodity. Over those hot flatlands some powerful thunderstorms can develop, with appalling vertical currents. Airborne radar, which was just coming on line, was not in general use, and without it there was no way to judge these hazards to navigation on a dark night. One night, over the bone-dry state, some of the chaps were hauling just such a cargo when they unwittingly flew into one of these storms. The Liberator got torn apart and was scattered over miles of prairie that was now irrigated with ninety proof. This event even caused some trouble as far up the line as Congress, but the final outcome was never discovered. Neither was the finale of another rather interesting episode at this frontier outpost.

By now the war was stabilized enough for the military to become infested with every specialty known to man. One that was much resented by the aircrews were the Jock Straps. Muscles were their business, and the not so apocryphal story was that one of these beauties upon reporting for duty as an athletic officer exclaimed, "Jeez, yesterday I couldn't spell Enswine and today I are one." The one giving the base in the boondocks the benefit of his act was a genuine famous big-league football coach who preached the doctrine of fearlessness in the face of the enemy. His fame in the civilian world was such that he had been commissioned as a senior-grade lieutenant. These valiant commandos who would never fire a shot in anger were just considered a part of the acute inconvenience of serving one's country by the resigned airmen. Love and respect they would have to do without.

One night this redoubtable hero was in the bone-dry town where the base was located and unquestionably had had a few when a local cop approached with nothing particular in mind. The lieutenant panicked and took off in his car. Careening through the gate of the base with the now interested cop in hot pursuit, he skidded to a stop in front of the officers' club. There was a formal party in progress. The jock dashed in and, placing himself in the prone position, seized the commanding officer's legs and beseeched him to not let them take him away. Pretty damn embarrassing, but the end remained shrouded in the same mystery as the great whiskey rainstorm.

The cloying atmosphere of a noncombatant naval installation was inducing a feeling of claustrophobia, and it was time to seriously consider the options. Although the people of the United States were not as government-dependent as they have become in the present age, the regular military establishment and those aspiring to become a permanent part of it were fully subservient and nauseatingly obedient. I recalled the adventures in getting out of instructing in the RCAF, and there had to be a solution here somewhere. Of course, it might result in getting separated from the marines, but on the other hand, what was so fearsome about that? There were plenty of jobs in the flying business, and combat had already been visited. No doubt some absolutely obnoxious conduct would send the training command down memory lane and let the chips fall where they may.

Once firmly committed, the final act just sort of materialized. Going down to the flight line early one morning after a late night in town, the Threadbare Buzzard found the line chief running up one of the FM-2s. Climbing up on the wing, the Buzzard motioned the chief out of the cockpit. When he appeared in front of the airplane, he was signaled to remove the chocks. This airplane had previously had some brake troubles, so, not thinking anything was unusual, the chief complied.

To see out of a fighter properly, it is necessary to be sitting on a parachute. Unfortunately, there was no chute in the kite nor anyone to help with the shoulder harness. The hell with it. The fine little

FM-2 practically leaped into the sky. A wingover and a daisy-cutting pass produced a fine audience. Then, without chute or safety harness, it was not easy to see out, and all of the maneuvers from then on, especially the slow rolls, had to be made very smoothly to avoid falling out of the speedy little bird. That also negated the thought of flying inverted under the wing of a B-24. Besides, it wouldn't fit. Upon reparking the machine, it was personally met by two naval officers of equal seniority. They were also bigger.

This certainly stirred things up, and many of the other officers even seemed to be very frightened. The establishment appeared to be somewhat dazed, and it took awhile to determine that a general court-martial was just the thing for the mutinous rebel. This was a very interesting and in some ways amusing episode. Back at JAX Main Side, where this event was scheduled, the accused gained some insight into the souls of the heroic administrative officers. Many of them were pointedly aloof and some would even scuttle by when encountered. Obviously they were hoping that nothing would rub off on them that might compromise their opportunity to become the next Hornblower—or at least to be considered for a regular commission with its regular paycheck when the war was over.

The general court-martial itself didn't take long and was a formal assemblage of nonflying nonentities who were pathetically impressed with the gravity of the occasion. Not so was the defendant, who had a hangover, and the lieutenant colonel from VF-4 who was the only witness the defendant requested. He, more or less, gave the impression that a bunch of feather merchants judging a genuine combat veteran was somewhat ludicrous. The verdict was guilty and the sentence was to lose the monthly flight pay of $100 for five months. This was certainly a bargain since the desired result was achieved. The criminal would be sent back to the United States Marines, where it was supposed such antisocial conduct was tolerated.

Without any military ambitions whatsoever and never believing that a commission was a sacred possession, complete separation from the service would have been quite acceptable. At any rate it was said that the admiral (whoever he was) would probably suspend the sentence when it was reviewed. Unfortunately, a clumsy student in a fighter out of Main Side chose that time to instigate a midair collision with a civilian airliner in the vicinity of the municipal airport. (It was another one of those "giant airliners" with seventeen passengers aboard.) The navy's political sensitivity to taxpayer outrage at this event extended to the Threadbare Buzzard. Therefore, the $500 fine was *not* suspended and went a-glimmering along with the airliner's passengers and that accursed student pilot.

There was actually another valid reason for this drastic action to escape training command. Although the army was still using up a lot of pilots, the navy-marine requirement was shrinking. As the formerly high educational standards were greatly lowered, there was an equal increase in available bodies to be trained to fly. The Japanese, for all intents and purposes, no longer had first-team pilots, and their nearly adolescent replacements were so undertrained that they were actually just furnishing target practice for the Americans.

As for the Americans, there were so many trained naval aviators (as previously noted, the marines had over ten thousand by then) that in many cases they had little more to do than keep training and sharpening their skills before being deployed in startling numbers. The navy, which only a short time before had felt an urgency to acquire more bodies, was now, in the closing months of 1944, initiating a program to administratively wash out students in proportion to the numbers in each stage of training.

One clean-cut young officer, who didn't look the type, was encountered falling-down drunk in the officers' club one evening. He had just been cut from operational training after all of the struggle to get his wings and commission. Although the combat veterans present tried to explain his good fortune to him, he was inconsolable. The worst thing for him was to face his family and their high expectations. Life just wasn't fair for some of these chaps whose only crime was getting into the program too late. It underscored the point that any more procrastination by the Threadbare Buzzard in getting out of there

would result in ending the war at JAX along with the other dissatis-
fied marines. Following the court-martial and orders back to the
marines, a large group of the now jealous fellow instructors threw a
going-away party that slopped over into town. This would all have been
delightful if it hadn't resulted in a near-fatal car wreck that also wiped
out some commercial real estate. After escaping this unpleasantness,
it was time for a leisurely journey back to the benign landscape of
southern California.

XX

Westward in the United States has historically carried the connotation of the path to freedom. This was truer in the days of World War II, before the vast improvements in communications and transportation led us into modern secular society. Escaping exile on the East Coast to the civilized West was, for a Westerner, just as good as escaping from a maximum security prison. The first place to report for further orders was the marines' reception center at Miramar, just in back of San Diego.

In those days the field adjacent was known as Kearny Mesa, and one of the activities used navy patrol planes. A navy friend from the Navy Operational Training Squadron at JAX was training for deployment in a brand-new type of aircraft. Actually, it was a B-24 with only one tail, and as such was designated by the navy as a PB4Y-2. Not doing much while awaiting orders, I accepted an invitation to go on a practice sortie with him and his crew one Sunday afternoon. This hop wound up over at the Salton Sea behind the mountains, which was a bombing and gunnery range at that time. Riding in the jump seat between the pilots provided some excitement when faulty stops in the top turret allowed the guns to depress too far. This caused a burst of gunfire that came very close to terminating the whole flight. The day was not over, and when the lumbering machine

was homebound in the gathering darkness the pilot was advised that
the West Coast was socked in and he was to land at Holtville, close
to El Centro.

There was no surface transportation at that time of night, and the
aircraft was going to stay there to repair the damage the next day. That
night a ride via truck was arranged clear to San Diego. Since gasoline
was so rigorously regulated, the main vehicles to move were trucks. This
one resembled the type of livestock trucks ridden in while in the military. In Canada a sheep truck and a cattle truck had supplied needed
transportation, and this one fittingly enough had a load of pigs.

The rush to get back by 0800 hours Monday morning concerned the unfortunate administration in place at Miramar. Whereas
the marines used to have 100 percent combat troops, that was no
longer the case. At this late date in the war they had expanded to include dogs, women, and some noncombat men officers in administration. The combat marines usually excused the arrogance of these
feather merchants by saying that the trouble with those stupid bastards was that they hadn't had the crap (approximate word) scared
out of them. There was to be no antagonizing these unmentionables,
if the desire to get back to El Toro was to be realized. That was a fortunate decision, and the very next day that ambition was fulfilled. El
Toro was a fine place to be, but a return to instructing posed a clear
and present danger. This led to an opportunity for a fine new di-
mension of flying.

Beginning with Tarawa, the general dissatisfaction of the marines
with navy invasion support had broadened to include air support. The
marines being an oftentimes resented part of the navy were accus-
tomed to being shortchanged in both equipment and air support.
Bloody Tarawa with its shocking casualties indicated an obvious need
for improvement before the marines' manpower was depleted faster
than they could be recruited and trained.

One significant change that had to take place was in air support.
The ground-shy and safety-conscious navy was leaving a great deal
to be desired. Ideally, if a bomb is to be used, it required one foot of

altitude per pound of bomb to provide the delivering aircraft absolute safety. In other words, a 1,000-pound bomb would require a pullout altitude of 1,000 feet. This altitude was, apparently, also used by
the navy in strafing and demonstrated a reluctance to give their all for
the marine troops.

Marines used to fly from carriers before World War II, but in the
hectic early days of the war this no longer applied, because their limited numbers had to be committed to the land. Now, under severe
pressure and with a surfeit of marine aviators available, the unwashed
were being returned to carriers to still the complaints about the air
support. By Christmas of 1944 the first two marine squadrons were
on the *Essex* and entered combat at the very beginning of 1945. Hastily
trained for carrier operations, they nevertheless gave a brilliant account of themselves despite serious casualties.

More squadrons were then assigned to the big "bird farms" (a
term developed for carriers after the war). There was also a program
being developed for complete marine air groups using "Kaiser Jeeps."
These CVEs were just slightly larger than the first small carriers, but
their low speed still required them to come into a stiff headwind to
supply the speed over the deck to land and take off a Corsair. When
they came on line, they would be used primarily to afford air support
for ground troops.

Before the war, some of the best movies on the then unbelievable glamour of flight were done with the navy and carrier aviation.
In those days the better-organized and-funded navy enjoyed a great
advantage over the army and their aviation branch. This had instilled
a desire in the Threadbare Buzzard to someday fly from the deck of
the ships. This desire lay dormant while other more realizable avenues
to the sky were pursued, but now it looked possible. Being back on a
civilized Marine Corps air station, he didn't have to do much politicking to get into the carrier program.

Another old acquaintance from the Solomon Islands had qualified for a unique position for a marine. He was a "flag waver," not as
in "patriot" but as landing signal officer, or LSO. These chaps were

equipped with two flags on the end of short handles, and by positioning the flags and even performing occasional wild gyrations, they helped the pilot land in such a fashion that he could pick up an arresting wire with a tail hook he lowered from under the tail of the aircraft. Before doing this for real, a lot of practicing was done ashore, and was called FCLP, which means field carrier landing practice. This flag waver had been a fine combat pilot and obviously had some reservations about the adaptability of his old comrade-in-arms to this different way of flying.

The practice was carried out at an auxiliary field at Twentynine Palms. After a few passes he signaled for me to land and suggested that observing some of the students might be instructive. He had one student whom he seemed to be quite proud of, and he said to watch closely as he waved this paragon in because this was the way to do it. Unfortunately, a short distance from touchdown the lad's Corsair spun in. After that it became increasingly easy to master the technique to a degree of competency. If short of star quality, it was at least serviceable.

One day after a sketchy briefing the Threadbare Buzzard was given charge of about twenty second lieutenants, who were also undergoing carrier qualification. The instruction was to get them out to the Marine Corps Air Station at Ewa Plantation on Oahu. Of course, getting there was not that simple and entailed getting up to San Francisco, where Fleet Marine Force at 100 Harrison Street would arrange transportation overseas. These fine people, pending transportation, had assigned quarters in the Fairmont Hotel on the crest of Nob Hill, but these quarters were not so opulent as the address might suggest. Actually, they were in the lower regions of the hotel in what had been the old California Room and consisted of rows of double-deck bunks. Across the passageway was the swimming pool. After the war this pool and the surrounding area were converted into The Tonga Room, a really unique nightclub with a created tropical setting that could cloud up and rain just like down in the islands. For now it was still a swimming pool.

The young lieutenants, finding themselves free of firm discipline for the first time since the beginning of their cadet training, were rather creative with their newfound freedom. A riotous nude swimming party with a bunch of San Francisco's giggling beauteous belles was just one event that caused the management to get testy with their captain (me). In order to maintain the appropriate distance between ranks, the captain embarked on his own amusements.

One late afternoon, over at the Top of the Mark, a casual conversation with a navy lieutenant led to an interesting adventure. The lieutenant turned out to be a chaplain with a very distinguished accent and grand manner to match. He said that over in the Fairmont and in the vicinity of the swimming pool there was a fine large club for officers. He also waxed poetic in describing the beauty of one of the hostesses for whom he apparently had plans. After a few drinks he said he must be getting over there and why not come along? When he stood up to go it turned out that he was a very large, athletic-type cleric.

The club was indeed a fine place. It was huge with a big band and a lot of excitement. There was also a large representation from a marine fighter squadron that had converted to carriers and was on the way overseas. Some of their senior pilots were Solomon Island veterans who welcomed their old comrade and inducted him and the chaplain into their roaring party. The chaplain's girlfriend was unquestionably a thing of beauty, with her upswept blond hair and a class act all of the way. She sort of joined the party as her duties as a hostess permitted, and was obviously smitten by the chaplain. She also had an unbelievable fixation with the glamour of flying. This led to stretching the truth a bit, and she somehow got the impression that she could be given a ride in a navy airplane at the Alameda Air Station across the bay. Since the pilot had never even been on the Alameda Naval Air Station, this was, to put it mildly, a damned lie, but it certainly did pique her interest in the miserable-looking young marine. The liberal libations having already fueled this descent to the role of depraved liar, a further blasphemy was considered.

Why should the chaplain be so lucky? After all, he should be out ministering to the sick and miserable or saving souls or something. Besides that, he was in the navy. It was going to require the intervention of the god of aviators to solve this problem, and produce he did. Magnificently. When the midnight closing came, the party was planning to go on to an after-hours club where the welcome mat would be out despite the restriction in force on drinking hours for the armed services. The chaplain took this precise time to visit the head and left instructions to delay the young lady until he got back.

Fortunately, she returned first and seemed dismayed that the chaplain was not there. This was the time for action. It was explained briefly and forcefully that navy chaplains were men of God and of such dedication and purity that they had forsworn the base conduct of lesser mortals. Although they could, and did, kid around, it was unthinkable for it to go any further—especially, a navy chaplain. Therefore, he had requested that the marine should make his apologies and become her escort. While speedily vacating the premises and securing a taxi, another thought occurred. That chaplain was surely going to head for the after-hours club when he found himself all alone in the closing officers' club. It is the philosophy of the working fighter pilot to take care of the immediate, since the future may never come. To this end the lady was informed that it might be possible to take her for that airplane ride at Alameda NAS early the next morning, but, in the interest of getting some rest, it would be impossible to go on to the after-hours club. This was reasonable and the driver was directed to the young lady's apartment, which turned out to be on one of those steep streets running down Nob Hill. She warned that the doorman would not permit men friends above the lobby. This was not, at first, believed, but the belligerent old goat was adamant. Returning to the street with the young lady in tow, this matter was taken under study. A fighter pilot must be knowledgeable, and it is a known fact that apartment houses must by law have fire escapes. Further, they must be accessible from the inside of the building. This can be through a one-way exit door or just an unlocked window at the end of a hallway. To provide security, the last run of the fire escape is raised with a counterweight that allows it to be lowered in times of emergency.

In the steep alleyway beside the building this ladder was located, and due to the steeply sloping terrain the counterweighted section seemed out of reach. A fighter pilot must be resourceful, so the end of the ladder was finally reached by standing on the young lady's back and making a determined final leap. This brought it down with a terrible screeching of rusting pulleys in the foggy night.

The two disheveled conspirators now ascended the rest of the way to the desired floor and sure enough, the window at the end of the hall letting out on the fire escape was unlocked. It took some further effort to free it up. The young lady had just unlocked her door, when all the night's celebration and recent exertions suddenly took their toll. Bushusuru!!!

Right across the hall and by the elevators was a stairway. With hand over mouth and in panic these were rapidly descended and the lobby crossed. The curb was gained just in the nick of time. The old doorman had followed close behind and said, "I'll be damned." Slowly walking off into the enveloping fog, with a clearing head, it was painfully clear that there was a bathroom just inside the lady's apartment. No doubt that damn chaplain had employed his spiritual connections to place a curse on his not-so innocent victim, causing him to panic at a crucial moment in the proceedings. Such are the rewards for protecting a man of the cloth from sin. A fighter pilot, however, is also a philosophical pragmatist and understands that often elaborate preparations lead to meager results.

The transportation out to the islands was a piecemeal affair as air transportation became available. With some little manipulating, the unwitting clerks down at 100 Harrison assisted in the realization of another youthful dream that only the war could make possible.

Pan American Airway's history was part and parcel of the great romance of flying that was current before the war. Under an incredibly ambitious and ruthless leader, they had written some of the U.S. foreign policy and pioneered overocean flying that was then considered as impossible as going to the moon was later. It was really an incredible accomplishment. Their aircrews were the product of the most rigorous training in all of aviation. Charles A. Lindbergh, the Lone Eagle and undisputed idol of all aspiring aviators, was an integral part of it. He, with his wife, had done a lot of the route exploration, and to make it even more glamorous, she had written bestsellers about these trips.

Pan American originated transpacific air routes using what then were really giant flying boats. It was only on November 22nd of 1935 that the first regularly scheduled airmail flight across the Pacific to Manila departed from San Francisco. To put that into perspective, it must be remembered that the Japanese attack on Pearl Harbor took place only six years later. Perhaps the best descriptions of this event are to be found in the old newspaper reproductions that surface in museums and historical celebrations. The thousands of witnesses crowded every housetop and there were fireboats, fireworks, bands, and ceremonies. Other millions of people were glued to their radios. Not even the astronauts bound for the moon many years later received such attention. It must also be pointed out that this was at the height of the Great Depression, and aviation and the movies provided the most promising rays of light to the demoralized population. This was also accomplished by free enterprise and not by the stunning government costs of the space program.

The airplane on this first flight was named the *China Clipper,* and its captain was the World War I marine aviator Ed Musick. Those captains were as famous then as any movie star. They ascended to the exalted title of Master of Ocean Flying Boats and as such, must be forgiven their sometimes arrogant attitude.

The war brought most of these routes to an end as the Japanese dominated the Pacific. However, the route to the Hawaiian Islands remained open with these same flying boats in service. Enjoying this plush passage on the remaining Pan Am boats was usually reserved for high-ranking military and prominent politicians. Judiciously sending the lieutenants out on military flights made it possible for them to enjoy these luxurious flights.

The base of this operation was at Treasure Island in the middle
of San Francisco Bay, at what was for that time an impressive terminal. With the throaty roar of four mighty reciprocating engines, the
hull smashed through the chop until the great machine lifted into the
sky. This was indeed a genteel way to travel, and the passage had cost
what had been a fortune in the depression days. The ship of the air
had a wardroom amidships and individual bunks for the passengers.
There were several passengers wearing stars on their shoulders and a
few important-looking civilians. The meals were gourmet and the
sheets starched, and they even had a chief steward. If there was a drawback it was the speed of advance.

A great percentage of Pan American pilots in those days were former naval aviators, and the master of this one had also been a marine
many years before. This led to an invitation to the command deck,
which was not referred to as the cockpit, as it is today in the plebeian
airliners, but as the bridge. These aristocrats of the air were organized
along the lines of ships, and bear the responsibility for the modern
habit of calling the pilot and copilot a captain and first officer. The
only anomaly here is that on a real ship the captain (who is much
closer to a god) would hardly dirty his hands on the helm and has well-
trained lackeys to perform any mechanical chores.

The master proudly pointed to the tachometers for the engines.
These were turning at an incredibly slow speed, which kept the fuel
consumption to a minimum for the long flight. He pointed out the
window at the propellers and with a straight face claimed that if one
had good eyes he could read the Hamilton Standard labels on the
blades as they went by. That was not really true, but the big bird was
moving through the air at a very deliberate pace. It took eighteen
hours to reach Hawaii. That was a high point in the Threadbare Buzzard's collection of airplanes flown, or failing that, flown in. The pilot did not offer to let anyone else touch the controls, so passenger
status was maintained. This Master of Ocean Flying Boats did, however, rather wistfully want to discuss the Corsair fighter at length.
Time marches on.

XXI

The Marine Corps Air Station at Ewa Plantation on the island of Oahu was no longer recognizable as the same place where VMF-214 had been formed a few years since. The navy field at Barbers Point almost interlocked with it, and the facilities could hardly be believed.

While the old officers' club had given the impression of having been converted from an abandoned chicken coup, the new one was an architectural triumph. The story was that a famous architect had been issued a commission in the marines for the specific duty of designing it. With the abandon with which the armed services were now scattering money around, there was no reason to doubt this. The masterpiece was an obtuse L shape with the lounge on one leg and the semioblong bar extending from a wall that featured a hugely blown up life-size photo of a formation of Corsairs on the other leg. The sides were rolled up for the warm Hawaiian air, and it surrounded a swimming pool with a truly extensive patio. They had dancing on this patio with name bands. Not only that, they sometimes had afternoon *tea dancing*. The marines were still engaged in vicious fighting farther out in the Pacific. Had it not been for that, a disinterested observer might well have deduced that the "Devil Dogs" were now the "Lap Dogs."

Checking in as per orders to VMF-213, there was another surprise in store. VMF-213 had already been one of the first two marine squadrons to see action on the big carriers and was now being used as a carrier replacement training squadron. Its normal squadron commander was supposed to be another old Solomon Island friend, one Major Lou Smunk. As luck would have it, while in the PX he suffered a collapsed lung. He was temporarily attached to the air group, and he introduced the acting squadron commander, Major Don Frame, who was trying to join or rejoin VMF-123 on the carriers. This caused the new arrival, me, to be assigned as the squadron CO, although still a mere captain and the recent veteran of a navy general court-martial. The leadership in those parts seemed to think this was hilarious. Some of the senior officers in the marines either had or were developing a somewhat dim view of the navy, and some might say for many good reasons.

At Wake Island the timid support and recalled re-enforcing task force had caused the loss of the island and doomed the United States to some of its early failures. The contemplated abandonment of the marines at Guadalcanal was down to the wire, and had it not been for the tough Admiral Halsey, it would probably have taken place. The poor planning and the overriding of marine concerns at Tarawa contributed to the bloodbath. Peleliu, which was one of the bloodiest and least publicized campaigns, was carried out despite the fact that collapsing Japanese airpower made it redundant. Overriding Halsey's objections, his majesty, Admiral Nimitz, found it inconvenient to cancel.

The marines were, at this time, involved in the liberation of the Philippines and had a lot of marine aircraft ashore doing air support. Since his majesty, Dugout Doug, was doing his "I shall return" act, anything that wasn't U.S. Army was having its contribution ignored in any publicity releases. This reaffirmed the old Marine Corps adage: The army gets the medals, the navy gets the queens, and the guys that get the (deleted) are the United States Marines. However, some disgruntled marines had managed to slip in a few signs that expressed their disgust. These read: "With the help of God and a few marines, I, Douglas MacArthur, will retake the Philippines."

The squadron, with its mission focused on training replacement pilots for carrier operations, was very large and mustered at times over seventy pilots. The field carrier-landing practice was carried out at a strip on the other side of the island, and actual landings aboard ships were done on CVEs. Since they had a top speed of about eighteen knots while straining all of their rivets, they needed a substantial headwind to land Corsairs. For practice their deck was kept clear, with no aircraft parked ahead of the barriers.

The airplanes would form the "Prep-Charlie" (prepare to land) pattern on approaching the ship and then drop into the "Charlie" circle. This was limited to two aircraft and required some judgment by the pilot. Going downwind at about one hundred knots, he would be off a distance that would allow a continuous one hundred eighty-degree turn, which was initiated as he was opposite the stern of the ship. The pilot would fly this at as low a speed (about three knots above stalling speed) as was safe for the type, and pick up the signal officer on the last ninety degrees of the approach. The best aid for assuming the downwind distance off was to visually place the top of the carrier's smokestack on the horizon while getting the gear, flaps, and tail hook down and the prop in low pitch.

The LSO would be signaling on the final approach with his flags. These guys were able to judge the correct attitude and speed of the approaching airplane so the pilot could concentrate on the approaching deck. The LSO's signals would advise if the speed was too low or too high, if the airplane was skidding or if it wasn't lined up. He had two signals that had to be obeyed absolutely and promptly. The first was a waveoff and the other was a cut. This was before the day of the angled-deck aircraft carrier, so it doesn't take much imagination to realize what havoc might ensue if he didn't have this absolute control. The waveoff consisted of waving both flags across each other in front of him and meant "Pour on the coal and get ye hence without delay." Before the wing-root stall characteristic of the Corsair was cured, this could initiate a slow roll if the throttle was added too quickly. Fortunately, the Corsair was now idiot-proof, if not entirely sailor-proof.

The most welcome signal was the cut. This was performed by dropping the left flag down alongside the signal officer's leg while drawing the right one across his throat. He had a little helper looking back up the deck to advise him if he was in any danger of landing the approaching aircraft on top of another one that was already aboard but not yet clear of the arresting wires and far enough forward to have some barrier wires erected behind it. Naturally, under the existence of combat this could get a bit sticky. The necessity of trying to land a large number of aircraft returning from strikes that were extremely low on fuel and somewhat shot up, with dead or dying onboard, would result in management speeding up the deck. If night had fallen, this could get even hairier. Under such circumstances, sometimes fewer barriers where in place before the next kite was "cut."

Once in a while, one of the CVEs that were being practiced on would be visited when they were in the naval shipyard. This was done mostly to see up close, rather than from the perspective of a Corsair's cockpit, what the arresting gear and barriers looked like. The air officer on one of them had a very interesting story to tell concerning the navy's ally, if not bosom buddy, the United States Army. It had been previously determined, including Doolittle's Tokyo raid, that land-based aircraft could be launched from carriers. It fell to this chap to participate in a familiarization episode with army P-51 Mustang fighters.

The army chaps were, not surprisingly, somewhat skeptical of the whole business, but their airplanes were hoisted aboard and out to sea they went. The navy air officer showed them the catapult and explained how they would be positioned and how their airplanes would be hooked to the bridle. The bridle led down from just aft of and under the leading edge of each wing. It formed a V with the point attached to the traveling block in the catapult track. With full flaps down, the pilot would wind the engine up and place his head back on the headrest while standing on the brakes. When in all respects ready for the ride, he would look down at the launching officer and taking his hand off of the throttle, raise it across his throat. The launching officer then gave him time to regain his death grip on the throttle before dropping the flag. The air officer was disturbed by one thing. These guys didn't know at what speed their aircraft stalled.

The air officer did commend the army squadron commander for his high courage in allowing himself and his airplane to be hooked up as an example to his shaky troops. Then, however, with his engine running flat out, he refused to look at the launching officer. After a period of time with the launching officer vigorously flapping the aileron on the wing nearest him, which beat the hell out of the pilot's knees with the stick, that worthy did look at him. The flag dropped and the kite went halfway down the catapult track with the tires smoking from the unreleased brakes. The pilot apparently didn't keep the stick firmly neutral as instructed, and the Mustang didn't even use up all of the track before going almost straight up in the air before leveling off at a couple of hundred feet. Naturally, this threw away the bridle, which is supposed to be retained at the end of the track. Throwing away the bridle was regarded as damn poor form in naval circles, but in this case nothing but relief was evident as the P-51 flew off. With this awesome demonstration of the airplane's power and stability, the rest of the pilots, being pretty tough guys anyway, gained immeasurable confidence and turned incredible performances. Try that with a Corsair—even the new models that could be flown by little old ladies in tennis shoes—and sayonara.

Although I had no military ambitions and was totally unimpressed with being the squadron commander, it did have one great positive. A squadron has some jeeps assigned along with its airplanes, gas trucks, bomb trucks, and other miscellaneous rolling stock. Any CO gives himself a jeep as a personal perk. Another advantage of the jeeps became apparent when dealing with the squadron adjutant. He had been a very big time New York lawyer with a partially bald head, thick glasses, and a rather intolerant attitude toward the young squadron commander. This came from a rather strange ambition that he entertained. Also being a captain, he thought that he should have been placed in charge of the squadron when Major Smunk collapsed. This guy didn't even know how to fly.

A jeep solved everything. That and those officers' club dances. The island of Oahu's atmosphere was a far remove from that existing when VMF-214 was formed there after the attack. A lot of civil servants were now present, and none more welcome than the bright young girls at Hickham housing. Naturally the jeep was the sports car of that environment, and invitations to the dances were popular, even from a slightly balding, myopic, bad-tempered shyster.

As the squadron adjutant was returning from Hickham housing to Ewa one night in a squadron jeep, his eyes failed to detect a dignified old Japanese-Hawaiian in his ancient Chevrolet at a notorious crossroads in the two-lane highway. This caused some trouble, and with the military's fear of bad public relations, it came all of the way down to the squadron level, with instructions to take strong disciplinary action. The poor chap was very obviously fearful and probably regretted his previous contempt for his commanding officer. The squadron commander, in his role of martinet, decided to administer commanding officer's punishment rather than refer it to higher authority.

The squadron adjutant was instructed to personally type up the whole proceedings to send to the air group so he wouldn't be disgraced in front of his troops. He was sentenced to two weeks of "hack," which meant confinement to quarters except to perform his duties. Further, he would have no driving privileges until further review. This was the maximum punishment that a commanding officer could award an officer. With these papers in hand he was instructed to stop by the officers' club that evening before starting his sentence. This would allow him to buy his commanding officer a drink out of gratitude for his leniency, before entering durance vile. He was so grateful that he docilely agreed.

The first sergeant was, fortunately, an old acquaintance, and after a somewhat hilarious session with him, all was in readiness. That evening at the officers' club after the contrite adjutant had purchased several drinks, not only for his commanding officer but for some of the other young scalawags who were with him, he got a further surprise. I opened a large manila envelope supplied by the first sergeant and produced an official document stating that the entire sentence was being suspended by his commanding officer. This, it said, was done because of his impeccable performance of duty and his outstanding loyalty to, and popularity with, his fellow officers.

It got to be quite a party, and now the squadron did have the most loyal and strongest advocate of immature fighter pilots for an adjutant, not to mention his popularity, which grew in proportion to his investment in drinks. He didn't even suspect that the air group was satisfied with a simple endorsement stating that unspecified action had been taken.

There was another jeep episode, and this one concerned the commanding officer's personal jeep and a happy young friend who had enjoyed the mud, mosquitoes, lousy food, and exciting lifestyle of the Solomon Islands. This guy was called "Bluie" in Australia, as befitted his flaming red hair. He had done some legendary thing down in the Solomons, which either included flying home with an incredible amount of one wing missing, sinking a Japanese destroyer by hitting its depth charges while strafing, or perhaps both of these things. At any rate, he was extremely young and enthusiastic, and when he showed up he also had a monumental cast on one leg.

He explained that he had just been repatriated from doing ground support in the Philippines and told a harrowing and heroic story concerning his injury. He, along with a lot of others, were getting a little sick of the tiresome tales of the heroism of marine fighter pilots. Once he had his audience mesmerized, he broke out in raucous laughter and admitted that he had fallen off of a water trailer that was affording additional seating while being towed by an overloaded jeep on the way to a movie in the jungle. True, this did take place in the Philippines. And speaking of jeeps, he had found out that his very best buddy (not true) had a jeep of his very own.

Naturally, he and the damn jeep didn't surface for a considerable time. He was traced back to Aiea Hospital, where he had been AWOL. The surgeon in charge had restricted him and made dire threats, but as usual his luck held. The Marine Corps' favorite admiral made an inspection up there and enthusiastically greeted the rambunctious young rebel, whom he knew well from his exploits during the time of terror. That took care of the chief-surgeon problem, but he couldn't remember what he'd done with the jeep. It was finally located in some widow's garage in greater downtown Honolulu. Now, having certain privileges not accorded to anybody who wasn't the admiral's buddy, he again surfaced at Ewa and again borrowed the jeep from his other "best" buddy.

This was beginning to be an interesting job, and the next chore was a dandy and involved one of the squadron's enlisted men who was serving his country as a corporal. At least that was how he was carried on the squadron roster. On the island of Oahu there was a vast U.S. Army presence, and of course they had an appropriate ration of generals. One of these generals had a daughter who somewhat resembled a friendly pig, and this caused her to lack popularity amongst the legions of young officers available.

When she acquired a handsome young marine aviator as a suitor, her cup did runneth over. Her fond father was actually no fool and knew what he had. It didn't take the old boy long to get suspicious and quiz the young man on his background and place of duty. The young man proudly admitted to being a fighter pilot in the carrier program over at Marine Corps Air Station Eva. To avoid discussing all of the tiresome details, it will suffice to say that a search of the corporal's footlocker revealed uniforms with stripes up to master sergeant and an officer's uniform with insignia up to captain.

Before the Uniform Code of Military Justice was adopted after World War II, the naval services operated under a system roughly patterned after the British Navy's Code of Oberon. That code was devised to protect His Majesty's property and enforce discipline with a cat-o'-nine-tails at the commanding officer's pleasure. In fact he could even hang the offenders for such crimes as making love to the livestock carried for rations on long voyages. Although somewhat modified in the course of time, commanding officers were given much wider authority than now.

In the Marine Corps, a squadron commander could be directed to convene a summary court for serious crimes committed by enlisted personnel, which, of course fell just below general court-martial status. Impersonating an officer was such a crime. Then the commanding officer would assume the duty of recorder, which made him both prosecutor and defense lawyer and left the victim helpless. For a chap with no military ambitions and fresh from the Jacksonville court-martial, this posed a very unappetizing dilemma.

This problem was fielded by the now loyal adjutant (may his tribe increase). Although a prominent lawyer in civilian life, he apparently held certain reservations concerning military justice. These may have been exacerbated by his recent difficulties over the jeep. He brought over a grizzled old marine major who had come up from the ranks and, although no lawyer, had developed a fearsome reputation for defending guilty enlisted men over the years. He laid out a course of action that solved everything satisfactorily.

Due to the overwhelming body of evidence, the young man was subsequently found guilty. This evidence included a deposition from the maiden who had been trifled with and was of a viciously acrimonious nature. This was all fine, since the wily old major had helped with the many errors in the transcript that caused the whole matter to be thrown out on review. It also included a rebuke for the squadron commander for all of the sloppy procedures. As the old major explained, "What do they expect from you stupid damned fly boys anyway?"

Aside from the carrier training, the squadron was called on to participate in some exercises because the marines were getting lined up to invade Iwo Jima. Later, those marines did get some preinvasion air support from marines flying off carriers there, but then had to rely on the navy. Students of that fearful campaign estimate that great numbers of casualties would have been avoided if the troops had enjoyed marine air support all of the way.

One afternoon while doing fighter escort for a formation of dive-bombers on a practice attack, one of the dive-bombers had a very interesting adventure. These bombers were not the old, reliable Speedy Dees, but the large, modern brutes, the SB2Cs. They had some birth pains that, just like the Corsair, had to be ironed out. One thing that troubled their pilots was a tendency of the fabric-covered elevators to leak in air and shred while in the dive, which made recovery difficult, if not impossible. That is not what happened to this one. The formation was returning to Ewa and was over the gorge that runs across the island, when one of the bombers got on the horn and announced, "I've just lost my engine." Upon looking down on the bomber formation it was confirmed that he had that right. The engine had literally fallen off the airplane. This presented a ludicrous, albeit terrifying, sight. He was too low to bail out and did the only thing he could do. He skidded through a cane field without hitting one of those stone dikes that run through them, and fell into the gorge. Unaccountably, he escaped this spectacular demonstration uninjured. That night at the club he gave up his youthful predilection for sobriety for good.

These exercises served as a reminder that the war was getting into the final innings, and it was time to get moving before it ended. Ewa was pleasant enough, but this was actually just another training squadron. The sympathetic management recruited a stray major who, although a dive-bomber pilot, could substitute for the still-rightful squadron commander who was still mending. Upon being issued three second lieutenants to form a regular fighter division and some rather ambiguous travel orders, I was off across the blue Pacific to explore the next chapter.

XXII

The navy in all of its wisdom had its very own airline. Its designation was Naval Air Transport Service, or NATS. To demonstrate that they could do something right now and then, they had the right man in charge of the Pacific Division. In civil life he was known as the dean of the airline pilots during the crucial formative years of the industry. An Annapolis graduate many years before, he had originated the first and greatest navy aerobatics team, the Sea Hawks, back when it took a great deal of flying skill. Once in his checkered navy career he was told that he was a gentleman by an act of Congress and a pilot by an act of God. Of course, any pilot of his ability and stature was bound to come to cross purposes with the navy's battleship admirals. Now for the time and place, he typified the reason that America could win a war— that was by utilizing the progressive civilian brains that had made the country what it was.

The NATS airplane was a far cry from the Pan American flying boats. The navy designation was the R5D, and it was actually the civilian successor to the old DC-3 Gooney Bird and designated the Douglas DC-4 on the civilian side or the C-54 in the army. This marvel of the modern age (then) landed only four hours west of Hawaii at a place named Johnston Island. This was a runway that was literally manufactured by scraping up enough coral to make a runway with an equal amount of space for the support facilities. There were some rock-happy troops stationed here with the equally rock-happy ground personnel for the search aircraft based here. (Rock-happy refers to those poor souls who found themselves stuck on some remote island in the boundless ocean. During World War II there was no catering to any candy-assed troops, and they could spend the whole war there with no relief.)

With the aircraft fueled with aviation gasoline and the passengers with a few cold beers, the show took to the air again. Eight hours later it lurched to a stop on Kwajalein in the Marshall Islands. "Kwaj," in the vernacular, had been wrested from the Japanese in the recent past, as evidenced by its torn-up real estate. From here it was another eight hours to Guam in the Marianas Islands. This place had belonged to the United States before the war. They had taken it away from Spain and then lost it to the Japanese at the beginning of the war. Now it was American territory again, and scenes of the recent recovery were everywhere, especially Agana town, which had been flattened by vigorous U.S. Navy shelling during preinvasion.

The place was now considered so safe that the navy had moved its Pacific headquarters out here from Pearl Harbor. Now, in the early months of 1945, America had such resources in equipment and manpower that there was no doubt that the outcome of the war was already determined. However, due to the optimistic Japanese philosophy and propaganda that their civilian population suffered, there was still going to be some more real bloodshed and desperate battles to be fought.

The good news was that first-team Japanese aviation was a past number after the Solomon Island campaign. The bad news was that this didn't prevent them from putting immature boys into airplanes in a bitter, last-ditch demonstration. A lot of these (not always willingly) were made into kamikazes, whose sole mission was to dive into American ships. This, of course, killed them and didn't do the ships much good either. Although shooting them down, if the sporting aspects were to be observed, really amounted to murder, it was absolutely necessary.

The marine colonel in charge in those parts said that the division would embark on one of the CVEs (jeep carrier) that was following the fleet around with spare airplanes and pilots to replace the losses, which were running pretty high right then. Meanwhile, there was a marine activity here, with Corsairs to use to maintain proficiency if it were felt that this was necessary due to any delays getting to the ships. Meanwhile, the colonel offered the use of a real jeep to get up to the big officers' club on the hill. He also managed a slight smile and advised carrying a side arm up there but didn't amplify this ambiguous remark. That officers' club was something else. It was housed in a giant Quonset hut and was divided into three parts. A really huge area was devoted to the common junior officers. The next space was a great deal smaller and was for field grade, who were those wearing a gold leaf or up. The last very small division was for flag officers, which had no "or up," just stars. The realistic wearers of the stars had thoughtfully stationed armed troops in front of their section.

The clientele represented a good cross section of the officers of the armed services. There were navy officers of every stripe, who came from battleships and carriers down to minesweepers, not to mention aviators. There were army chaps, marine officers, and even Seabees. The crowds were huge, frantic, and well oiled. To add to all of this, some idiot had designated the drinking hours to conform to the British or Australian system. This schedule had the bar open for a limited number of hours in the afternoon and again in the evening. When the closing time approached, a lot of the customers would stockpile drinks. Then it was a matter of "use 'em or lose 'em" before the joint closed.

The great diversity of interests among the drinkers, who tended to resent the other services' attempts to corner all of the glory for any military successes, was a recipe for dissension, especially after they had hastily downed all of the surviving alcohol in sight. Given the time,

place, and fine physical condition of the patrons, episodes developed
that made the colonel's oblique remark about carrying a pistol quite
understandable and reasonable.

The crude living arrangements were in tents at the airstrip. With
the army B-29s now infesting the Mariana Islands, they often landed
here. One of these giants inbound one night didn't quite make it and
crashed at the end of the runway. A hot fire soon turned the hulk into
a charred piece of completely consumed junk, all except the tail, which
miraculously remained intact. Astoundingly, the sole survivor crawled
out of this section.

Just as crude as the quarters were, the dentist's office was in a
tent that boasted the refinement of screened sides. His equipment
was designed for the field and included a real believe-it-or-not contrivance that required a hospital corpsman to pedal madly to drive
the drill. Getting a wisdom tooth removed was quite an experience.
So was the experience of being immediately pushed out into the
blinding hot sunlight. That guy lacked any vestige of bedside manner, probably hated marines, and may even have been a quack. At
any rate, the troublesome tooth was gone and complete healing was
effected by prolonged soaking in whiskey at the aforementioned officers' club.

With a little more time to waste, my flight borrowed four Corsairs and took to the air one morning to explore the area. Partway between Guam and Saipan to the north was a very small island named
Rota. Since it was deemed unimportant in the grand scheme of things,
it had not been occupied, and there were still some Japanese in residence. The flight had heard the local gossip about an old sugar mill
that was sometimes used as a target. With the airplane's guns full of
ammunition as was customary in those parts, it seemed like a good
idea to give this place a few rounds. On the way home, one of the guys
got on the radio and swore that he had gotten some return fire from
an upstairs window in the old building. When this tale was laughingly
repeated to the local boys, they became both concerned and angry.
It seems that sometimes there *was* return fire from this building. Not

only that, they ran attacks up there for fun and decorations. When that caused considerable amusement, they produced evidence that the forlorn holdouts up there had actually shot down some casual strafers. Good grief. Fortunately, it was time to go, and just in time; the welcome mat was showing signs of wear.

One day a boat from Agana harbor deposited the division on the CVE *Bougainville*. On this jeep carrier was another marine captain, John Morgan, with his three second lieutenants who were also to be replacements when needed. He was a fellow Solomon Islands veteran from the old air group with an extremely distinguished record and the surname of an equally distinguished pirate.

These "old-timers" who had survived the Solomons were beginning to trickle back out to combat as senior pilots among the hordes of well-trained but "virgin" fighter pilots. Since they were few in number and had shared unique experiences in the days when the United States had held a thin deck of cards and few pilots, they were drawn closer together.

In short order the ship weighed anchor and proceeded to sea with the support component of Task Force Fifty Eight, which was divided into three task groups. This allowed some elements to rendezvous with the floating reserves to replenish fuel, ammunition, planes, and sometimes pilots, without breaking off their continuous operations. During this sortie some pilots from the big carriers were highlined aboard and catapulted off with replacement aircraft. No replacement pilots from the *Bouganville* were required, and the ship proceeded to the fleet anchorage at Ulithi atoll. This anchorage featured "murderers row," which was a line of *Essex*-class carriers. The *Essex* was queen of her class, and these were the world's largest carriers at that time. There was recreation ashore which, due to its distilled nature, led to some interesting scenes when the liberty boats were boarded to return the celebrants to the ships. These weren't the only confused troops on scene. There was a stray Japanese pilot who came by to play kamikaze. Trouble was that in the moonlight he mistook a small islet with the surf creaming on the barrier reef behind it for a major ship underway. This brave warrior failed to sink the island but got his ticket punched for the trip to visit his ancestors.

After the anchorage at Ulithi atoll, the *Bougainville* steamed back to Guam and anchored one afternoon with its eight marine fighter pilots still aboard. The next morning in the wardroom at breakfast, the ship's executive officer informed the captain with the distinguished pirate's surname that he had been mentioned in dispatches from fleet headquarters, which was just up the hill.

It developed that when attempting to return to the ship the previous evening there wasn't a liberty boat convenient enough to suit his desires or those of a friendly motor machinist's mate who happened to be with him. The machinist's mate knew how to start a very large Higgins landing craft that was just sitting there. The descendent of a pirate, although a usually very quiet and reserved chap, proclaimed himself to be captain of the Spanish Main. He must have been as confused as the kamikaze pilot at Ulithi, because any fool could easily see that this was Agana harbor on Guam, far removed from the Spanish Main. Taken alongside with grappling irons by the outraged harbor patrol, they were returned to the ship in disgrace, although not in irons. The ship's captain, under pressure from far above, still had great admiration for the Solomon Island ace and inquired as to what he thought the punishment should be. After mature consideration the erstwhile pirate suggested restriction to the ship. However, he stipulated that this restriction was not to start until the ship sailed a few days hence. Done.

Soon after this, my four-pilot division was sent over to the *Admiralty Islands*, another jeep carrier, to continue our role in the floating reserve. When we had been not very long at sea, a destroyer came alongside with the other four pilots from the *Bougainville* aboard. Johnny Morgan, the Solomon Island friend, using a borrowed loud hailer, announced that they were going over to the fast carrier *Bunker Hill* as replacements in a Marine Corps squadron aboard. That was to be my last time to see him alive or any other way. Not long after that he answered the last bugle call in the sky.

Now it was the turn of the *Admiralty Islands* pilots, but we walked into an unfortunate circumstance. The ship got a message asking if they had any Corsair pilots aboard. The ship said yes, but they are marines. "We'll take anything" was the ungracious reply from Air Group 83 on the *Essex* (CV-9). Their Navy Bombing-Fighter Squadron VBF-83 had been aboard only a short time and had already arranged for some trouble that in an unfortunate strike cost them some pilots. We four marines from the *Admiralty Islands* would be the only marine replacement pilots sent into a navy squadron during the war, and we suffered the consequences, one of which was to be ignored in "official" histories.

Being ignored in the official histories is really not surprising, when it is considered that for fifty-six years the participants had never even inspected the records. For a participant, perusal of the historical versions of World War II can be startling. The records were no doubt strongly influenced by all of the divergent services and organizations that, in their ongoing public relations campaigns, stridently claimed to be solely responsible for victory. Any published myth or distortion becomes credited as an indisputable source for future historians. At this remove, the inaccuracies and the incompetence of research are actually quite amusing. A parable of the Oracle of Poverty Flats stated: "He who is born in a barn shall remain immune to the braying of the jackass."

XXIII

In short order, the *Fletcher*-class destroyer *Haynsworth* came in parallel and close alongside the fantail of the *Admiralty Islands* and fired over a messenger line. This was followed by the heavier highline that was bent onto the messenger. One end of this line had been made fast to the destroyer's superstructure and on the carrier's end was led through a rolling block hung under the overhang of the flight deck to a line of sailors manning the tag end. A navy chief was in charge of this line which, of course, was subject to the different motions of the two ships. The management liked to conduct these replenishment operations in whatever bad weather was available. This provided some cover from attack during this vulnerable operation. Fortunately, this day was not as bad as it could get.

A breeches buoy was rigged to a traveling block with a tag line to pull it back and forth between the ships. The chief standing on a capstan attempted to maintain the highline in a desirable configuration by bellowing at his troops, "Take 'er in, lads" or "Let 'er out" to keep the line from sagging into the sea or fiddle-stringing it at the other extremity. For the passenger in the buoy, this could provide an exciting ride, the excitement being proportional to the sea state and the motion of the ships. In practically no time the four marines from the *Admiralty Islands* had been deposited, one by one, on the deck of the destroyer. The jolly destroyer men congratulated them for being so dry and suggested that had they known that their guests were to be marines that might not have been the case. A pox upon them.

The destroyer boiled off on its merry way and wound up opposite the fantail of the *Essex*. Here the process was repeated in reverse and, after all of the training and inconvenience, here at last there was a major carrier underfoot. There was no question that this was one big mother. This was a different world entirely from the lean days of the Solomons. The squadron, VBF-83, alone had fifty-four pilots. Most of them weren't from fighter backgrounds and had not been onboard long. In the short time aboard they had suffered some bitter losses and didn't appear to have much of a gung ho attitude.

The quarters were great, and I was assigned to a two-man stateroom. The other tenant was a navy lieutenant who was the nightfighter pilot aboard. There was something almost weird about fighting a war with clean sheets and room service to come home to. Of course, to keep it available, it was necessary to come home. The three second lieutenants did not get such lavish treatment, but it was certainly better than anything available for shorebased pilots. Rank has its privileges, and in the navy the delineation between grades is pronounced and inflexible.

There was a vast wardroom with white linen and sparkling silver and food that a hungry marine found fabulous. Still, the navy officers managed to find fault with it. The cleanliness of the premises and food, as well as the many mess attendants in white starched uniforms, was a far remove from the Marine Corps in the field. It was indeed an atmosphere in which "The officers took the slack and the enlisted men took the strain." This is, of course, diametrically opposed to the Marine Corps philosophy in the field.

The other space on the ship that was of the greatest interest to the pilot was the ready room, and each squadron had its own. This space was immediately below the flight deck, and in addition to serving as a comfortable lounge it was efficiently set up for briefing and squadron flight operations. The individual chairs faced the front of the room, where there was a blackboard and a microphone with which a briefer would deliver the target information, scheduling, and other bad news to the pilots. They could even produce a chaplain if the news was grim enough.

The navigation information was posted here and included the "point option" data. Since the carriers were moving, this point is where they were supposed to be when the airplanes came home to roost. Also posted was weather information with estimated winds. Each pilot had his Mark Eight plotting board—for some vague reason, everything in World War II seemed to be a "Mark Eight"—which had a movable Plexiglas screen over a compass-rose-centered grid. On this screen he laid out the point option data and the wind line. Once that was done, if the flight was to be a search, the course and distance line was laid in, depending on if it was to be a relative (to the moving point option) or a geographical search and if it had a cross leg at the end of it. If the ocean was visible during this flight, the wind speed and direction could be observed and corrections made en route. This was the stuff of intensive training for navy pilots. Since the marines had not been back on carriers for long, it had been largely neglected.

There was a homing device in use, the YG-ZB, that was good to the sightline limit of VHF (very high frequency) radio transmission. This was about one hundred miles at twenty thousand feet and encompassed a circle divided by pie-shaped sectors every fifteen degrees. Each sector had an individual letter signal that was changed every day to prevent it from becoming compromised by attacking enemy planes.

The pilots' flight gear was also kept in the ready room, although they were usually wearing it. As launch time neared they would strap into their QAS harness. This harness was actually the parachute harness. This rig would be clipped to the parachute and its life raft, which remained in the aircraft. The QAS was clipped onto the chute only after the airplane had cleared the deck. No doubt it would make escape from the kite much easier if there were an accident before or during launch. The downside was if later in the day the pilot, finding himself in urgent need of his chute, leaped out only to find that at the busy time of takeoff he had neglected to fasten the clips. One navy pilot had done just that at the invasion of Guam and survived a fall of a couple of thousand feet into the ocean wearing only the QAS harness. He may have been the only one to survive this inattention to detail.

The navy pilots were hardly effusive in their welcome, although a few of the more mature were certainly friendly and went out of their way to be helpful. The unfriendliness no doubt was due to their inexperience in combat and self-protectionism arising from their early fright. It was only normal that some of them would be suffering from the "them or us" syndrome. The second lieutenants reported that in the anonymous environs of the community showers assigned to junior officers they had heard some disturbing remarks. Not being familiar enough to their new squadron mates to be recognized in the altogether, some of the navy squadron pilots had said such things as, "All right, if those [deleted] marines are so hot, give 'em all of the long-range searches." Needless to say, those searches were considered undesirable and rather hazardous given the current state of navigational aids and the ofttimes sketchy weather information provided.

That was certainly nothing to worry about, except for the reserved attitude of the squadron commander. He was a prewar Annapolis officer who was a deck officer before going to flight school. He had this in common with his executive officer. What he didn't have in common with his exec was flying ability or enthusiasm. The exec publicly stated that he intended either to get the Navy Cross (a decoration) or get killed trying. He managed both.

By this time in the war there were a lot of deck officers trying their hand at aviation in the belief that it was a better path to promotion. For the regular officers a few decorations were deemed essential for their future careers. All of the publicity that had been accorded aviation early on may have given them the false impression that it was easy. Although airborne Japanese pilots were no longer much of a threat, there was nothing wrong with their antiaircraft fire. Also, in that era there were the inherent dangers of flying, especially off carriers. Some of the navy pilots, despite their inexperience, overcame their reservations and did quite well. A few, regretting their pact with the devil, toughed it out anyway. There were cases where fear caused problems with leadership because the navy's inflexible rank structure sometimes left incompetents in leadership positions. Some of these finally quit flying or, if members of the "trade school (Naval Academy graduates) protective fraternity," were relieved of commands without loss of honor.

There was one continuing terror for all aviators. That was the unremitting fear of capture by the Japanese. The one ray of hope in the Solomon Islands had always been the old saw that "Those damn Japs can kill you but they can't eat you." This was no longer valid. At the war crimes trials conducted at Guam in 1946, some troubling information was brought to light. Twenty Japanese officers were convicted and the five senior ones were sentenced to be hanged. Their crime was devouring aviators shot down at Chichi Jima. The record is silent on whether they had wished to acquire the attributes of the brave enemy or were just hungry.

The Japanese, despite the overwhelming odds, were demonstrating their determination to fight to the end. Their submarines were a diminishing threat, but the kamikazes were becoming more popular as a ticket to joining their ancestors. Not long after coming aboard, I learned a lesson about the well-justified terror that these suiciders had instilled in the navy.

A navy pilot had offered to provide a checkout on some unfamiliar radio gear, and this was taking place down on the hangar deck. As I was head-down in the cockpit of a Corsair with the navy chap standing alongside in the step, the General Quarters alarm went off. Some quizzical comment about it being a drill went unanswered, and a quick glance revealed that the erstwhile instructor, in common with great numbers of other sailors, was racing across the, in places, slippery hangar deck. They were headed for what were known as "light locks," which were small compartments at the edge of the deck. Leaping from the Corsair and beating out a respectable number of other panicked heroes to one of these compartments before it was dogged down provided the Threadbare Buzzard with an explanation. The attacks were becoming so frequent and intense that no warning was ignored. The results of the hellish fires had been witnessed by many of these people, and these small compartments could possibly afford some protection from the raging fires. The sounding of General Quarters was most impressive, especially when followed by the announcement, "This is no drill!"

A great number of ships were now being hit. Whatever else can be said about the navy, they must be admired and given eternal credit for just how fast a fighting carrier could sustain a grievous hit and raging fires and get back into operation. A lot of the smaller ships got sunk. Oddly enough, the carrier that sustained the most crippling damage was not hit by a kamikaze.

This ship was the USS *Franklin*. It was not hit by kamikazes but two rather small bombs that penetrated to the hangar deck, killing almost everyone there as well as starting great fires on deck. To make matters worse, the *Franklin* was carrying what were probably the first of the Tiny Tim rockets to be deployed. These superrockets were about twelve inches in diameter and were launched from a yoke that swung down to clear the prop of the Corsair before lighting off. They had a fearsome warhead, and as these cooked off and self-launched in the inferno of the hangar deck they didn't do the ship much good. Seven hundred and twenty-four people were killed in this attack, and the good Lord only knows how many hundreds were burned, maimed, and crippled.

The latest version of the Marine Fighter Squadron VMF-214 had recently come aboard the ship and had the shortest combat record of the three incarnations of the squadron. The original VMF-214, named the "Swashbucklers," had the longest combat run, with the second version, the "Black Sheep," much shorter, and the carrier bunch lasting only a few days. There was only one member who had served in the other two incarnations, although there were some members from other squadrons from the old days in Solomons. Several pilots were re-placements who had recently been undergoing training at the carrier checkout school at Ewa Plantation on Oahu, which made the episode more personal. The *Franklin* presented a spectacular sight as she was taken out of the combat area. There was a possibility that she was saved only for reasons of morale, being one of the "unsinkable" *Essex*-class carriers. She eventually was gotten back to the States.

With bloody Iwo Jima now secured, the fleet was ready to take on Okinawa as the final steppingstone to the home islands of Japan. Marine air support was now more important than ever. It has been pointed out in historical studies that if marine air support had been present throughout the whole of the Iwo Jima operation, the horrify-ing casualties could have been substantially reduced. In fact, in the history of marine aviation it was clear that preinvasion bombing and naval shelling got its worst black eye in the Iwo Jima show.

Okinawa was destined to be the largest invasion of the entire Pa-cific war. The assemblage of support and invasion ships was a stag-gering sight from the air. There were a thousand carrier planes in the air over Okinawa and its auxiliary islands or on attacks on the home islands. Carrier Task Force 58 was steaming about ninety miles off to the east. Its point option (the navigational point that would be made good to recover aircraft) moved on alternate days on a course of ei-ther 90 or 270 degrees. Every day there was a permanent CAP (com-bat air patrol) over the fleet to deal with the constant kamikaze attacks.

At a significant distance from the capital ships were the picket boats, destroyers. Because the U.S. planes were showing a radio code called IFF (identification, friend or foe), the Japanese would attempt to follow returning strikes inbound for the carriers. These picket ships suffered grievously. In a fine example of graveyard humor, some of them posted large signs on their superstructures. The signs generally bore variations on the theme, "Attention Kamikaze Pilots, Carriers This Way." This was followed by a large arrow pointing to where their crews suspected the bird farms (carriers) were doing business. Few Japanese understood English anyway, and the destroyers' mission was to "delouse" the returning carrier planes by checking for following enemy planes. In this enterprise some of the destroyers underwent vicious attacks and paid with their lives and their ships. They also rescued pilots whose shot-up planes could not make it home.

On the other side of Okinawa was the wall-to-wall invasion fleet of every conceivable type of ship afloat. For a working fighter pilot with a real interest in the Pacific campaigns of the marines, this was the one show not to be missed. Neither was the opportunity to fly off of carriers, despite the unfortunate circumstances.

There was plenty of work to be done with the constant CAPs and increasing preinvasion strikes on Okinawa and farther afield. The Corsairs were heavily loaded at launch and provided some new experiences. They could be carrying all or any part or combination of the following: 5,600 rounds of .50-caliber ammunition, a large auxiliary fuel tank on one wing pylon, a 1,000-pound bomb or a napalm bomb on the other pylon, and eight 5-inch rockets on the rails under the wings. For a former strictly fighter pilot, bombing was something new, as was dropping napalm. The first napalm drop I flew was on a small islet just off the island of Okinawa. The whole flight made drops, and the flames going up the side of the hill that was struck were rather frightening. This same islet was the scene of Ernie Pyle's death.

This man was perhaps the most famous of the intrepid war correspondents. His genuinely humble attitude and real sympathy for the unfortunate grunts of the infantry in the European Theater of Operations had won him great fame. With that phase of the war recently won, he came to the Pacific. Perhaps due to his great respect for the army ground pounders, he had speculated that perhaps the Marine Corps grunts were overrated. They were to be his final comrades.

D-day at Okinawa was a long and difficult day. That morning's launch was long before dawn and afforded another not entirely

welcome experience. With the assigned Corsair pretty well forward on
the deck, it would be catapulted. This was something different. The
signal man with his illuminated wands would keep the airplane taxiing forward from "Fly One" until the right wheel hit a guide, and then
the signal man would cross the wands for stop. The bridle was hooked
up while the instructions on a board held up in view of the pilot were
complied with. The first was "wings locked." There was a large handle in the cockpit that was put in the forward position, causing the
wings to fold down and lock. There was a final safety pin that also
should be operated and was indicated by a small metal flag sticking
up at each wing root. Fortunately, this was a redundancy and all too
often, after becoming airborne and after daybreak, it would be observed that the flags were still up. Delicately raising the operating handle and watching the flags go down produced a great feeling of relief.
The next important instruction was "IFF on." That signal might save
the brave aviator from getting shot down by some well-meaning
friends.

Then, with the flaps down full, the engine at full power, and head
back against the rest, it was time to look at the launch officer. Taking
the left hand off the throttle, it was raised across the chest. The launching officer would then allow enough time for that hand to get back to
the throttle before he signaled launch, with a light wand if by night or
a flag if by day.

By night, the sensation of being at rest one moment and flying
in an overloaded airplane at just above stalling speed on instruments
the next would indeed provide one of life's profound moments. That
was just the beginning. The airspace at the end of the deck had to be
promptly vacated in order to clear the slipstream that could cause the
next plane taking off serious difficulties. There was one more consideration, because the task group would be steaming line abreast and
other ships could be launching simultaneously. This necessitated a predetermined launch lane that extended from right ahead to a given
number of degrees to starboard.

While flying in blackness, turning to this heading while getting the wheels up and dealing with trim changes and with other complications called for some skill. If for no other reasons, the carrier pilots had to be accorded some respect. However, the catapult did get the airplane into the air in short order and even, in some cases, provided more air speed when airborne than a regular takeoff run from "Fly One."

With several flights that day, the division flew right around fourteen hours. That is a long time in the confines of a fighter cockpit, especially under these circumstances, and requires the resilience of youth. It was long after dark when the last mission was to be landed. Already low on fuel, it was not welcome to receive orders to orbit awaiting further instructions. What had happened was that a navy pilot had somehow either not engaged his tail hook or had it broken off. He wound up inverted, with the wreckage jammed in between the flight deck and the carrier's island. Fortunately, he didn't burn, and by some act of God and sailors, was extracted with only minor injuries. It took a considerable time to scrape up the fighter and shove it over the side. Being jettisoned was a standard fate for damaged airplanes, especially when it was necessary to speed up the deck.

Now it was the marines' turn, and I discovered that none of us had ever made a night carrier landing. On the final approach in the "Charlie" circle the lower extremities were shaking so badly from fatigue that it took a "Benny" to steady down. This stimulant was carried for just such emergencies. All four marines made flawless approaches and landings. The only problem came in forward spot after the fearless leader, having cleared the arresting wires, had one barrier raised behind him. The signal man with his illuminated wands was a bit hasty and before throwing them away and hitting the deck had caused the leader's prop to shear off a small bit of the tail of the plane ahead. Don't count your losses.

Happily the marine grunts walked ashore in their sector of the Okinawa beaches. Things got tough after that, but this was only day one in what turned out to be a long and bitter campaign. The next day there was sad news. The marine captain from the Solomons who was the leader of the other four marines on the *Bougainville* was dead. He had been killed by antiaircraft fire on D-day while on an attack from the carrier *Bunker Hill*, where he and his division of replacement pilots had been assigned. He was as good as they get, but war and flying steel respect neither youth, talent, courage, ability, nor integrity. He possessed a large ration of all of the above.

The Japanese, as was their custom, bitterly resented the invasion and produced several weapons of desperation. One was the Baka bomb, which was a bomber-dropped missile with a unique guidance system. This guidance system was a real live Japanese, and this obviated a lot of technical failures. The Baka never posed much of a threat, and neither did the miniature submarines, but these all required taking out. The kamikazes were the real threat, and they arrived in great numbers. However, not all of the Japanese pilots were gung ho. One chap, shot down by the night-fighting roommate, was flying a Betty bomber and became that genuine rarity, a prisoner of war. When interrogated, he indignantly denied being a kamikaze and insisted that they were a great deal lower on the social scale of heroes than he, a real live officer of the regular Imperial Navy. An even rarer prisoner of war was a real kamikaze pilot who, lacking the courage or insanity to make his dive, ditched when he approached the fleet. By some divine intervention, his welded-on bombs did not explode. When picked up he had an interesting tale to tell.

With only sketchy flight training he had been abruptly sent to an outfit where he discovered, to his dismay, that he was a volunteer to die for the emperor. What really ticked him off was that he didn't get the final benefits for his impending heroism, which usually included a final sendoff heavy on saki and the services of a charming female. Instead, he was really shaken up when, on the final morning, he was given the prayer-inscribed *hachimaki* headband and put into a Zero fighter with the already armed bombs welded onto it and the landing gear fiddled so once retracted it would not come down again. With little enthusiasm, he took a chance on ditching and lived to tell the tale.

This whole Okinawa operation was a show of unbelievable action, with the ships under attack and air operations at full bore. As explained before, any aircraft damaged on landing would be pushed over the side if it looked like it would slow up the speed of the operation. That and the tremendous expenditure of bombs, ammunition, and fuel made resupply crucial to continuing operations. For this purpose, the task force was divided into three task groups, permitting one task group to rendezvous with the reserve ships frequently. This would mean that one group could resupply every third day, and sometimes that seemed to be the schedule.

For this vulnerable period, the group would endeavor to find bad weather to shield itself from possible enemy attack. This could get rather exciting, with a fleet oiler or ammo ship on either side and a destroyer at the fantail to transfer pilots via highline. These pilots would be bound for the jeep carriers to fly replacement aircraft back aboard. One exceedingly foul day back at the fantail waiting to get the exciting High Line Thrill Ride, a TBF pilot wandered over and identified himself as another survivor of Poverty Flats, Montana. While commenting idly on the seamanship of the destroyer trying to position itself on the port quarter in the raging sea, the situation suddenly deteriorated. The bouncing "tin can" rolled some of her superstructure right under the overhanging ramp of the *Essex*'s flight deck. The destroyer got the worst of it and sheared off and really did look like a tin can—one that had been stepped on. That ended the attempt for that day. The collision was not that common, but failure to complete transfers happened rather frequently. Altogether, the ship handling of the destroyer skippers, who commanded awesome horsepower and maneuverability in extremely close quarters in violent sea conditions, was impressive, to say the very least.

The pace of the battle may be judged by the rate of human casualties. In short order the TBF pilot and a fighter pilot who hailed from a town close to Poverty Flats were dead, and the other representative of the place was missing.

On a mission to supply air cover for a TBF strike at an island close up to the home islands, the squadron leadership showed its colors. This day set a record for kamikaze attacks, with a total of over seven hundred for that day and the next, and the show was spectacular on this beautiful, clear day. The antiaircraft fire and burning planes in the air were most memorable. On launching, a collision with a plane approaching head-on was narrowly missed, and it was thought to be some confused pilot from another ship. A F6F Hellcat was the next to launch, and being directly behind made no such mistake. Still only a few feet above the water, he lowered his nose and blew this kamikaze to hell.

Immediately after I joined up in the escort formation, the shipboard fighter director was issuing orders to the combat air patrol for intercepts. It was assumed that just like in the marines an assigned escort meant protecting the bombers. This didn't seem to apply here, and the squadron leader promptly rolled out of formation and dove on some approaching kamikazes. Apparently he was suffering from buck fever, since his tracer fire missed badly, so the Threadbare Buzzard, following along with his division, tore up the unfortunate Zero, which hit the drink. Right then the fearless leader, identifying himself, shouted "Splash One" (a claim for a kill). This caused the marines, now back in a close formation, to exchange startled looks, but not for long. Rolling out, the fearless leader was observed missing another kamikaze, who was then given the same treatment as the first one. The leader, again identifying himself, shouted, "Splash two!" This wasn't taken seriously at the time, since there were other matters at hand.

Another kamikaze turned away and started running all-out right above the waves. Giving chase and going into water injection to give the Corsair an additional kick in the butt, we closed the distance. Right then the Zero pilot did a very strange thing. He pulled up like he was going to do a wingover and a head-on run, but settled for a ninety-degree turn. The wingman was now inside of this turn and over the radio expressed a sincere desire to shoot this Zero down in order to rid himself of his status as a virgin fighter pilot. That was certainly reasonable, so now, becoming an observer and running full-out in water injection, it was a simple matter to pull up on the Zero's wing. This was a mistake that would last a lifetime.

Crouched in that Zero was what looked like a fifteen-year-old boy staring back with a look of terror that can never be forgotten. Just then the wingman got the range, and the Zero exploded into the water. In his exuberance, the victor initiated a victory roll and actually disappeared into the flying junk. Great relief was felt as he continued flying. This turned out to be the last murderous episode participated in during the war and forevermore.

Back aboard the ship there was plenty more action. Despite testimony to the contrary, the leader continued to claim the kills, and although we contested them, there was really little enthusiasm. Not only that, the skipper of the TBM squadron whose escort had abandoned him to shoot at kamikazes was in a rage. A rightful rage, it may be added. The fighters had no right to chase off without being directly ordered to do so. The navy policy, it turned out, was the same as the marines, to protect the bombers. Obviously somebody was looking for some easy glory, with future promotions in mind. A lot of this stuff in the waning days of the war was just murder anyway and had little to do with the glorious knights of the air jousting for fame and perhaps a maiden fair. However, until the fanatical Japanese surrendered, it was going to continue to be necessary, and somebody was going to have to do it.

On the ship there was a group of Marine Corps mechanics left over from a previous squadron who were Corsair experts and intensely loyal to the marine fighter pilots. The four pilots and a large group of these guys were down on the hangar deck that evening examining the wingman's Corsair. It was somewhat dinged up from its encounter with the flying parts of the Zero and even had one of the Zero's wheels embedded in the wing root. Everybody had heard about the dispute over the kills, and the marines were not pleased. In fact, some of them muttered that the next time his majesty took off he might encounter terminal mechanical difficulties. A stop had to be put to that, and the troops were ordered in no uncertain terms that no matter what happened to the marine pilots, they would never, ever, entertain such thoughts. It turned out that including the future in this instruction was indeed prophetic.

XXIV

It was now more than a rumor. The super Japanese battleship *Yamato*, which was about the last of the fearsome Imperial Navy, was on the move. With her attendant screening ships but without air cover, she had departed Tokuyama Bay and transited Bungo Strait. With her senior officers suffering from an excess of saki the night before, she was headed for the action off Okinawa. This was obviously going to be a final suicidal run, hoping for divine help or, failing that, a glorious end. It turned into a contest between the carriers and other navy ships to see who could put paid to what would be the last action of the Japanese Fleet.

Task Force 58 had a plan to locate her and finish her before surface ships could come up or the shadowing submarines copped the glory. Interservice competition for glory was not only intense, but so was the rivalry between the surface ships, submarines, and carriers within the navy. To this end the carriers launched their surface searches to maximum range. These searches, due to the bad weather, would be flown at low level. That was fine except that radio communication was done by VHF, and the nature of that method is that the signals are sight line. In other words, a transmission on the surface can only be heard to the horizon, while an aircraft at 20,000 feet can be heard about 100 miles distant due to the curvature of the earth.

To overcome this difficulty there would be two communications relays employed along with the Combat Air Patrol, which was either over or in close proximity to the carriers and would do the final relaying of any messages. Since this patrol alternated divisions at 10,000 and 20,000 thousand feet, they greatly extended the sight-line distances. Of the two relay teams, one would be at 150 miles from the force, and the other 300 miles distant. This outlying team would be in contact with the searches flying underneath the weather. All contact messages would be relayed using a simple security device known as a "Shackle Code."

Given the bad weather obscuring the ocean and the vagaries of winds aloft, there would be no opportunity for the relay teams to correct the navigation they had laid out on their Mark Eight plotting boards. There were bound to be changing wind and weather conditions over the considerable distance and extended time period involved. The outlying station was going to be very unappetizing for any carrier pilots interested in longevity. Naturally, and in accordance with the previous stated aim of giving "those damn marines" the tough searches, there was little surprise when this assignment was made at the briefing. The marine division of four planes would be sent as a unit in case they encountered enemy aircraft and had to shoot their way out. Not long after launching and gaining formation, it was necessary to enter the overcast for the long climb-out to station. This was a thick overcast, and it took a long time before coming out into the clear "on top."

Much later at 0823 hours, a search team far below and under the weather sent an urgent message. Unshackled, it reported a latitude, longitude, and course and speed of a group of ships. Prominent was one BB (battleship) in addition to lesser screening ships. Beyond doubt this was the *Yamato* by a process of elimination, if nothing else. When the information was relayed, some instructions came back after an appropriate time lapse. Instead of navigated time as briefed, the outlying relay team would maintain station until relieved. This was considered necessary for contact to be uninterrupted until all of the strikes were launched, in case the enemy force was changing courses, speeds, and dispositions.

Finally, long after the original time planned, the force gave the division permission to start home. After the many hours grinding around at altitude on oxygen, where fuel consumption is necessarily higher, it was going to be dicey at best. Some of the fuel-consuming altitude had to be maintained to receive communications, and it was hoped that the YG-ZB Homer broadcast by the force, with a range of 100 miles at 20,000 feet, would get through. No signal. Then a few hopeful suggestions for different courses were received from the force, and finally a message wishing the division "Good luck." Now, tucking the division into tight formation, a descent through the weather was initiated.

This descent continued to a very minimum altitude before breaking out over an angry sea. The smart thing to do would be to ditch in a loose formation. This plan was disrupted when the Tail End Charlie apparently ran out of gas and went in. Despite the extremely rough ocean, he got out of the Corsair but didn't seem to have his raft out. While circling him with the intention of dropping a spare raft if necessary, the section leader called and said that his engine was cutting out and he was ditching. He came into wind and hit the water in a burst of spray. Looking over where he had gone in caused the division leader to lose the location of the Tail End Charlie in the rough sea. Now, with nothing left, the division leader and his wingman decided to ditch in formation, and the kites were brought onto the wind line with gear up, full flap, and tail hook down. The ammunition had already been fired off to lighten the ship. Now the QAS harness that was clipped to the parachute and life raft in the seat was released to minimize impedance if things really went to hell on impact.

Even with the considerable sea running, she went in easier than the Corsair did in the Solomon Islands two years before. After bouncing off two succeeding waves, she plowed into the third. Getting out was also better, and after the rather rough impact, she was floating with the engine down. This allowed pulling the raft out before she sank.

Now there were complications. Only half of the Mae West life jacket inflated. As I was wearing heavy shoes, pistol, and other weighty gear, this half-inflated life jacket didn't furnish enough flotation to stay on top of the raging sea. The raft now seemed to be missing, and something kept banging my left leg. Always fearing the worst, this was taken to be a shark. Here was better luck and the "shark" turned out to be the life raft attached by a forgotten lanyard to the belt buckle. Locating the CO_2 bottle on the raft, I activated it, and this led to a further problem. On the surface the wind was really screaming and blowing the tops off the waves in white foam as well as making the inflated raft unmanageable. The battle went on for an indeterminate time before the raft could be wrestled into the right position for the wind to catch it and flip its aspiring passenger into its modest confines.

Those one-man rafts certainly illustrated the old sailor's plaint: "Oh Lord, Thy ocean is so vast and my boat is so small!" However small, it was a lot better than what was in second place. After a very long period of recovering from severe exhaustion and throwing up, some stock of the situation was possible. First and foremost, there seemed to be the sound of a police whistle. This was not a hallucination, and upwind a short distance away another raft heaved up atop another wave. It was the erstwhile wingman blowing the whistle from his survival kit. Getting the rafts alongside and lashed together took most of the remaining daylight and was complicated by the fact that his raft seemed to have a leak and demanded periodic reinflation. Naturally, the saltwater patching kit that cost the taxpayers a bundle did not work and neither did the alleged pump. This called for desperate efforts to keep his raft afloat by blowing into a tube. Fortunately, the wingman was a rugged former football player of some note, with good lungs. Still suffering from the reccurring malaria contracted in the Solomon Islands, I wasn't all that much use in the endurance department.

Then it was dark and the misery increased. There was some desultory speculation on the fate of the other two guys and the unlikelihood of much of a search being made by the embattled task force.

It was also speculated that any dispute over the claims for the downed Japanese kamikazes the previous day would now be resolved. Unfortunately, this would be in the favor of the navy chap, whose chief talent appeared to be screaming, "Splash one for me!"

That night had to set some kind of record in the undesirable category. The arrival of dawn in a cold, rough sea with a cold, gray sky wasn't all that much better than the darkness. The leaking raft needed continual attention, and after being well purged with salt water, I found that hunger didn't seem to be much of a problem. Sparing use of the pitiful amount of canned water in the rafts apparently took care of that need, especially in the cold wind. The results of a few years of recurring malaria were taking their toll, and so was the submersion and exposure. There was probably some madness creeping in. This was evidenced when a sea gull appeared and I endeavored to shoot it with the .38 pistol as the pièce de résistance for a gourmet meal, feathers and all.

The only problem was that, as the wingman forcefully pointed out, there was no sea gull. By the time this was acknowledged, it was dark again. Now really exhausted and with the raft still demanding attention, we agreed that this was probably the last night. Long after dark there seemed to be the roaring of engines. The wingman being still in possession of his senses and with a strong will to live, unlimbered his .38 pistol. Most pilots carried tracer ammunition in these side arms as an emergency signaling device. This ammunition was classified under the Geneva Convention as dum-dum and was illegal. However, since the honorable enemy didn't give a fig for civilized conventions anyway, it was considered a good tradeoff. Almost immediately after he fired, the engine noises faded and then suddenly increased in volume. Out of the blackness, what seemed from our low level of observation to be a huge hull came smashing through the waves, nearly running over the rafts. The wingman, still being in possession of all of his faculties and mindful of the terror of capture, said, "It's a light Jap cruiser." And then with great gravity amended his assessment, "No, no, its not! It's a Japanese heavy cruiser." At that time a blinding light hit the huddled survivors, and a loud hailer bellowed some good old American profanity.

Making another pass, the vessel came around again and with no mean feat of seamanship, parked alongside the rafts in the angry sea. The last lucid memories were of getting hit with a life ring, to which a desperate attachment was forged, and of being jerked from the raft, smashed into the pressure hull, and being hit in the eyes by the search-light. The next memory was of lying on a bunk with a stocky chap looming overhead holding a bottle and a tube. He appeared to be en-grossed in fitting a large needle in the end of the tube. He nearly leaped out of his skin when asked politely just what the hell he was doing. This obliging chap said he was trying to revive the patient. He also said that the patient had shown little sign of life since he had been jerked into the hull, where he had managed to get such a death grip that his fingers had to be pried apart with a spanner.

It was established that this was a day later and that the USS *Sea Devil*, a distinguished boat (a submarine, not a ship), was playing host during this unexpected career move. It seems that the wingman and the section leader were both aboard and doing fine, and they soon trooped in. The *Sea Devil* had been searching for the Tail End Char-lie with great diligence but was being forced to give up. By now the likelihood of anybody surviving in those circumstances was unrealis-tic. The boat was on the way home after a very full war patrol. They had three Japanese prisoners aboard from some ships they had sunk in a recent desperate action. They had one more aboard until recently, but they had buried him at sea. With their newfound expertise gained in this endeavor, they figured burying the failing marine pilot would be a piece of cake. However, they really didn't take it too hard when the rascal rejoined the living. Instead, they produced a message from the Commander of Submarines Pacific congratulating them for their humanitarian gesture. They had the three survivors sign this message as a permanent part of the history of the *Sea Devil* (SS400).

After an interesting war patrol, the sub now made her approach to Saipan. This was now a forward submarine operating base and boasted a mother ship. The crew was conducting field day to make a good impression when they docked. The Japanese prisoners were put to work along with the crew in this enterprise. Having gotten over their original fright at the terrible fate in store for them if captured, one of them indicated that he would commit hara-kiri (suicide) rather than turn-to with mop and pail. He changed his mind when the cook handed him a large butcher knife and regarded him expectantly.

When the sub was tied up, the prisoners' fright returned. They were blindfolded and placed on a bunk in the forward torpedo room to await the medical authorities. The feeble marine was also waiting for the medical chaps and therefore sat down beside them. With the hatch open it wasn't particularly warm, but they were sweating profusely, and it was actually possible to smell their fear. What a difference if roles were reversed. Instead of being starved, beaten, and tortured as our prisoners were, they would be given humane treatment and good food and sanitary conditions. They would surely survive the war. They probably became executives with Sony eventually.

The submarine men were not only the most heroic and effective of the entire navy during the war; they were also the most unheralded and self-effacing. That went for their admiral who received his guests on the mother ship. He speculated on what he might have done if he had gotten some friendly aviators aboard who had attempted to sink his sub at the Battle of Midway, or so he said.

There were a few days in the transient officer's quarters at Saipan while Air-Sea Rescue did their interviews. They had a joint venture there, with an Army Air Corps colonel and a navy commander apparently in joint charge. Although their main line of concern was the rescue of downed crews of the B-29 Super Fortresses now raiding the home islands of Japan, they were interested in everything. There seemed to be many problems, both mechanical and weatherwise. In fact, if the U.S. Marines hadn't made the terrible sacrifices in capturing Iwo Jima for an emergency refuge for B-29s going to and coming from their targets, casualties of those aircraft may well have been unsustainable.

The Air-Sea Rescue officers had some very disturbing information on the weather picture. As impossible as it may sound at this remove, meteorology was practically in its infancy. They said that the Superforts were running into winds of unpredictable direction and unbelievable velocities at altitude. This was the beginning of the appreciation of the jet-stream winds, which now have a great deal to do with modern airline operation and weather predicting.

These two knowledgeable officers were of the opinion that the outlying communications team, being above a solid overcast at altitude for hours, had indeed encountered this phenomenon. This would certainly explain a lot about not being able to find the carriers again. They also decried the habit of the various branches of the service of not sharing such crucial information. In fact, interservice communication was so poor that they frequently attacked each others' ships and aircraft. However, it was a big war and, in retrospect, what are a few people more or less? Especially if they are marines.

XXV

fter the Air-Sea Rescue chaps finished their interrogations, arrangements were made to fly me the short distance down to Guam, where there was a considerable Marine Corps presence. It was assumed that they would arrange transportation back to the *Essex*. This was not to be. Instead, a whole bunch of people got involved and the local authority said in effect, "No way." The reason given was, considering the great surplus of trained pilots now available, the division had done more than their part, not to mention our less-than-enthusiastic reception by VFB-83 on the ship. The flight surgeon they produced waxed wroth that anybody with a history of the famous Solomon Islands malaria would even be allowed close to combat anyway. When he was told that down in the Solomon Islands malaria was considered only as an inconvenience and the main concern was to get the patient back on line with dispatch, he really got vehement. That, he said, was then, when things were a lot grimmer and it was necessary to squeeze all the work possible from the critically short supply of aviators available. Now he was going to throw his weight around and forbid it.

There was also a chaplain present to reinforce the surgeon's argument. The clergyman was informed that the *Essex* offered a tempting opportunity to discuss the matter of who shot down a couple of kamikazes with some unfriendly people in an unfriendly environment. He, in turn, declared that the whole killing business was beginning to look increasingly immature. He had a point there, and all resistance ended. It was time to go home.

There was now only one more thing to do on Guam, and that was unexpected and impressive. A major showed up and extended an invitation to a party with a bunch of ground officers. This major, Joe Quilty, had been one of the great Wolf Pack pilots from Guadalcanal, and he had a tale to tell. The survivors of the Solomon Islands campaign seemed to be coalescing into an exclusive society, perhaps because their numbers were small. The members, whatever their squadron had been down there, were always happy to see others of the group who were again overseas. The major was frankly looking for the company of aviators rather than the ones he was currently involved with.

The party was in a wooded area where there was a large camp of marine infantrymen. They were recently from the victory at Iwo Jima, what there was left of them. The major had been shanghaied to be this lot's forward air controller for air strikes. This required being accompanied by a sergeant equipped with an SCR-3 (Army Signal Corps radio) and taking a position as far forward on the ground as was possible. It was his duty to call in the planes for air support of the infantry. This is just what Chuck, the ill-fated brother of Yamamoto's slayer in the Solomons, had been doing. Apparently, getting out of this assignment alive required something of a miracle. Handicapped by a lack of marine aviation to direct in support of the troops, it had not been a pleasant experience. The torn-up dead and wounded bodies all around afforded an experience never encountered in air combat. Surprisingly enough, the surviving officers of this battalion seemed normal enough, and the flying major was even critical of the lieutenant colonel, who, despite being a legendary hero in battle, suffered a serious flaw. According to the major, this poor chap had committed the unforgivable sin of washing out of flight training. This didn't seem to worry the colonel too much, and he returned the major's insults with some severe criticisms (probably well deserved) of aviators. When one of these jolly officers was pointedly asked just how in hell a sane person could charge one of those beaches, and especially Iwo Jima, he said he owed it all to a canteen full of brandy.

There was one tale about the navy they couldn't wait to lay on me. It seemed that on the approach to Iwo Jima in the face of heavy fire, the navy coxswain of a landing craft panicked while still quite a distance from the beach. He started cursing and screaming at the marines that he was going no farther and ordering, "You bastards, get out of the boat." When he started to turn away from the beach, the marines all jumped into the water to get to the beach as best they could, burdened down with their equipment. No sooner were they out of the boat, which was now fleeing crazily, than an artillery shell found the range and blew the boat and the coxswain straight to hell. According to the marines, it sure lightened up what was otherwise a rather depressing day.

Life was a different matter in those days, and on Iwo Jima the marines suffered 25,852 casualties with 6,821 killed, while the Japanese lost 21,000 dead; only 200 surrendered in that one campaign. However, there was a newspaper correspondent at the party who had been on the B-29 raid that had recently done a low-level fire bombing of Tokyo. The best estimates, which were largely confirmed after the war, was that 85,000 Japanese were killed and 41,000 injured in this raid.

The next day an R5D was boarded for the long return flight through Kwajalein and Johnston Island to terminate on Oahu. Now there didn't seem to be any hurry to do anything. The war raged on at Okinawa, and the marine carrier replacement training squadron was sending out more replacement pilots, but now only to marine squadrons. All of that was now the concern of other marines.

Part of the indolent lifestyle included getting a tan lying on the grass in front of the BOQ (bachelors' officer quarters). Now and then a white balloon could be sighted far up in the sky. These rather pa-

thetic attempts at a secret weapon by the Japanese were launched in
Japan loaded with incendiaries to drift to the West Coast of the
United States. The balloons were too high for intercept in the little-
understood jet-stream winds. Some of these actually arrived at their
destinations and even caused some fatalities and minor fires. When
sighted, they did serve as a grim reminder to the three sea survivors
that up there were unknown winds of remarkable velocity.

There was another reminder of the recent past that was somewhat amusing. By that time in the war the island of Oahu was nearly
sinking under military equipment and installations. The U. S. Army
was flying a diversified assortment of aircraft from their own fields.
One army outfit was equipped with the P-47 Thunderbolt, a hefty
fighter that could come down like streaked lightning in a dive. One
morning the three survivors were still lying around in the double
bunks of the transient officers' quarters when an army pilot determined to give the marine air base a thrill and initiated a dive right overhead. The rising crescendo of his big reciprocating engine running flat
out was deafening and unfortunately didn't quit until there was a
thunderous explosion. He probably got into compressibility and
couldn't get the Thunderbolt out of the dive. One of the lieutenants
was asleep in a lower bunk, and this rising racket jackknifed him erect,
and he hollered "kamikaze" before knocking himself out on the up-
per bunk. It was a perfectly synchronized maneuver, with his impact
and the P-47's arrival in a parking lot matching perfectly. Some memories die hard.

Another grim reminder of the recent past was a visit to the big
hospital up on a hill overlooking Pearl Harbor, now known as Tripler
Army Medical Center. Some old friends and other contemporaries
from the carrier checkout squadron were there. These were chaps who
had been on the ill-fated carrier *Franklin* when she was struck. The
unit they were attached to on the ship was none other than VMF-214.
This was the squadron's second resurrection following the original formation on Oahu in 1942. By the time of the *Franklin*, none of the pilots who had been present at 214's birth was a member.

These chaps had suffered grievously but were still in good spirits since, with the war still on, they were considered great heroes. The war would soon be over and that would radically change. Their misfortunes would become only an embarrassment to the vast majority of the citizens whose nonparticipation in combat inevitably engendered a massive guilt complex. Wars were ever thus. If this were not depressing enough, an impromptu tour of a ward containing survivors of Iwo Jima would break the strongest heart. Just as bad was the apparently high morale and humor shown by some of these truly mutilated human beings.

One day I was directed to an office in the control tower at the navy field on Ford Island. Present here were a number of high-ranking navy officers of the icy-eyed persuasion, who would always take their responsibilities too seriously. Happily, the marine member of their staff was an ex-fighter squadron commander of great fame from Guadalcanal, Duke Davis, who was genetically unable to take anything much seriously. The question of the day was to find out what happened to marine pilots who were sent as replacements into navy squadrons in the fleet. This practice had not happened before, and since they seemed to be in charge of these matters, they wanted to find out how it had happened in the first place. Since they seemed to have a lot to do with high-level decisions, it would seem more than passing strange that they wouldn't know. Employing strict honesty and aided by some sarcasm from the marine colonel, a considered opinion concerning the whole mess was delivered. It may have done some good, since it never happened again during the war.

This report seemed to warm the personages up slightly, and one of them inquired, rather sympathetically, as to what the future held. The colonel took this opportunity to interject that these guys were going back to the States to indulge in such pleasures as appealed to young marines everywhere. Actually, he was rather graphic in his remarks and on this note the once again constrained meeting broke up.

The flight home was in a four-engine navy flying boat of impressive size. This Consolidated Aircraft Company PB2Y-5 was a great

deal cruder than the Pan American flying boat on the outbound trip
had been. On the plus side, it took only about twelve hours to San
Francisco in its noisy, cold, vibrating interior. This inconvenience was
negligible considering the destination.

San Francisco was even better than it had been on departure,
although that time seemed much longer ago than it really was. This
was probably because the interval had been such a busy time. Now
there were no responsibilities, as there had been in the recent past,
for a group of wild young pilots who were on their way overseas. The
fine people down at Fleet Marine Force Pacific, headquartered at 100
Harrison Street, arranged quarters back in the Fairmont Hotel, despite the greatest earthshaking event transpiring in San Francisco
since the earthquake of 1906. Now underway in "The Cool Gray City
of Love" by the bay, the United Nations was being formed to bring
everlasting peace and tranquility to the shattered world. Bah, hum-
bug.

The three ragged marines looked disgraceful in their salt-stained
khakis while waiting for the tailoring of the new green uniforms to be
finished in a fashionable haberdashery. Some of this waiting was being done in the famous Cirque Room cocktail lounge of the hotel. An
impressive-looking civilian gentleman in a blue suit came over and sat
down unbidden and ordered drinks. He seemed to know a lot about
aviation, and it was a great shock when he identified himself as the
flag secretary for Admiral Halsey, the Marine Corps' favorite admiral. He was of great stature in the government and had been a leading candidate for president of the United States. Now, as an important
man in forming the United Nations, Harold Stassen was on leave from
his navy duties. His practiced eye had identified the ragged marines
for what they were. After exchanging a few sea stories he took his departure. This left his new friends considering the possibilities of re-
taining their shoddy dress. Who wants to be just another pretty face?
With new uniforms in hand, there was no other excuse for sticking
around. One Hundred Harrison Street issued travel warrants to Miramar, the marine aviation reception center in back of San Diego. The

wingman, being an upright chap and a married man, proceeded to carry out the Marine Corps' wishes in this matter. The gallant leader and the section leader got to talking with a stunning young lady in the travel office who thought marine fighter pilots were "just divine." This indicated that San Francisco still had a lot to offer.

This resulted in the wingman taking just any old passenger train south on schedule. The two mutineers were given berths on the Lark as far as Los Angeles; it was a lush, all-compartment train favored by movie stars and other privileged citizens. However, this was some days later, when exhaustion and lack of funds dictated this move. Finally, arriving at Miramar the wingman was found to be mired in the usual paperwork to get his thirty-day repatriation leave.

The marines, as a result of the great wartime expansion, now had a lot of officers who were not combat veterans, and the personnel administering this sewer were a sad lot. The man in charge took it upon himself to take the matter of the late arrivals very seriously. The Threadbare Buzzard, entertaining no intention of suffering any abuse from this feather merchant, caused some verbal unpleasantness to ensue. These smug administrative types were equipped with neat uniforms and the certainty of never being shot at. They gloried in their small authority and fit the description of the Oracle of Poverty Flats for all minor bureaucrats: "As happy as a dog rolling around in a dead skunk."

This unpleasantness was certainly beneficial to the two criminals who were soon banished from sight by being hastily sent off on leave while the upright wingman was still caught in the machinery. The orders, when the leave expired, were to Marine Corps Schools at Quantico, Virginia.

It was time to revisit Poverty Flats, Montana, where one end of the horse was a head as opposed to those infesting Miramar.

XXVI

No great attempt was made to secure air transportation back to Poverty Flats and, despite the wartime impairment of the trains, it was a pleasant journey. The slow, uncomplicated atmosphere of Poverty Flats provided a welcome change from the recent adventures.

In no great hurry and with a reporting date for the start of the assigned school in hand, I determined to travel to Virginia by train also. It was a fortunate decision, since this would be the last time the transcontinental journey would be undertaken by this gracious mode of transportation. As any personal feelings of war-related expediency faded away, a leisurely stay in Chicago at the Palmer House was one of the pleasant breaks in the journey.

Quantico, with its great golf course and Waller Building officers' club, seemed to be every bit as charming as it had been when I was fresh out of the RCAF in what now felt like the distant past. It was more extensive than remembered and boasted a number of schools.

The school assignment was the Air Infantry School, and its student body was unique. They were more or less equally divided between ground officers and aviators and had in common one qualification: they were all combat veterans of the tough battles in the Pacific. Part of the purpose was to expand even further the already close cooperation between air and ground troops. The importance of this was the impending invasion of the Japanese home islands, where these officers' experience was going to be necessary in increased leadership roles. Even to these somewhat fatalistic veterans, the projected body count predictions were hardly reassuring.

Almost all of the management was in the hands of nonaviators, and some of these really disliked everything about the pilots, and who could blame them? These grunts had gotten the worst of everything, taken the most brutal losses, and then been accorded little credit, not much glamour, and—unkindest cut of all—much less pay than the dashing aviators.

Way back when flying airplanes was a much more dangerous occupation than just hanging around the barracks and marching in the mud, it was determined that flyers should be compensated for the added risk. This took the form of "flight pay," which amounted to an addition of one-half the regular base pay. With an all-out ground war in progress, this now hardly seemed fair, but change comes slowly to any governmental enterprise.

Anyway, the motto of the marines is "Semper Fidelis," which is interpreted in the vernacular to mean, "I got mine, screw you." So, a plague upon the mud-marines.

To collect this 50 percent added onto base pay for flight pay, it was necessary to fly only four hours a month. To make this convenient, there were some of the old reliable SBD dive-bombers stationed at Brown Field, which was part of the Quantico base. This made it possible to take the nonflying contemporaries in the class for rides. Some violent aerobatics or giving some exaggerated dive-bombing demonstrations to these chaps often terminated their complaints while disposing of their groceries.

Many of the aviators in the class were old acquaintances, and there were some ribald comments on the subject of my having only dropped four brand-new Corsair fighters in the drink. Present was the marines' all-time champ in the formation-ditching business. He had been in a flight of twenty-three Corsairs that were being ferried between islands in the central Pacific. Through command goofs that failed to supply a transport aircraft for an escort, and almost ludicrous weather reports that were fourteen hours old, and lack of communication information, this turned out to be a fool's errand. Operations rivaled the *Indianapolis* sinking for incompetence. By the time the leadership of the flight had devolved on the Quantico classmate, it was too late for him to do much of anything. He decided to ditch the last fifteen fighters that were in this group. Two of them wandered away, but he got thirteen of them in the drink in a group. For two days, with only twelve one-man rafts, they survived and were picked up. Out of the twenty-three Corsairs, twenty-two were lost and six young pilots had answered the last bugle call in the sky.

With the ever-jealous navy always trying to steal the Marine Corps' records, this mark was exceeded. Just how many airplanes went to Davy Jones' Locker during the war is obscure but impressive. One whole carrier air group got lost in the soup and ditched every plane save one that was piloted by an ensign right out of flight school. Since he didn't know any better he flew back to the carrier.

Of course, ground warfare was the mud-marines' domain. It soon developed that these people were doing a lot of interesting things, and many of these things required a high degree of skill. In no time at all most of the differences between the officers disappeared and friendships were forged, since there was one common denominator. Simply stated, a war can get you killed whatever your specialty.

Some of those ground officers came complete with legendary reputations. Despite their often inoffensive appearances, some of them were tough guys that really didn't give a damn.

A memorable captain was assured of no further promotions due to a slight misunderstanding at the battle of Tarawa. When a senior officer didn't provide his frontline company (or what was left of it) with some requested support, he made his way back and in a very physical confrontation took charge of it himself. In addition to not having to worry about future promotions, he was awarded one of the nation's highest decorations. It didn't matter much, since he was planning on going back to his old job as an elementary school teacher if he happened to survive the war.

Another officer was said to have gotten a reputation for exercising undue caution on Iwo Jima, where the Japanese were well dug into caves. It was known that the Japanese also had saki in those caves. He was known to call up flamethrowers to burn the defenders out. According to his bloodthirsty troops (or what was left of them), the flamethrowers raised hell with the saki. They would prefer going in with bayonets and "forget the casualties; save the saki."

One running mate at Quantico had made a fearsome reputation as an artillery officer on Saipan. When some badly trained troops that were involved in the action had their line cave in during some middle-of-the-night banzai charges, he had some 105 howitzers, or whatever the grunts call those cannon, stuffed with canister. This canister resembles a cheesecloth bag full of ball bearings. And then he jacked the tailpieces up to level. He literally waited to see the "whites of their eyes" before giving the order to fire. This stacked the dead enemy up in front of his positions while the guns were reloaded to coolly await the next charge. When the class was given a demonstration of this technique in the field, the weapons instructors respectfully let him conduct it despite his status as a student. In this demonstration they lined up some of these cannon and stuffed the canister in on top of the powder increments. For a target they hung up some sheets at very close range. After the roaring detonations, and as the smoke was settling, it was frightening to see the shredded rags that had been sheets fluttering to the ground.

Although this young man and an impressive number of others of his type were the products of "field commissions," they soon became thoroughly integrated with the aviators. A field commission meant simply that after the officers and senior noncoms in their outfit had been killed off or severely maimed, then they became the leader. This may have been doing it the hard way, but it saved the Marine Corps the expense of field-testing their officers for courage and dependability under fire.

The aviators, however, became the leaders in a field where they held the undisputed superiority. This was in the weekend festivities in Washington, D.C., which was close at hand. There was one well-known hotel that was managed by a former marine officer, and he was generous in providing quarters for the weekend revels, despite the tight hotel market in the wartime crowded capital. In this large establishment the corner suites were distinguished by having grand pianos. To add to this touch of class, the officers' club at Quantico seemed to be able to furnish inexhaustible supplies of booze. This was of inestimable value with the shortages and national rationing. Unrationed were the nubile young ladies whose numbers in the paper-passing halls of government rivaled the ranks of the ladies in the West Coast shipyards. However, despite all of this, there was work to be done.

Some of the work down at Quantico encompassed participating in field exercises. These were carried out in a large area of wilderness that was charmingly named "Guadalcanal One." There was one huge exercise that included everything from artillery to infantry charges. My assignment for this problem was both interesting and instructive. In fact, it was a simulation of what Major Joe Quilty, who had issued the invitation to the party on Guam, had been doing for real on Iwo Jima. The job description was forward observer. The position was in a foxhole on a down slope that was shared by a sergeant with a SCR radio. The forward observer was equipped with an area map of the slight valley immediately to the front. He also was equipped with a transparent overlay with a grid to place over the map to reduce its geographical features to grid coordinates. Back in what the gravel pounders love to call a defile, which in English means a depression in the earth's surface, was the artillery and also the canister man of Saipan note. He was in charge of the mortars, which were just tubes into which a sort of rocket is dropped to be fired aloft for an impressive distance.

When the forward observer had determined a target to be marked with phosphorous smoke, it would be relayed as map coordinates back to the mortarman by radio, and that worthy would, by some obscure magic of aiming, fire the mortar rounds. Since there might be some discrepancy in accuracy, the procedure was to do "ranging fire" first. That was the classic, one over, one under, and one right on, approach. Then, "fire for effect," which would draw down a whole flock of projectiles, hopefully on target. This guy was uncanny with those mortars and was said to have the skill to ignore the ranging fire and hit the coordinates with no further ado.

Down below the forward observer were some ancient farm buildings that the marines were apparently very fond of, judging from the prohibition of ever using them for targets. How many of these exercises they had survived must have gone back into prehistory.

As the hot afternoon wore on and the flies became more insistent, the forward observer and his loyal sergeant with the radio were becoming bored and increasingly irritated. The final problem would call down a massive air attack by a flight of Corsairs that were flying all of the way up from Cherry Point, North Carolina, for the occasion. The predetermined target for their attack would be merely a spot where the white phosphorus smoke rounds from the mortars were directed by the forward observer.

The radio sergeant and I had, on occasion, covered the coordinates of the farm buildings with the plastic overlay and inspected each other tentatively. This time, after placing the grease pencil position on the overlay some distance from the buildings, a finger was placed on the buildings themselves. The sergeant nodded slightly and said, "You're the officer." In the complicated language of the marine this meant, "I ain't gonna talk." The coordinates that fitted the buildings were relayed back to the mortars with the instructions to "mark target" with white phosphorous using battery fire. It was sarcastically added that, no doubt, he would need ranging fire to correct his aim. The rather belligerent answer indicated that they were ready when ordered and the ranging fire could go to hell.

"Fire!"

Overhead was the swishing sound of the mortar rounds that could actually be seen on their descent. Jeez! Down in the valley there erupted a very stirring scene. Ancient boards intermingled with top-soil and the thick white smoke were flying everywhere. Sirens sounded to suspend the drill, and surprise, surprise: they even had a fire truck out there that started for the blazing buildings with some other random vehicles in pursuit. Or they did until the Corsairs announced their arrival by initiating a spectacular attack.

A sedan with a flag decorated with some stars on a flag affixed to a running board came bouncing right over the rugged terrain and skidded to a halt by the forward observer's position. The line overlay with the position thoughtfully placed some distance from the buildings was seized and with much cursing and hollering, the sedan crashed off in the direction of the mortarman's position. Apparently the mortarman was of resolute character and didn't even bother defending himself. The marines were trying to get this genuine hero to join the regular establishment, so nothing ever came of this. He was even able to join in the laughter when spurious decorations for this caper were passed out in one of the corner suites, the ones that had the grand pianos in them in the hotel in the nation's capital.

Just as the class was about to matriculate, some fine army chaps, flying from Saipan with a newfangled type of bomb, disposed of Hiroshima and, just to prove the point, followed it by wiping out Nagasaki. Suddenly the war was over and the nuclear era had dawned. The scene of mass hysteria in Washington, D.C., that night would have to be seen to be believed. All of the toilet paper in the hotels seemed to be floating down on the crazed citizens who were dancing and rioting in the streets.

The next day wartime gas rationing, the most restrictive and hated symbol of the war, was repealed. That morning driving back down to Quantico through the gigantic traffic jam with some of the class that included the mortarman and other distinguished gravel pounders, a new side to the nation's gratitude to the veterans was revealed. The traffic was stop-and-go, and one of the stops was right beside another car with a couple of somewhat drunk and beefy civilian war workers. One of them shook a large fist and hollered, "Ah right, you fancy sons a bitches, the party's over. Now you can take off your pretty little suits and go to work for a living." The gravel pounders, who appeared to be very good at this sort of thing, were energetically dealing with this heresy when the state police arrived. The heroes of the home front were led away, but it was a sobering lesson that indeed the war was over. Back in Quantico the change was unreal. People actually looked younger and somewhat shocked. After all of these years, there would be no more next invasion, no invasion of the Japanese home islands, no more question of dying. Life could go on.

Since the war, there has been the recurring question of whether it was a moral thing to use nuclear weapons against Japan. It would be ridiculous to ask that question of anyone embroiled in the Pacific war and whose life could now begin. Besides, a bemused weapons instructor with a bent for history summed it all up. He said that since the stone ax was invented, there always had to be a weapon developed to counter the next invention, and so on. It was always almost predictable what weapons the next war would be fought with. He went on to say that it was still predictable now, even to the war after the next one. That one would be fought with stone axes.

Although the war in Europe had been over for some time and the demise of Japan had been a foregone conclusion, the peace was actually awkward at the beginning. There was the matter of getting shut of the service. After some consideration, a plan was worked out to award points for length of service, combat decorations, et cetera. I later learned that this solution was not absolutely foolproof. The former adjutant from the carrier checkout squadron at Marine Corps Air Station Ewa beat the system. Since he had very few, if any, points, he was put in charge of the discharging activity at Miramar. Being a lawyer by profession and harboring the opinion that *military intelligence* was the world's greatest oxymoron, he promptly discharged himself.

With plenty of points, it was still necessary for me to go down to Cherry Point, North Carolina, to get separated. While waiting for the paperwork, it was still possible to do a little flying. Upon going over

to an air group commanded by an old CO from the Solomon Islands
to borrow an airplane, he had a fine tale to tell.

In his air group they had a squadron of B-25s, the same type of
aircraft with which Jimmy Doolittle had bombed Tokyo. A couple of mechanics fantasized about flying one for a long time, since they were always taxiing them around and riding in them. One day, while taxiing,
they decided that since the war had ended, now was the time to get the
B-25 into the air. As the colonel explained, "They would have made it
except for a mistake that was hilarious for a couple of experienced mechanics to make." They forgot to remove the "gust locks," which keep
the control surfaces immobilized while the aircraft is parked. They
emerged unscathed from the total wreckage of the airplane after a takeoff run that included taking out a fence at the end of a very long runway. When quizzed as to their fate, the colonel laughed heartily and
opined that they were a couple of fine guys who would soon be going
home after long and valued service. Who gave a damn about one of the
thousands of expensive new airplanes destined for the scrap heap anyway? He seemed quite pleased that they hadn't gotten hurt.

It was not long before papers replacing active duty orders with
reserve duty orders brought blessed freedom—well, almost freedom.
There was still the matter of getting out of this swamp to some civilized place to catch an airplane. This was solved handily while at a
party at a senior officer's on-base house. He was of the type of regular officer who was married to a lady from an impressive Detroit family and fortune. He was also that type of well-connected senior staff
officer who kept in touch with his flight pay by flying passive aircraft
the minimum four hours a month. In order to transact some business
out in Detroit, he was going to fly an R4D (DC-3, or "giant airliner")
transport with some troops out to the navy field at Grosse Ile the very
next night and he needed a copilot. Well, well, well. There are small
lies, white lies, and damn lies.

The next night was very dark, and seated in the unfamiliar copilot's seat a remarkable fact came to light. It appeared that his majesty
didn't know much about flying this damn thing either. Fortunately,

those "giant airliners" were simple machines that any little old lady in tennis shoes could probably fly. However, the little old lady in tennis shoes might have a little more difficulty if it were at night, the machine were heavily loaded, and it had some weather coming at it en route.

One lesson I learned about that rugged Douglas was that it was just amazing how many alarming bounces (resembling modified crashes) it could take before coming to rest, with the wings still attached, in the even darker night at Grosse Ile. It didn't seem to be much of an occasion for lingering farewells and, before the passengers could recover, a taxi was leaving all of this far behind.

It took quite a bit of relaxing in Detroit before it was at least partially possible to realize that after five and a half years of war with the RCAF and the U.S. Marines, it was all over. The time frame in a lifetime was from late teens to the very early twenties and had become a way of life. However, it had been such an intense period that it would forever remain fresh in memory.

There was one more duty prompted by concern and common decency that could not be avoided. The mother of squadron mate Chuck, who was the brother of the army pilot who killed the Japanese Admiral Yamamoto, lived in the area. When contacted, she confirmed that, according to a surviving fellow prisoner at Rabaul, the Japanese had starved and beaten Chuck to death.

After extensive adjustment to the civilian world, it was deemed safe to board another "giant airliner" to continue onward. This aircraft had two freshly scrubbed, well-barbered little men wearing shined shoes and their company uniform, in charge of the machine. A cute little hostess to reassure the nervous passengers that flying was indeed safe was included. This would appear to present a reasonable risk.

XXVII

Now that the war was over, it was found to be necessary to make some adjustments. The prevailing opinion of the local peer group was that, now that the nonsense had come to an end, it was time to conform. This seemed to call for a rather desolate future. Veterans were supposed to rejoin the real human race by way of a rather unappetizing and extensive initiation. There was room for only minor flexibility. It went something like follows.

Forget that hero crap.

Finish education if required.

Get married.

Find as good a job as possible.

Get a house and prepare for a long, boring, useful life as a substantial member of the community (church optional).

When the *first* War to End All Wars (the one immediately preceding World War II) came to a close, there was a popular song titled, "How're You Gonna Keep Them Down on the Farm?" It referred to the returning soldiers who had gone from the farms to the great outside world and found *sin*, especially in France, which signified major debauchery to the bumpkins of the time. It is doubtful that the average doughboy of that era got much exposure to sin, but the suspicion was prevalent. The majority of the veterans of the current "War to End All

Wars" were very grateful to be "back on the farm" or whatever comprised their dull equivalent, and were willingly conforming to the approved life. A few free thinkers said, "The hell with it," and lived happily ever after.

After I had gotten in a few quarters at the University of Montana and built a house, it became apparent that this was not going to work. Selling out, it was determined to go out to Seattle and go to school there. At least it was a bigger place. It also possessed an unexpected treasure of inestimable value. Having absolutely no military ambitions despite a still-lingering love of flying, I considered the marines as part of a past life, so much for that.

Soon the postwar Seattle housing shortage was circumnavigated. This was accomplished by moving in with a friend from pre-war Montana, who had inherited his parents' apartment. His father, a noted straight arrow who was on loan from the U.S. Forest Service to the War Assets Administration, was transferred to Los Angeles to clean up the corruption engendered by the huge sale of surplus war materiel. This apartment was traded for a more modest one, which was more conveniently located to the university.

The university was staggering under the weight of the returning heroes who were enjoying the largess of a grateful nation by way of the G.I. Bill of Rights. This legislation to educate even the marginally intelligent offered an attractive alternative to facing life and going to work. This experiment in mass education did more than any one thing to increase the American middle class and lead to the long and sustained prosperity of the country just emerging from the war. Ironically, this entitlement had been crafted by that distinguished World War I veteran, President Harry Truman. The redoubtable Harry Truman was the only president in the twentieth century who did *not* have a college degree, probably because the veterans of the First World War got damn little pampering.

Not long after these arrangements were in place, and having achieved the top of the list, a new Ford convertible was mine. The time had come to enjoy and participate in the rewards for having won the war. There was more to follow.

Seattle owned one of the really fine old naval air stations, Sand Point. It was practically in town, and the postwar air reserve was based there. Not only that, a fine Marine Corps Reserve fighter squadron was included. This VMF-216 was skippered by a jolly chap last encountered assisting in the decoration ceremony in the hotel suite with the grand piano in the nation's capital. He was now in the employ of Pan American Airways flying the Nome Road and was being transferred to Mills Field at San Francisco to fly the Pacific runs.

He explained that they were provided with a lieutenant colonel of the regular establishment and a couple of continuous active-duty helpers, both officer and enlisted. The squadron pilots were all experienced combat troops, so that was no problem. The lieutenant colonel's title was inspector instructor. Since he was of the generation who had been flying mostly transports, et cetera, he was blissfully ignorant of the world of fighters, so that wasn't any problem either.

The squadron had weekend meetings and did a two-week maneuver every year. Quite a few of these guys were going to school or were already out in the world working. Of course, the splendid new F4U-1D Corsairs they were flying were available at any time. Corsairs cost a staggering sum of money per air hour to operate. This group of pilots really didn't need any more fighter training, so this actually was a magnificent flying club funded by the taxpayers, who had it coming anyway. The only downside was that it was on a base that was infested with the U.S. Navy, but that could not be helped. Soon the Pan American chap was on his way to San Francisco, and here was a newfound command for the Threadbare Buzzard.

In addition to the squadron and school, Seattle was a magnificent place to be during this reconstruction period. It was always the gateway to Alaska and had a very salty working waterfront. It was a great navy town, with the installation at Pier Ninety-One in addition to the Sand Point Naval Air Station. Across the sound was the large Bremerton Naval Base. Seattle was well represented in aviation as the home of mighty Boeing Aircraft (originally known as the "great wooden airplane company").

The rapidly expanding University of Washington with its hordes of GIs (this term had originally been applied to the standard grunts as a diminutive for "government issue" but now applied to all veterans) was a mess, with the rampant construction, muddy paths, and overcrowded classrooms. There was some speculation by the learned professors as to whether educating this vast array of young savages was possible at all. The papers of these aspiring intellectuals bore a red stamp reading "veteran" as a warning to the professors and was referred to as the "mark of the leper."

The postwar social ramble was vigorous even in the face of the remnants of the bluenosed local society. There were only beer and wine bars available to the peasants, and these were closed on Sundays. About this time the song "Gloomy Sunday" became popular. This caused a rash of desperate winos to hurl themselves off the Aurora Street bridge. This prohibition also caused the skid row around Pioneer Square to resemble the Bowery awash in human wreckage.

This hard-liquor aberration didn't extend to the more affluent. At the bottom of this layer of society were the bottle clubs of First Avenue. Above that were "private clubs" that were really not so difficult of access and were actually lush cocktail lounges. Well up on this scale were the naval officers' clubs at Sand Point and Pier Ninety-One, the homes of the hard-drinking naval establishment. The officers' club of the U.S. Army at Fort Lawton was not so fortunate. They were actually only a bottle club and as such were several pegs down from the more enlightened navy clubs.

The Naval Air Station at Sand Point was a gracious prewar establishment with fine brick buildings, which gave it a feeling of permanence. It did have one drawback. Jutting out into Lake Washington was a single runway, and that was not all that long. Airplanes had developed rapidly to meet the demands of war with exponentially increased weight and horsepower, leading to much higher takeoff and landing speeds requiring longer distances to take off and to stop on landing. This led to some amusing incidents, especially amongst the more cumbersome flying machines, of which the Lockheed Hudson bomber seemed to have the worst luck. With a significant load, its twin engines would be straining as it thundered down the runway. One unfortunate lad had his copilot bleed off the flaps instead of pulling up the landing gear at the wrong time and greased the airplane into a perfect landing. Unfortunately, this landing was effected on the calm waters of Lake Washington at the end of the strip.

Another chap, seeing that he wasn't going to achieve flight before the end of the runway arrived, pulled up the wheels on purpose and skidded to a stop with spectacular sound effects just short of the lake. This crash was witnessed by the commanding officer of the station, who raced his car to the airplane. Leaping out, he approached the pilot's window, which, without the wheels extended under the kite, was at eye level. Thoroughly upset, he shook his fist and delivered himself of some profane comments to the already shocked young pilot. Those naval officers of the regular establishment who commanded these small fields were a weird lot by any standard and, at any rate, were probably on their preretirement tour of duty.

The only regular naval activity operating out of Sand Point was VR-5, a navy transport squadron equipped with R5Ds (the military version of the DC-4), which were the four-engine successors to the R4Ds. Among other assignments, they made the long flight to Adak, Alaska, which was far out in the Aleutian Chain. One of these pilots was the same chap who a few years ago had lost an engine while taking off in a "Baltimore Whore" target-towing airplane at Jacksonville, Florida. His close call with destiny hadn't changed his approach to life. The wing of the bachelor officers' quarters he and his mates occupied was infamous as "Point Desperation."

This group had to be admired for their skill as instrument pilots. In a dense fog, anyone looking down on the airstrip from the picture windows of the officers' club could often hear, if not see, them. They would effect landings and takeoffs, day or night, in these conditions if necessary. Sometimes the requisite relaxing from these rigorous duties would become a bit boisterous.

When school would become a bit much, I would drive out to Sand Point and strap on a Corsair. The area encompassing Puget Sound, the Cascade Mountains, and the Olympic Peninsula and its snowcapped mountains provided a splendid and relaxing sightseeing flight. All alone and with no constraints, it was fun to kite around through the mountain passes and over the towering peaks with only the flashing shadow of the Corsair for company. Then, roaring out to where Puget Sound meets the mighty Pacific Ocean at Cape Flattery, I would buzz the sea-foam-smothered rock of Tatoosh before thundering down the wide beaches. With plenty of horsepower to pull over any obstacle, the feeling of mastery was complete. As a courtesy, it was possible to give some yachts, fishing boats, and ships on Puget Sound and out in the open ocean a thrill, wanted or not.

Perhaps the most satisfying activity was possible when there were towering cumulus clouds available. Playing a solitary game of tag, racing around the white monsters and watching the perfect reflection of the airplane in the center of its own completely circular rainbow was an experience not enjoyed by many humans. Stunting over, around, and falling into the deep caverns in the clouds and occasionally diving through the clouds with their clammy gray interiors and bursting once more out into the brilliant sunlight certainly shook off the "surly bonds of earth," as the lost young American pilot in the RCAF expressed it in his memorable poem, "High Flight." Of course, these flights were logged as familiarization training flights, and it was best not to bother officialdom with the nature of the familiarization. Few of these exuberant activities had been available during the war when most flying was done encumbered with formations and heavy responsibilities. Now, with the regular military still in a disorganized state, it was time to use the kites for pure pleasure before the establishment recovered from the war and got uptight.

Being in the reserve produced other rewards in the freedom-of-flight department. In the organization of the reserve, the main overhaul base for Corsair airplanes was at Jacksonville, Florida. This necessitated literally ferrying the Corsairs across the diagonal breadth of the U.S.A. It also required putting any reserve pilot who volunteered for these flights on active duty for their duration, and also paid a stipend for expenses. If he overnighted at military bases, this amount was much less than if he was forced to stop at nonmilitary fields. In cases where the pilot wished to stop at a civilian field, he would (if experienced) put a bottle of whiskey in his flight bag, which was placed behind the cockpit armor plating on top of the radio installation. This was in case his wanderings led him to stop at a nonmilitary field in a dry state. Although there were no constraints on the route taken, it generally went south by easy stages to Red Bluff, California, and on to Alameda at San Francisco and Los Alamedas near Los Angeles.

Turning eastward, the route led to Litchfield Park outside of Phoenix, Arizona, where the navy maintained a facility to place unused aircraft in preservation. With the war of recent memory, there were certainly plenty of them. That paled to insignificance when the seemingly endless rows of army airplanes parked on the dry desert were viewed from the air. Nothing gave a more graphic illustration of the might of U.S. production during the war. Heroics and public relations aside, this production was what had won the war for the allies.

Onward the route led across the desert to El Paso, Texas, then to Dallas and onward to Jackson, Mississippi, before the final destination of the Naval Air Station at Jacksonville. Or at least that was the prescribed and recommended route. However, there was one proviso, and that was that ferrying was not supposed to be done during the hours of darkness or in instrument conditions. The individual pilot therefore had plenty of latitude to pursue his own agenda.

The first visit to Naval Air Station Jacksonville after the war produced an eerie feeling. The frantically overcrowded installation and all of the activity and excitement and the round-the-clock roar of aircraft engines during the war was no more. It felt like one huge haunted house. Up at senior BOQ most of the rooms were closed off and the few tenants were the staid and humorless members of the regular establishment. Having finished the paperwork late on the afternoon of arrival, this circumstance led me to a desire to depart early to start flying at that very favorite time of day, just before daybreak, with its early light and subtle promises of the day to come. Managing to get down to operations that predawn Sunday morning produced another shock. There was nobody around. This was a weekend! Well, there *was* one person around. He was a civilian security guard of the Florida cracker persuasion. Although communication was difficult due to certain language barriers and the lack of organized coherent thought, he was finally checked out on holding the fire bottle, and the engine was started. Fortunately, those nice, modern F4U1-Ds had electric starters and didn't require shotgun starts.

Operations was unmanned and all of the formalities of departure were ignored. As day broke somewhere over the Florida Panhandle, a flight plan was filed with Airways with a request to notify the navy if possible. Next stop was Jackson, Mississippi, a place it was thought impossible to miss. It later turned out that it *was* possible to miss Jackson if the right man were involved. Although all of the pilots were fighter trained, some had been qualified late in the war. The old-timers didn't have much trouble finding their way around the United States. This was done by just picking up a course and following it for an estimated period of time. Then when in the vicinity of the desired destination, they would refer to the *Airman's Guide*. In the center of this estimable publication were all of the identifications and instrument letdown procedures for the old Adcock radio ranges.

However, one young man from VMF-216 who volunteered to ferry one of the Corsairs occasioned a rather interesting episode. Fortunately, he didn't have to take an airplane to JAX, just bring one back, so he went that way by transport. For some reason, on the way back, he failed to raise Jackson, Mississippi. A lot of the rural south looks the same, and finally giving up before he ran out of gas, he determined to land while he still could. The main problem was a lack of available airstrips, just expanses of loblolly pine trees. Necessity is a great sharpener of a pilot's skills, and discerning a narrow road down among the pines, he did a commendable job of landing the fighter. Of course, he did run the surprised driver of a big lumber rig off the road.

When ferrying airplanes the pilot always took along a supply of navy purchase orders, which can buy literally anything. With these, and his natural talent for making hasty decisions, the pilot proceeded to engage the big rig and with its driver, and with some incidental help and equipment, got the wings off and the Corsair loaded on the truck. After trucking it to the nearest railroad he was, at first, in a quandary as to what to do with the damn thing. Then it came to him that the Marine Air Reserve was headquartered in Glenview, Illinois, so he addressed the airplane there.

This was still before the candy-asses took over, and this activity was commanded by a general who was practically a founder of marine aviation. Not only that, he acquired the Medal of Honor during his career and would be a hard man to shake up. He proceeded to send the squadron a message commending the lieutenant for his resourcefulness, but wished to express the thought that perhaps better navigational skills might have avoided the whole expensive episode. Besides, what the hell was he supposed to do with the airplane the lieutenant was thoughtful enough to send him, especially since the wings didn't seem to be attached.

One navy chap ferrying a TBF torpedo plane out to San Diego had a sailor approach him for a ride at a fuel stop in Dallas, Texas. He stuffed this chap out of sight in back where the gunner would normally be. After encasing him in a parachute and checking him out in its use, he discovered that the intercommunications system didn't work. He told his passenger that there wasn't a chance of anything going wrong, but if it did he would open the bomb bay doors and that no time should be wasted, just jump.

Hours later, droning across the desert, the pilot became bored. Forgetting that he had a passenger, he started fooling with various controls. One of these was for the bomb bay doors, and when the airplane's performance indicated that he had inadvertently opened them, he hastily closed them. Much later he landed at North Island at San Diego and was almost ready to leave the airplane when he remembered that he had a passenger. No passenger. This caused quite a flap and fortunately the sailor was ultimately rescued from the rattlesnakes and Gila monsters. He was last seen hunting for the pilot.

There were other interesting adventures to be had out on the ferry routes in the days before aviation became as familiar as horse manure in a Texas town. One story that was uncovered quite by accident was greatly appreciated but never revealed to higher authority. It concerned a flight of some little twin-engine Beechcraft airplanes known as the JRB in the passenger version or an SNB if it had a glass nose and was used for bomber training. A group of highly competent and fun-loving members of the squadron volunteered to simultaneously take delivery of a number of these kites and bring them back, possibly as a flight.

They were doing well and determined to remain overnight in El Paso, Texas. They had a fine party in a local hotel, and one young lady in attendance complained that she was going to be late getting back to her home in Arizona. One pilot quizzed her on the availability of an airfield at her destination, and she assured him that indeed it did have a field. Hauling unauthorized civilian females around in navy airplanes was more than just frowned on, it was downright illegal, but what the hell.

Encased in a flight suit to avoid the possibilities of embarrassing questions, the young lady and the rest of the party arrived out at the army field the next morning via taxi. Strangely enough, they couldn't find an airport listed on the maps at the Arizona town she named. The lady became adamant, so the kites fired up and departed. After some concentrated effort they located the named town, but it certainly didn't appear to have much of a presence out there on the desert. They did locate a rock-strewn resemblance to what could have been an incredibly short, narrow strip complete with a wrecked shanty and what could have once been a windsock.

"Don't do it! Don't even think of doing it!" the other pilots shouted on their radios. Too late. The nice new navy JRB blossomed out with landing gear and flaps and was doing a wrapped-up carrier landing approach. While the other chaps orbited and watched in horror, the JRB landed and practically ground-looped to a halt. The door flew open and the young lady emerged. Wasting no time on maudlin farewells, the young Romeo bent on the throttles and, blowing up great clouds of dust and avoiding all of the boulders, staggered into the air in full view of his stunned friends. Whoever the pioneering aviator responsible for that primitive airstrip was, he and his primitive airplane were long since gone.

Those JRBs were not a bad way to travel if one desired to go somewhere with other people or transport people. One afternoon, a large navy sailor stationed at Sand Point, who had been needed at home in Pasco in eastern Washington due to a family emergency, wished to return to Sand Point. He had a friend who was a pilot in VMF-216, and this friend was also a budding airline pilot. This chap called up and said that he would like to log a cross-country flight to go over and pick the sailor up, but there was a problem. The only airplane available that could accommodate a passenger was a JRB, and he had never been checked out in one. With little else to do, I agreed to go along with him and incidentally check him out in the airplane. It didn't seem worth mentioning that the personal checkout had been accomplished by merely having him read the handbook and declaring this to be a fact.

Pasco is located east of the mountains, where the mighty Columbia River makes a huge bend to the north. Never having been there before, I performed the navigation by flying in that general direction until late afternoon, when the big bend was sighted and an airstrip appeared. The copilot, in the interests of checking out in type, initiated the landing approach, which was to the west. All went well until raising the nose, just before touchdown, when he let the airplane drop with a thunderous crash. It continued to bounce until a determined wrestling match brought the show to a halt. All in vain, a guy in a car came out and said that this was the first military airplane to land at Kennewick in some time. *Kennewick?*

Kennewick, indeed. Pasco was just across the river. In grim silence the young airline pilot was relieved of his duties. The JRB hastily pulled off of this field and proceeded across the river, where sure enough there was the former field of the navy's wartime "E" base. Approaching the end of the runway and pulling the nose up to land, the full rays of the setting sun were blinding. This caused an exact repeat of the performance at Kennewick and provided the now insufferable copilot with a good laugh. "Sun got in my eyes too," he chortled.

No further time was wasted, and having sufficient fuel to get back to Sand Point, the sailor was boarded and the airplane was soon in the air again in the oncoming dark. The plan was to go west until the Boeing Field Adcock range was raised for the approach to Seattle in what had been predicted to be deteriorating weather. The radio reception was also deteriorating. Above the gathering overcast the snow-covered top of a peak was located in the dusk. Believing this to be Mount Rainier, the JRB was pointed in that direction.

After it had been full dark for some time, the copilot observed a startling sight. The tops of fir trees seemed to be flashing past nearly between the starboard engine and the fuselage. Wasting no time, he pulled up and to the left, which turned out to be a very fortunate direction. Now with a doubtful position, it was time to start worrying about the amount of fuel aboard if any extended orientation was necessary. Both pilots, as one, turned and looked down the aisle of the passenger compartment where the parachutes were usually stored. Alas. There was only one parachute aboard and the sailor, who must have been psychic, was strapped into it. A large, tough-looking specimen, he was staring belligerently back at the pilots. Back to work.

Finally, working a very faint range signal, we determined that the airplane was a considerable distance north of where it had been estimated. The fir trees must have been on Mount Baker. Turning south in the now really lousy night weather, we raised Sand Point. Here they had a GCA (ground controlled approach) truck manned for those incomparable transport pilots of VR-5. The copilot justified his airline training by making a flawless approach and greasing the JRB on the all but invisible runway. Fortunately, there was still enough fuel in the tanks to permit taxiing to the flight line, but not much more. Over in the officers' club with large glasses of courage in hand, we agreed that the less said about this caper the better.

These fine little airplanes were about the size of Amelia Earhart's Lockheed Electra 10E and were actually a real lady's airplane. It was even possible to take one of them over to Poverty Flats to the old dirt airstrip. This was where the chaps who did the Forest Service flying had introduced the whole adventure of flight.

An impressive bunch, they had been the originators of dropping firefighting equipment and supplies. They had, in conjunction with some brave Forest Service employees, originated the "smoke jumpers" before World War II. Their work had contributed greatly to the development and refinements of the wartime parachute troops. They were true pioneers of flight and had barnstormed with all of the originals.

One of the barnstormers of their era was a chap answering to the name of Cupey Lynch. He, at that time, had a young man who did the parachute jumping for him, and he was teaching this young fellow to fly. It was Cupey's opinion that the youngster would never make a pilot. This fellow finally went to army flight training. His name was Charles A. Lindbergh and everybody has heard of him. Whatever happened to Cupey Lynch?

They were about to move the old Ford Trimotors and their increasingly newer equipment across town to a new airport with genuine paved runways. After first buzzing this dirt field and then making a hairy carrier approach down the side of the bordering hill, I skidded the SNB (the bomber training version) to a stop in front of the gas pumps and the four-stool restaurant. The grizzled founder, who was a genuine legend, came over with a frosty stare and said, "Boy, you had better look out. The state director of aviation is in town, and that was some approach you made after that stupid low flying." Just then, "the director," who held pilot's license number 527 signed by Orville Wright, put in his appearance.

"Man, I can really teach 'em how to fly," enthused my once-upon-a-time, legendary instructor. Then he and the godfather of mountain flying enjoyed a good laugh and said it was a damn good thing that the culprit was one of theirs. This was considered most flattering.

XXVIII

One ongoing chore for all of the armed services is recruiting. It is necessary to continually attract new blood, and getting a youngster's signature on the papers by any means is considered cricket. Once he is in hand, there is, of course, no real obligation to keep any promises made to him, real or implied. One attraction, and especially right after the war, was the association with aviation. It didn't matter that the route to flying the machines was now a long, stony path. The path to enlistment was short and well greased.

Seeing the military airplanes flying had the attraction of an open flame to the moth. One way to increase this attraction, if possible, was to put on a show. Stunt teams had a good run before the war, and the most famous was the navy's Sea Hawks. This led the Marine Air Reserve Command to encourage the formation of such a group. This was when the Blue Angels were being considered. They, of course, were experimenting with exceedingly stable aircraft. The Corsair was considered impossible, if not suicidal, for such action.

While doing a barrel roll one day, it was observed that the wingman did not drop back as was usual in tail chases, but stayed tightly tucked in the wing position. Well, now! A few more maneuvers and there he stayed. Of course, this young man was an unusual pilot and was still a first lieutenant, and for a very good reason no longer in the regular service. The versions varied, but the central facts remained: upon landing after a wild action at Rabaul during the war, he had been involved in a violent and, some said, physical confrontation with a squadron leader. Unfortunately, marine officers in aviation were promoted only on seniority, and not proven ability and courage, as were the army's pilots. From time to time, this would lead to an unfortunate aberration of leadership, but discipline must be preserved. Now, with this one pilot, Phil Talbot, who was widely recognized for his talent in dealing with the Corsair in all of its moods, and possessing the guts of a bandit, some thought was given to the feasibility of following in the footsteps of the leader of the Sea Hawks, who was the best of his time and later was the greatest innovator of the infant airline industry. However, that leader had had three planes in his team, and that was going to be the pattern. Where to find the third man? Easy. The squadron had a very unusual man, Dick Francisco, who was very nearly overlooked because of his many other accomplishments, like having been prominently mentioned as the next heavyweight champion of the world before the war interfered. After a series of tryouts with other good pilots, the project was nearly abandoned, due to some close misses. Then this chap casually mentioned that he would like to take a shot at it. He was incredible. To get away with doing close-formation aerobatics in the Corsair required a completely unflappable attitude that didn't admit to the concept of "quit." Soon the three airplanes would start with a formation takeoff and proceed to do their act.

The largest audience the team played to was at the big celebration of the crew races on Lake Washington that year. There were many other shows and invitations. Soon one of the navy's best reserve pilots formed his own team with Corsairs and provided formidable competition. This lad had a lot of flying time while quite young and due to his experience had entered naval aviation directly in what was called the AVT program. Unfortunately, he was not a combat pilot, which combined with being an AVT reserve officer was the kiss of death, carreerwise. This young man was completing his education as an aeronautical engineer at the university. He went on to not only be involved with the design of the nation's first rocket airplane, he did the test flying. He might well have been the first American in space if it hadn't been for the pesky Russians. Their successes caused a badly shaken United States to hastily place some lesser test pilots in what amounted to rifle bullets and fire them off. Some of his records still stand.

A pompous ass in the local navy chain of command disbanded this excellent team, probably out of jealously. This should serve as an object example of the navy's impeccable judgment. When this outstanding aviator was getting ready for his epic flights in this rocket plane, he suffered further complications. The brand new U.S. Air Force (a service that did not exist in World War II) was fighting a gallant battle for publicity in the lucrative postwar aviation industry. Busy manufacturing a reputation as the sole defender of the United States in the sky, they even opposed the idea of anyone who wasn't "one of theirs" test-flying this revolutionary machine into the headlines.

This did leave the field to the marines, at least for the present, and the enthusiastic marine command recommended that the stunt team participate in the Cleveland Air Races. During the depression, these air races were about the biggest deal around, and now they were being revived big time. Now the navy put a stop to that by declaring that it didn't believe that intraservice competition in this department would be productive. In other words, in the postwar battle of public relations the regular navy wasn't welcoming any comparisons with the unwashed reserves and particularly the marines. At this remove, with the once famous Cleveland Air Races as dead and forgotten as the extinct dodo bird, it is to laugh.

The administrative side of the peacetime military rapidly became apparent. The first visit from a delegation of staff from the headquarters in Glenview, Illinois, had some interesting points to make. The first comment was that the pilots were to start thinking of greater responsibilities, since this flying was really immature. None of these staff types had been prominent in the shooting phases and had probably been frightened by the Corsair anyway.

They also wanted a detailed accounting of the ammunition and practice bombs on hand. The squadron was administratively well organized due to its nonflying adjutant. He was a professor at the university and an expert on foreign affairs. He spoke a bewildering assortment of strange tongues, including an uncounted number of Chinese dialects. That was certainly handy in interpreting the wishes of the regular Marine Corps.

The report on the ordnance and the estimate of having enough of this surplus stuff on hand for years to come brought down wrath. These grim warriors instructed their audience in the economics of governmental affairs and said that it must be expended and the sooner the better. *They* would have to go to Congress for next year's allotment, which would be based on this year's expenditures, and that had damn well better be plenty. Accordingly, the airplanes were kept busy racing out to Cape Flattery to fire off the .50-caliber ammunition and pickle off the practice bombs in the blue Pacific.

The next chapter opened when the time came for the squadron to go to the Marine Corps Air Station at El Toro, California, for its two-week maneuver. This was the first postwar maneuver, and all of the reserve squadrons west of the Mississippi would report. During the war, an entire marine air wing had been moved from Cherry Point, North Carolina, to the West Coast by a single memo to the general commanding stating that on or about a certain date he was to accomplish this. By rail, by air, by truck, and God only knows what other forms of locomotion this was done and hardly noted. That was during the war.

Now was peacetime, and the squadron received an operations plan for this caper about the thickness of a mail-order catalog. It certainly demonstrated the diligence of the planners from the regular establishment who missed nothing, including the number of rolls of toilet paper required. Working many nights with the splendid adjutant, the conditions were finally met. The trouble was that those regulars did it for a living and the reserves did it out of a desire to keep in touch with the airplanes.

Eighteen Corsairs were flown down and the rest of the muster went down in transports. The Sand Point R4D (military version of the "giant airliner") was taken along. The weather was clear at El Toro, but the famous smog kept flight operations to a minimum. However, the partying of the assembled squadrons was reminiscent of the "rendezvous" conducted in the spring by the old-time mountain men who came down out of the hills to sell their pelts, drink rifle whiskey, and fight. Facing a sharp reduction in demand after the war, the El Toro officers' club was disposing of great quantities of booze. The canny adjutant negotiated a good deal on a large amount of this to fuel squadron parties of the future. It was loaded on the Sand Point station R4D on the return, and the pilot was warned that if he got involved in any crash he had better make sure that he perished.

There were still some things to do, and the stunt team was providing some interesting episodes, but that was coming to an end. It started crumbling when the whole air group at Sand Point received an invitation to appear at a celebration at Astoria, Oregon. The airport was on the Oregon side of the Columbia River, where the Tongue River flows in from the south. With the field awash in navy airplanes, they got a huge turnout. The marines were forced to follow a civilian stunt pilot with their act. This lad had a twin-engine Air Commodore, not what would be thought of as an acrobatic airplane. He proceeded to perform such impossible and precise maneuvers that he left the marines literally breathless.

"Not to worry," said a grizzled old pilot standing nearby, "you guys go a lot faster and make a hell of a lot more noise." That is certainly a valid premise in the world of public relations.

When we finished the regular stunt routine, we were to the south of the field in the vicinity of the Tongue River. What better finale than to use the river. Accordingly, the three Corsairs managed to hide in between the trees and proceeded downriver full bore. Opposite the end of the runway, we executed a left-hand barrel roll, changing heading by ninety degrees to dramatically spring out of this concealment and come parallel with the runway. Witnesses later reported that it was quite effective, and the marines, deciding not to wear out their welcome, did not land but headed back for Seattle.

With the air group still mainly in Astoria, Sand Point was nearly deserted. However, there was a car down at the flight line when the three Corsairs taxied up (in formation of course) and shut down their engines. Out of the car stepped the wife of the former champ and one of the world's bravest men, Dick Francisco. She marched up to the Corsairs and reaching up to the intercooler intake in his port wing root pulled out the top of a pine tree. Apparently the barrel roll out of the river had been initiated a bit low, and that plane was on the inside of the roll. There ensued a quiet, logical discussion with only the lady contributing her thoughts. They were quite valid. A grown, mature man who had a growing family and responsibilities would no longer be racing around the countryside with his irresponsible little friends giving the bumpkins a thrill. So now there were two, but it would never be the same again. Anyway, a master stroke was conceived by the three rover boys. Boeing Field was being replaced by the great new Seattle-Tacoma Airport, and the stunt team was invited to participate in the opening ceremonies. A plan was devised to make a lasting impression, and it was a dandy. The third man would be allowed to participate in this as his last hurrah, but would only have a walk-on role.

His Corsair was to be fitted with one of those little pods used to carry practice bombs and also a device for producing smoke intended to hide infantrymen on the battlefield. To the west of the new Sea-Tac Airport and below some steep and rather high bluffs is Puget Sound. Over on the Sound and concealed by these bluffs, some fun-loving coconspirators would have a barrel containing oil and a hefty charge of dynamite. As the announcer would present the stunt team flying over, a midair collision would be simulated, some old rags would fall from the bomb pod, and the smoking Corsair would dive out of formation and disappear under the bluffs where the oil and dynamite would complete the tableau. Then the announcer would remind the vast audience that the United States Marines never counted their losses, so the remaining two planes would get on with the show.

The arrangements for this treat were extensive and, inevitably, leaked out. There was even some outrage expressed as to the image of safety this might instill in the timid hearts of the traveling public. So the plan was abandoned, and the stunt team with a man missing was no longer much fun anyway. The team was soon relegated to the dust bin of history.

Time sped by, and the nature of the marine reserve was changing. As new pilots were coming in to be checked out, the squadron was no longer composed of purely wartime fighter pilots. The whole tone was becoming more conservative and controlled by the uptight peacetime military. The magic was going, and worse still, school would soon be over and the necessity of "facing life" appeared imminent.

XXIX

A lot of the originals in the squadron were dropping out as they finished school and were getting more deeply embroiled with their growing families. What one of the more dependable pilots had to say when he quit was at first a shock and then commonplace. It turned out that he had never had any love affair with flying, but it was better than what was in second place during the war. Also, the reserve supplied some badly needed money for his growing family while he finished school after the war. Now that he was done with all of that and well into his chosen career, they could take their (deleted) Marine Corps and stuff it.

Although the service was becoming increasingly mundane, there was still some notion that there must be adventure left. Going into the airlines wasn't any better, since there is nothing more boring than flying a large airplane straight and level for prolonged periods of time. Their pilots also were required to fit the cookie-cutter pattern, with neat haircuts and shined shoes, and lead lives as irreproachable as monks. Although pay in the airlines was better, if they wanted to be bored most of the time, they might as well have stayed in the service.

For several years after the war there were vast numbers of surplus aircraft available at truly ridiculously low prices and equal numbers of young men who knew how to fly them. This combination led to some of the greatest and underreported adventures in the history of flight. Right in Seattle there were chaps who had acquired surplus DC-3s and DC4s and were engaged in any enterprise offering even a marginal return. With Alaska a virtual frontier, they were offered several perilous opportunities in that territory, and fish often seemed to play a part in these schemes.

One group acquired a four-engine Coronado flying boat that had been an admiral's private transportation. It boasted certain amenities, like a paneled lounge amidships. Most of the stockholders were former enlisted men from a patrol squadron, and the pilot was their well-respected former squadron commander. Needing more pilots, they uncovered a pair of ex-navy fighter pilots whose main qualifications consisted of cash they had managed to save during the war and were willing to invest. The business plan, such as it was, consisted of a sketchy dream of flying salmon directly across Canada from Anchorage, Alaska, to Chicago, Illinois. They even had obtained permission to overfly Canada.

With the bright new era of commercial aviation dawning, they got quite a bit of ink in the Seattle press. As a device to raise further capital through favorable publicity, the company invited the reporters to a maiden flight over Puget Sound. They had only enough money to supply gasoline to the wing service tanks to the engines, but this was considered enough. After the former lieutenant commander made a smooth takeoff, he turned control over to the two former fighter pilots and went below to entertain the honored quests in the splendid paneled wardroom.

Fighter pilots are, by nature, curious beings, and when they saw an unfamiliar ship on the surface they peeled off to go down and take a look. One does not peel off in a lumbering, four-engine flying boat. In the first place, it floated the honored quests, drinks in hand, to the overhead of the magnificently paneled ward room. In the second place, it floated the meager ration of fuel aboard to the tops of the tanks, and all four engines quit. By the time the commander fought his way back to the command deck and gained control, a lot of exciting things had happened.

With vigorous pumping on the emergency fuel pumps, the engines were restarted. The fine machine lumbered back to Lake Washington, where it landed before running out of gas, which it did rather promptly. The bruised reporters wrote some interesting articles. However, the nature of the publicity this generated failed to attract any more investors. This airplane may *still* be for sale.

Down at the south end of Lake Washington at Renton were some seaplane ramps at the foot of the field. At that time these were backed up by an immense hangar full of new but now surplus Martin Mariner (PBM) flying boats. These were long-range navy patrol planes. One of these PBMs mysteriously vanished in the search for the five TBFs that allegedly became victims of the "Bermuda Triangle." Any pilot believing in that myth would probably believe in the Amelia Earhart soap opera. That PBM, no doubt, blew up due to fuel leaks in flight.

These airplanes were for sale cheap, and a sharp young Park Avenue lawyer acquired a pair of them and engaged a navy patrol pilot from the reserve. This chap happened to be an acquaintance of mine, and he was again looking for a copilot, with in-type experience optional. Always having a fascination with flying boats, from the old PBYs at Corpus Christi to the most inspiring crossing to Hawaii on the Pan American flying boat, the Threadbare Buzzard had an excuse to postpone facing middle-class life just yet.

The PBMs were very large boats with a pair of 2,000 horsepower engines (more power than the four engines of the Pan American boat delivered). The sharp barrister convinced the government to license them to gross out at 50,000 pounds, albeit they were classified as "X" for experimental, so were limited to an N instead of an NC before their numbers. The first thing the creative New Yorker came up with was hauling shrimp from Mexico. It was to be supposed that during his dealings in the gray-market steel business right after the war and while developing all of the appropriate Mexican connections, he had seen

this opportunity. At any rate, he could work magic and had proved
this in the original operation, which was already history.

The plan was for the PBM to proceed to Carmen, Mexico, and
load up with 15,000 pounds of shrimp in burlap bags and deliver them
to the fish brokers in New Orleans at a huge profit. The interior of the
airplane had been stripped to accommodate cargo, and in order to
proceed to its destination it would accomplish the journey in stages.
The first one led down the coast to North Island, where the obliging
navy assisted in the fueling. There a used-car salesman and his girlfriend came aboard to continue on with the crew to the next fueling
stop at Corpus Christi, Texas. What their arrangement was was obscure but, as a matter of fact, most everything associated with that operation was obscure, and it is probably a far better thing that it remain
that way. Due to the slow speed of advance over the desert and the
primitive plumbing facilities, it was hardly a first-class passage for the
passengers.

The PBM landed and was beached at, of all places, the 18-Dog
seaplane ramps at the naval air station. During the course of this entire adventure it remained a complete mystery as to just what arrangement the Park Avenue lawyer had with the navy. Right after the
war there was a lot of confusion, and all things were possible, but the
degree of cooperation was astounding. No less astounding was the ensuing action. The attorney-owner said that since the airplane would
be going all of the way across the Gulf of Mexico empty, it would be
a fine thing to haul something. And what was there a shortage of down
there? Ice was the answer, and by some wild promise of profit the local ice plant owner was induced to deliver thousands of pounds of
great blocks of ice to the seaplane ramp. U.S. Navy sailors aided in
loading this in the PBM.

The next morning, departure was made impractical due to some
difficulty with the navy beaching gear (read: removable wheels) the
airplane was sitting on. In the hot Texas sun the ice melted. After
pumping the ice water out onto the hot concrete of the ramps, the proprietor of the ice works delivered the replacement stock, and the load-

ing process was repeated. Now, unfortunately, there was a hurricane warning, and the ensuing delay caused more ice water to be pumped out. Texans must be of a very tenacious nature, because, defying all logic, the process was once again repeated.

This time was the charm, and before the break of day the PBM was launched into the basin by the ever-cooperative navy, and it clawed its way into the air. With its burden of fuel and ice, it would be making a slow climb as the fuel was burned off. By the time a reasonable altitude was reached, the sun was climbing in the sky and the temperature had climbed with it, making the command deck so hot under the overhead windows that the crew was down to their skivvies. Now the plane commander pushed over slightly to get the flying boat on "the step." In the air, this minor change of attitude will actually increase the speed by a knot or two. This had a totally unexpected reaction.

Flying between the burning sky above and the molten sea below, the ice was once again becoming liquid. With most of the watertight integrity within the hull removed to accommodate cargo, an unrestrained tidal wave was generating in the long hull below the command deck. This caused the airplane to start to porpoise through the air as both pilots fought to prevent it from doing either an outside or an inside loop out over the lonely sea.

The flight engineer, being a veteran of the navy's rugged operations in the wartime Aleutian Islands, wasted no time. With a fire ax he chopped a hole in the after chine of the hull. Now, cold water was being poured into the hot Gulf of Mexico, slowly resolving the problem along with any contemplated use for the ice. This engineer then proceeded to patch the hole with *concrete*. "Sure," he said. "Did it quite often in the Aleutians." Not only that, this unorthodox repair lasted until more sophisticated remedies were available.

Carmen, in the state of Campeche on the Yucatán Peninsula, was a place where the shrimp boats came, and was equipped with a sandy plaza in the center of its unpretentious civic presence. The local wheeler and dealer was named Pico.

When the edge of an unexpected hurricane intruded onto the peaceful scene, it was necessary to weigh the PBM's anchor and stand off under power to avoid being driven on the beach. As it was, a shrimp boat driving wildly out of the storm managed to put a large dent in one of the twin tails. The unexpected delay also used up so much fuel that it would be impossible to get back to New Orleans, especially when hauling a heavy load. Acquiring 100-octane aviation gasoline at this place would, at first glance, appear to be impossible. Not to Pico, who, in the fractured language used to communicate, said he had some. The canny flight engineer said he couldn't possibly have 100 octane. Pico vehemently begged to differ and agreed to supply a sample. The flight engineer proceeded to pour the sample on the yellow sand of the plaza and toss a match into it. Studying the flame, and after much pondering, he agreed that it was indeed 100 octane. As he explained later, that was the best he could do in this game of bluffing.

Soon a dilapidated gas truck appeared and the PBM was tailed in close to the beach. It was hooked up to the wing service tanks with the damnedest assortment of decaying hoses in captivity, and, with the engineer straining the product through a chammy, a respectable amount was taken aboard. Much later there was some sort of a scandal about a Pan American Airways wartime gas dump in the vicinity having been raided.

The shrimp Pico supplied in large burlap bags were rotten by the time the officials in Louisiana caused them to be dumped into Lake Pontchartrain. For the remainder of the lifetime of the PBM there were 102 open bottles of AirWick present, for all of the good they did. What happened to those New Orleans fish brokers is unclear, but there were some rather serious threats. The PBM went to the Naval Air Station at Norfolk, Virginia, since the navy decided that it wanted to remove the gun turrets and fair over their locations.

On the field at Renton, Washington, the other PBM resplendent in gleaming white paint with American Flags on both of its tails stood ready for the next chapter. These machines were very close to new and had cost the taxpayers a bundle.

This next chapter would be to fly lobsters from Lewisporte, Newfoundland, (six cents a pound) to Rockland, Maine, to be sorted, and then continue by truck to Boston and New York in double ice barrels, with the price rapidly escalating. The route this time would go as was practical from Seattle to Rockland. Flying boats have two advantages over land planes: they are not encumbered with the weight of landing gear and can be landed on the water. That can be very convenient. On the downside, they cannot easily land where fueling is possible. The first available facility was at an aircraft maintenance outfit at Minneapolis.

The amount of fuel that could be carried was dictated by certain modifications made in the interests of cargo capacity. With a weather factor consuming more fuel than desired, it was determined to land in Lake Coeur d'Alene in Idaho and wait for things to improve. The instrument approach was a novel one and involved getting the high cone on the old Adcock radio range at Spokane and then flying outbound toward where the lake should be, until the outer fan marker was passed. After that, we would do a timed letdown. Fortunately, this letdown was completed just as the lake appeared out of the rain.

Fortunately, aviation still had a patina of glamour attached, and the natives were friendly. Locally, the PBM was referred to as the "giant flying machine." The stay in the lake at Sand Point, Idaho, was pleasant, and one local chap decided that when the weather permitted a continuation of the flight, he would go along as far as Minneapolis, whence he came. Best of all, he owned a fine local restaurant and was certainly a gracious and generous host to his newfound friends. Not so fortunate (for him) was the prolonged stay, which exceeded the time frame in which he could leave. Also not so fortunate was the actual departure of the big bird. There seemed to be some impediment to heaving the anchor home, but finally, by getting rough with it by use of the engines, it came free. Sometime later, Sand Point suffered from a persistent stench emanating from the lake. It was finally determined that the anchor had severely damaged the city's sewer outfall. Anyway, the "giant flying machine" and its gallant crew were long gone.

Fort Peck reservoir and its friendly staff were the next hosts before continuing on to Minneapolis. There the expedition received fuel and appropriate recognition in the press. It is just amazing at this remove that airplanes could command such attention. Onward to Rockland, Maine. It was apparent, even from the air, on the approach that this picture post card village on the rockbound coast was going to be a special place.

Anchoring inside the breakwater at this salty historical seaport was soon accomplished, and a large, salty character in a boat had the crew aboard and headed ashore. Here the new enterprise had a pier and, on the shore end, a lobster pond. This was in a building with running saltwater tanks, where the lobsters were graded and placed in double ice barrels. To command a high price from the gourmet, the lobster must be kept alive to the time he is to be devoured.

The crew didn't take long to get organized and had soon rented a cottage out at Owl's Head from the local pharmacist. At that halcyon period in the nation's history, the drugstore also had an original soda fountain and sold no lawn mowers or ladies' clothes. In those marvelous days before the overpopulation of the country got underway, the charm of the place cannot be appreciated in today's society.

A new and memorable chap now made his appearance: George Curtiss. He was a local aircraft mechanic of some note and had the all-important A&E (airframe & engine) license. He had spent the war as a flight engineer on flying boats with the Coast Guard. He lived in Maine by choice, and out by the cottage the crew had rented he had, with his wife and baby daughter, a marvelous old farmhouse. Very shortly, at the insistence of the in-place engineer, he was a member of the crew. Between them they could fix anything. This guy was also one of the funniest and most sarcastic humans on the face of the earth. It was a long time later, and quite by accident, that it was discovered that he came from an affluent family. Although on cordial terms with them, he preferred his own lifestyle.

Not long after this, some vacationing females from Seattle delivered the cherished Ford convertible to the New York attorney. He was pleased to drive it the rest of the way to Maine. Meanwhile, on going down to Norfolk, the other flying boat had been brought back and was also anchored out in the bay. This whole thing furnished a most gratifying substitute for real life. The oncoming summer is a time of magic in Maine. Even at Rockland there was a fashionable resort hotel that even had tea dances. Up the road a piece was the incomparable "Camden by the Sea." (Rockland, on the other hand, was known as "Rockland by the Smell" in honor of its fish-packing plants.)

Camden had a beautiful little harbor that hosted the "skin ships." These were the schooners that made the crew pay for the privilege of sailing around Penobscot Bay, with the wondrous places like Vinalhaven as their ports of call. This little pocket of charm harbored the first flower boxes ever encountered on lampposts. Before the days of pollution and too damn many people, the weather during the summer season was a dream come true. The natives were at first painfully reserved but soon came around; the cottage out at Owl's Head served some purpose as a social destination for the more liberal-type citizens.

Soon enough the real purpose had to be served. This was to get the cheap lobsters out of Newfoundland and to Rockland. The weather in Newfoundland lived up to its reputation, and very shortly the experienced ex-navy chap said he'd had enough and left to get married and pursue his career. This left me a fighter pilot with a nineteen-year-old chap with thick glasses and a private pilot's license from a Renton, Washington, high school in charge of the flying boats.

Actually, these machines were interesting but not difficult to fly, which is true of all big airplanes versus the agile fighters. However, operations on the water made a few different skills necessary. There was no way to brake or turn except by using the engines and rudders, and in a substantial wind this needed close attention to prevent fetching up on a rocky shore. Another technique was putting the boat on a mooring. These moorings were constructed by sinking a substantial concrete block to the bottom, with a scope of chain lying on the bottom and a hefty manila line leading to the surface. This line was fed through a fitted block in an inflated aircraft tire and was braided into a back splice above that, making a loop sticking up in the air. This resembled, and was called, a "cobra head." Under any condition of wind and tide the aircraft had to be maneuvered close enough to the cobra head for the flight engineer in the bow door to reach it with a boat hook and attach the bow pennant to it when alongside. To let go from this mooring required its own methodology.

Most interesting of all were takeoffs. To begin with, the airplane had to be carefully balanced and the trim tabs set accordingly. In a chop, a badly balanced, trimmed, or handled flying boat could start to "porpoise." This could ultimately throw the engines out of her, and that would be followed by the whole shooting match blowing up. If the water was smooth, there was the problem of breaking suction with the surface, and the preferred method was to have a speedboat break up the surface ahead of the charging aircraft. With the great overloads (in the interest of profit) usually lifted out of Newfoundland, this could take very long runs to get airborne. In a good chop, the crashing of the hull in the waves could be quite disturbing.

The automatic pilot had been removed, the wing deicer boots were inoperative, and the prop deicer reservoirs were empty. Gander Airfield's approach control was quite good at predicting the icing levels, since they had plenty of pilots' reports in those prejet days, when all of the overseas traffic funneled through Gander, Newfoundland. They also had a GCA (ground-controlled approach) capability, which was reassuring when arriving in seriously deteriorating weather. Although the flying boats couldn't land on their runway, Gander could, in a jam, direct a controlled letdown into the lake.

When gathering a load of ice on the wings and propellers, it was best to change altitude and run the engines up to full power to throw the ice off the props. This would cause a fearful din as the ice struck the fuselage. When finding the harbor at Lewisporte in bad weather, all sorts of creative strategies were employed. Once, it was even necessary to remain overnight at the old RAF Coastal Command base at

Botwood. Since all of the aviation gasoline for Gander Airfield came ashore at the long, modern dock at Lewisporte, this was a convenient fueling point. All we had to do was tail the boat into the end of the dock, and the real professionals there would do their thing. British gas was much cheaper, since it was both dispensed in the larger imperial gallon and had no airport tax, which was extracted in the States. Unfortunately, since the trip back carried the load, there was no possibility of using British fuel both ways. As a result, only the minimum amount plus the lawful reserve would be used on the trip up. This did not allow much room for error on arrival.

Right about then a prominent Rockland man joined the jolly outfit. He was a large specimen and a member of a clan of seamen whose lineage was long and distinguished. They owned an island off the coast that boasted an extremely narrow entrance to a small harbor protected from the wild Atlantic. Around the harbor were large Maine farmhouses. This chap more or less organized the Newfoundland end of things. Another factor in his immense popularity with the crew was the *Billie B.*, a large fishing smack that he probably owned and certainly skippered. Sometimes down in Rockland between trips and for just the fun of it, everybody would swarm aboard and go out for codfish. These were fished with hand lines equipped with several hooks baited with clams. When there was a tug, the line would be pulled in. There was often more than one large cod on the line. The rough ocean and the cutting wind would be forgotten in the warm, snug, albeit pitching and rolling, galley of the *Billie B.* Then the skipper would construct a codfish chowder with onions, potatoes, and anything else that came to hand. Perhaps it was the circumstances, but as other memories fade, those chowders will never be forgotten. They were truly one of life's finest hours.

XXX

It didn't take long after the ex-navy chap's departure to get comfortable with this new flying experience. A routine was developed for the trips so that we attempted to maintain a twice-a-week schedule. Since no partying was allowed at the cottage the night before departure, all hands would be up and down at the lobster pond before the break of day. Occasionally, some culprit in the crew would forget the all-important groceries for the gourmet flight rations to be prepared in the airplane's excellent galley. Then it would be necessary to break into the picking room and lift a carton of lobster meat with which hotels and restaurants would make lobster cocktails. This meat was picked by underpaid women from the already boiled "cripples" or "pistols," which are, in order, a lobster that has lost one claw or one that has lost both claws. This destroys his market value in the live-lobster trade. Chewing on this delicacy for five hours of, possibly, rough instrument flight will do irredeemable harm to an appetite for lobster.

A rowboat would afford transportation out to the moored flying boat, and was left tied to the mooring buoy after the crew had embarked. Using the flashing light on the end of the breakwater for a reference point, a takeoff would be effected. In the coming dawn, Bangor Approach Control would be called in order to file an airborne flight plan. Operations such as ours enjoyed an uneasy relationship with the government's minions. The scheduled airlines, after all, paid for expensive lobbying to shut down unwelcome competition. Avoiding official disapproval was a constant concern, so care was taken until outside U.S. airspace and under the jurisdiction of the laid-back Canadians.

The route led over Charlottetown radio on Prince Edward Island and thence across the Gulf of St. Lawrence past the Îles de la Madeleine. The western approach to Newfoundland was made at Stephenville on their radio range, and then picking up Buchans radio on Red Indian Lake. There, the slave labor (back then the pay was miniscule for the Newfie and his rights were nil) turned out the paper for Lord Beaverbrooks' *London Daily Mail*. On a rare clear day, a giant raft of logs in the lake could be seen, and the paper industry must have taken a lot of the modest-sized Newfoundland trees. The alternate route went to the east, raising Sydney radio on Cape Breton Island and across Cabot Strait and directly to the Buchans range. Reporting when overheading Sydney radio, the operator in a charming accent would report the wind as "camm" (calm) and always follow with the same question: "Are you the chaps who were flying lobsters out of Yarmouth last year?" Answer: "No."

Over the high cone of the Adcock range at Buchans, a strategy would be determined to let down to Lewisporte, where there were no radio facilities of any description. The range at Gander could be incorporated in this strategy, and the friendly voice of Gander Approach Control was reassuring, although it did have a pronounced Canadian or British accent. These approaches, depending on the state of the weather and amount of fuel left, could be wonderfully creative and sometimes hair-raising.

Only once on the return trip was it necessary to land in the Bay of Fundy to sweat out some weather covering Rockland. This turned out to be an interesting mistake. The PBM was anchored close to some rocks poking above the water. These soon disappeared in the rise of the famous Fundy tide, which can rise or drop fifty feet in the world's greatest tidal range. Actually, it is a tidal bore. When the tide is out, the canny fishermen actually pick the netted fish off the nets that are strung on posts from a wagon and this is *no* sea story.

Lewisporte had started life like most of the small Newfoundland settlements. Back in the bad days of the "Brutish Empire," Newfoundland was a fishing colony. The fisher folk were supposed to return to mother England with their catches and not remain permanently. The freedom lovers were willing to brave hardships to escape from their undesirable social position by settling in obscure coves where hopefully they would avoid discovery. This early colonial atmosphere still maintained, although Newfoundland was independent that year. The next year it would gain Dominion status with Canada, which was shaking off her own bondage.

Gander airfield had really made Lewisporte, because it was the nearest practical harbor at which to construct a modern fuel pier to put the product ashore to sate the huge demand created by the stream of commercial airliners going to and coming from Europe. These required great amounts of fuel upon landing at Gander. This fuel was transported by narrow-gauge railroad the not inconsiderable distance to the airfield from Lewisporte.

When the flying boat would splash down, the youngsters could be seen sculling (rowing with only one oar at the stern) their primitive boats at great speed for the mooring buoy. There was a good reason for this enthusiasm. Back in Maine the proprietors of any store vending comic books would give the back issues, which had only their front covers removed, to the crew of the flying boat. The crew, out of their own pockets, would invest in a few cases of oranges as their contribution. Distributing this great treasure in this primitive land was a real privilege. In this raw town there was a tireless Scottish merchant who had a wharf of rock construction backed up by a warehouse. He supplied the lobsters in lath crates holding 125 pounds per crate. After fueling was complete, these were hoisted into the hull during an all-night cycle. When there were about fifteen thousand pounds aboard and the airplane had been successfully balanced for takeoff, the outbound customs manifests were completed. Sleepy dawn was awaited for enough light to take off for the States—that was, if everything went as slick as a greased pig; it often didn't.

At first, lingering in Newfoundland was rather unappetizing, but growing familiarization revealed an interesting lifestyle. The Newfies were beyond any question the world's greatest seamen. They built strong, seaworthy schooners out of the local fir and employed them under sail for everything, including going up to the ice in season to club the baby seals. While watching one of these schooners enter the harbor in half a gale one stormy day, they were seen to perform an unbelievable feat of ship handling to park it neatly beside the wharf with the sails falling precisely at the right moment. "Oh yes," they said, they had "an engine, but the bloody thing had packed it in."

This led the flight engineers to go down and inspect this huge, great one-lunger that had been constructed in Bristol, England, at the turn of the century. The engineers, who routinely mended 2,000-horsepower, sophisticated engines, had a devil of a time convincing the Newfies that they could help. They finally got the head off, revealing the huge, single cylinder encased in many years of carbon. A massive cleanup of this followed, and with a new head gasket they manufactured, the whole thing was reassembled under the doubting gaze of the Newfies. It caught immediately and produced a satisfying "poceta a queep" to the stupefaction of the world's greatest sailors. "Bloody mechanical geniuses," they said.

Although the economy was lamentable by U.S. standards, the natives didn't know any better and were quite happy. One of them had a restaurant of sorts and owned an automobile, which was something of a luxury, considering the small amount of chuckholed road available. Since the crew brought him all of the latest records from "Bop City" New York for his jukebox, he would loan them the car to go fishing. The road went only a short distance back into the wilderness to a beaver dam. These large rodents abounded in their pristine state, and the fishing in this pond was spectacular, with resident moose often complacently looking on. This afforded some noteworthy fish fries

back at the cottage at Owl's Head at Rockland. But first the fish had
to get back there.

After about a five-hour trip, the airplane was brought in low over
Rockland with the props roaring in low pitch. This served to alert the
friendly village grocer to get the predetermined grocery list together
and the required cases of beer ready for the crew on their way back
to the cottage. Meanwhile, the airplane was unloaded with the 125-
pound crates of lobsters thrown right into the harbor to be towed in
rafts to the dock. Here they were hoisted up and dispersed according
to grade in the various tanks of the pond.

Before the next trip, the airplane had to be fueled, and this was
accomplished by tailing it in to a large granite boulder dock practically downtown. This was also the place where the Vinalhaven ferryboat docked, and this operation always drew a large crowd. Sadly
enough, there was a local pilot who had one of those small, single-
engine pusher seaplanes called a Sea Bee. Before the great flying boats
had arrived, he had been the local dashing aviator. Much to his chagrin, the fickle public had transferred its affections. This led him to a
reckless and ill-considered action before a sizable audience. That little seaplane had a reversible-pitch propeller, which could dramatically
slow the airplane to a stop on the water. He landed in the vicinity of
the fueling operation one day and charged the granite pier and reversed his propeller at the last minute. Alas, the propeller took that
time to malfunction. The violent impact of frail aluminum and granite wharf promptly sank the Sea Bee. The engineers always had an old
crane truck available to aid in the fueling operation. A local lad attached its cable to the sunken wreckage, which was then hoisted high
and dripping for the townspeople's admiration. The fortunately uninjured former hero slunk away.

The comparison of cold and cheerless Newfoundland and the
happy, sunny summer weather of Maine was always startling. This was
reason enough for considerable relaxing. However, the legal lobster
season in Newfoundland is short, so it was necessary to squeeze in as
many highly profitable trips as possible. With two flying boats avail-

able, the crew was actually kept quite busy. This operation was sufficiently interesting and the summer social life sufficiently frantic to
make the time pass all-too quickly. Soon the season was over.

The planning for the next year included facilities to haul the airplanes out of the water for preservation and maintenance. At
Ellsworth, Maine, near the causeway over to exclusive Bar Harbor,
the navy had a now surplus field with seaplane ramps. The brothers
who were operating this facility welcomed the flying boats, and the
engineers soon had rigged up the mechanical means to haul the boats
out. The only thing missing was the actual beaching gear for hauling
out. This consists of very large wheels and tires that were attached to
the hull. That solution was at hand, since the navy wanted the gun turrets back out of the one boat that did not have them already removed.
After the airplane was taken down to Norfolk, the Park Avenue attorney struck a deal for two sets of beaching gear. He also wanted a
"doghouse," which used to contain the radar right over the command
deck, removed. The brains at Norfolk told him that the airplane actually flew two knots faster with this construction in place. He replied
that if they believed that, he had an experiment in mind for them. Clip
off all of the fastenings, and the airplane would take off. If the doghouse moved ahead of the airplane at a speed of two knots faster than
the airplane, he would buy their argument. Ill-prepared for lawyer
logic, the navy removed the doghouse. While awaiting this work to be
done, we saw another PBM in very deteriorated condition on the seaplane ramps.

Upon taking the now turretless airplane back to Maine with both
sets of beaching gear aboard, both airplanes were flown up to
Ellsworth and hauled out on the new beaching gear. There was a nice
parking area right at the head of the ramps, and the two airplanes were
made ready for winter. The flight engineer from Rockland would come
up and periodically run up the engines. While the second airplane was
departing Rockland to fly the short distance to Ellsworth, an interesting episode happened. There was a group of interested local citizens who petitioned to go along on this flight. After they had signed

waivers, the group was embarked on the fishing smack *Billie B.* and taken out and boarded. This crowd appeared to encompass half of the population of the town. As luck would have it, the airplane was anchored far out from the dock, so as to not obstruct shipping traffic on the bay. Once everybody was aboard, the procedure to weigh anchor was initiated. With just one engine started, the flying boat was being walked down over the anchor to break it loose from the bottom. Suddenly there was a crash, and the flight engineer down in the bow door started cursing. The anchor winch had been torn from its mounts and was dangling over the side, restrained only by its safety pennant.

The *Billie B.* had long since departed, so the operation had to continue with the passengers aboard. Several life jackets were bound together to act as a buoy and attached to the anchor winch, which was taken off its safety pennant and tossed overboard. Ignoring the chilling thought of what a disaster this might have occasioned if the winch had punctured the hull, the crew started the other engine, and the show was on the road. Sometime later, a Coast Guard buoy tender took hold of the erstwhile anchor machine with its attached cable and heaved up the ancient sailing ship anchor that the PBM's anchor had come afoul of. This salty piece of history was subsequently transported to the Rockland village green.

With a natural aversion to spending winters in the boondocks, I had determined to do so in New York. While I was getting a large bite of the "Big Apple," a casual trip up to Boston changed this plan. Boston was quite civilized and its denizens were philosophically closer to westerners than those on the Hudson. Some friends there arranged recruitment into their reserve squadron at NAS Squantum. This provided a fine social base and the welcome use of Corsair airplanes for cross-country expeditions. Some of these trips did not require staying overnight or even landing. These were to Rockland, Maine, where the natives would be given the benefit of a personal aerobatic air show performed by the nimble fighter. These were followed by dragging the main street at minimum altitude.

It was readily apparent that the character of the marine reserve squadrons were undergoing radical change. Many of the genuine fighter pilots were hanging it up and being replaced by second-team types. The administrators were, of course, those who had stayed in the service. Too often they did so out of terror of the outside world and a need for security rather than the love of flying on the first team. As a result, not too much time was wasted with it. Anyway, Boston had a much superior reserve squadron compared to New York, and the company was more congenial. All in all, it was a jolly and interesting winter. There was ample opportunity to visit the places where U.S. history was made in this area. Strangely enough, only a few of the local lads and lassies had done this, or even knew where they were.

XXXI

With winter over, the second coming of the flying lobster was about to get underway, and it was going to be a beaut. During the last season there had been increasing mechanical difficulties. It must be remembered that airplanes that were purchased for a song (or at least a few dollars) had cost the taxpayers a fortune when they were built. Any replacement parts came at those figures. Although there were plenty of 2,000-horsepower fighter engines available, the same-sized engines for the PBM aircraft carried a different accessory section so could not be used.

The Curtiss Commando (the largest twin-engine transport of its day) used the same engine, but China National had grabbed up all of the spares for their airline. This airline was under the active management of Claire Chennault, Madame Chiang's pet aviator.

The Park Avenue attorney had a surprise in store for the reassembled crew. The dilapidated old wreck of a PBM seen on the ramp at the Naval Air Station in Norfolk had joined the fleet as spare parts. The wily legal eagle probably got it for nothing, since the owner had, no doubt, abandoned it and the navy wanted it out of there.

The reassembled crew was missing one man. The nineteen-year-old copilot had been drafted, and being of an extraordinarily adventurous nature, had ridden a powered bicycle clear back to Seattle. His glasses were too thick for him to become a military pilot, although he was turning out to be a fine civilian pilot. This caused him to get into army helicopters, and as a crewman (not a pilot) he was killed in one of the damned things in the Korean War.

The current problem was how to get the dilapidated PBM out of Norfolk and on the ramp at Ellsworth, Maine. Just go down there and fly it back, said the self-assured legal eagle, who was not a pilot, only a master of logic, to his skeptical crew that now had only one pilot but two mechanical geniuses. Down in Norfolk the wreck was checked out as thoroughly as possible. The magneto drop was not good but not prohibitive either. The engineers said that they were both willing to go, since one was needed on the engine control station and the other for various chores. The grateful navy hastened to load a spare set of beaching gear into the kite and hastily put the old crate into the water. Without even cushions, the crew was sitting on some doubled-up, moldy, heavy winter flight gear. A few full-power runs up and down the bay later, the valiant crew nodded grimly to each other and poured on the coal. Over on the strand across the bay and into the wind line were some very nice beach houses.

Just about the time the boat was up on the "step" on takeoff, the control yoke collapsed. Some control wires had parted. The mechanical geniuses patched them together. The second engineer was in the copilot's seat with instructions to deploy full flaps at a signal to help hurl the whole affair into the lowering weather. This signal was given after a long takeoff run toward the beach houses. Nothing much seemed to be happening, so the old bucket was horsed off the water in a semistalled condition. It then flew down some side yards of the beach houses on the strand before entering the overcast. Later the chap in the copilot's seat said *he* didn't see any signal for flaps.

The weather was plenty thick and wasn't topped until somewhere in the vicinity of Chincoteague. Now we were lumbering through a nice sunlit sky, and everything seemed fine, except for a minor periodic vibration. By the time New York City was in sight, this vibration was becoming more persistent and the crew determined to fly right over Park Avenue in case the worst occurred. Perhaps the lawyer, if he were home, could go to hell along with everybody else. The radios didn't work, so there had been no flight plan or clearances, and, in fact, the whole flight might be classed as a criminal enterprise. By that afternoon, with the welcome sight of Ellsworth below, the flying machine was shaking so badly that it impaired normal vision. It was actually difficult to line up for splashdown, which was done with great dispatch. This time the flaps worked perfectly. The crew agreed that once was enough.

Various copilots were tried out and, as might be expected, the good ones were unavailable. Some of the unfortunates occasioned unforeseen adventures. The one best remembered was aboard leaving Newfoundland with an overload in the face of some really despicable weather. Antithetically, the morning in Lewisporte was clear, the airplane was loaded with the live lobsters, and we had been waiting since dawn to take off. The holdup was becoming visible to the west, where there were mountainous cumulonimbus clouds building. The usual procedure was to file a flight plan with Gander Approach Control over the telephone. The chap there had been advising holding until the weather picture became clearer. If it got much warmer on the water, the lobsters would die, and that would be practically disastrous. The outfit's financial picture would deteriorate, along with the mechanical deterioration of the flying machines

Finally, the chap over at Gander said that he would like to put a Trans Canada captain on the line who had just come in from Montreal. This chap was obviously bordering on hysteria and said, "For God's sake, don't even think of it." His airplane probably had bent wings, the passengers were injured or sick, and the airline would no doubt get sued. He would probably get fired. He also commented that in his long and distinguished career he had never seen the like of this before.

Well, the damn lobsters were probably going to die one way or another, so why not try to find a way over, under, or around this menace. After all, airline pilots were usually the product of the lower one-third of the class at flying school anyway.

Soon the PBM was in the air and headed west toward the towering cumulonimbus over Buchans. There did seem to be a light spot in the ominously boiling mess. This turned out to be a "sucker hole" when probed, and all hell broke loose. There was a lot of electricity in there along with a lot of other stuff. The prop tips lit up with St. Elmo's fire, and a ball of fire seemed to be right on the nose of the airplane and keeping pace. The prop hubs, which had been painted red as an aid in detecting ice buildup, were rapidly developing what looked like snow cones. With the ice building and the airplane taking a fearful beating in the rough air, it was going to be necessary to get below the icing level to survive.

The current copilot was put on the controls, while the radios were manipulated in an attempt to keep track of the intermittent signal of the Adcock range. This former bomber pilot seemed to be able to maintain control on rough instruments but insisted on turning to the left off the course. It was very necessary to maintain this course. The aircraft had been let down so far in the interest of shedding ice that it was estimated that it was now flying down the low ground in the vicinity of Red Indian Lake. The first "A" quadrant of an Adcock range in the United States was to the right of true north. What the copilot didn't know was that, for some stupid reason, the Canadians caused this quadrant to be to the right of one hundred and some degrees. This did, in hindsight, explain the copilot's performance.

Since the Threadbare Buzzard did not wish to decorate the second growth with broken lobster crates and human remains, control was rudely taken from this, by now, well-shaken chap. The radios didn't need any further attention anyway, having been arc welded together by one particularly violent bolt of lightning. By mutual agreement this chap did not make any further trips. Actually, he had hardly spoken since the storm gods had spit out the well-chastened flying boat somewhere over the Gulf of St. Lawrence.

Some additional arrangements were being made by management. For one thing, the wily attorney had attracted a wealthy investor who now had a great say in the decision process. He wasn't a pilot either. This did lead to some interesting developments, such as selling whole loads of lobsters to other ponds around Maine. One of the favorites for the crew was Booth Bay, one of the saltiest and most beautiful places on the coast of Maine. It was incredibly small for landing the big boats, but by dragging over the houses and treetops, the PBMs could splash literally a few feet off the waterfront. Even so, the end of the landing run ended outside of the harbor entrance. This sometimes, if there was much wind, caused water to break clear over the engines.

This place was so picturesque that it prompted many revisits with the convertible and the enthusiastic girls of summer, top down, of course, in those wonderful but brief Maine summers. Sou'west Harbor on Mount Desert Island, the home of the fashionable Bar Harbor, was another fine destination.

The mechanical difficulties were causing the extraction of the lobsters from Newfoundland to lag, and, due to the short fishing season, a scheme to store these live crustaceans was developed. Back in a small cove off of the large main harbor of Lewisporte, some floating lobster "cars" were constructed to get ahead of the game.

Now, there was usually only one flying boat available, despite cannibalizing the relic flown up from Norfolk for spare parts. Sometimes a great cargo of bait fish was hauled up to Newfoundland from Rockland to sustain life for the captives.

The crates of lobsters would now be loaded at night in this small cove that had a narrow and shallow entrance. It was necessary to take a few turns around this small area at full throttle to gain enough speed to get the heavily laden boat up on the step. This was to assure, when getting out of there, that the hull had sufficient clearance to get over the rocks below the water. This caused the humorous second engineer to compose songs on the intercom to annoy his comrades. His country and western rendition of his original ballad, "My M Boat Is Sinking" was not all that well received, *M* being a popular contraction for

PBM. It was still better than the hymn of aviators that he insisted on singing when the overloaded flying machine was battling some particularly unattractive weather. That went something like this: "Oh the bells of hell will ring for you but not for me."

Mechanically, things *were* really going to hell in a hand basket, and it was time to consider the future. When it was discovered that the reserve squadron at Boston was going to make a two-week summer maneuver at Cherry Point, North Carolina, it was time for me to move on. Fortunately, it really didn't entail the rat leaving the sinking ship. There was a sometimes copilot who was obviously hard up, and although not being too bright, and despite his army background, he could get one of the machines off of the water. He was, with obvious ambitions to climb the golden ladder of success, also intent on shining-up to the increasingly demanding management.

It did not take long for me to remove to the friendly environs of Boston town. There were fine memories of the whole business and particularly of Maine. The incomparable summers and the charming towns and great people would be missed. No more parties at the Owl's Head cottage, which had been given up after the move to Ellsworth. No more of the shore dinners buried in the sand out at the second engineer's farmhouse. No more freshwater swimming and diving into pristine freshwater lakes from huge granite boulders. Also there would be no more romps around the countryside and forests in the top-down convertible, or the social affairs at the classy resort hotels. Life moves on.

As an epilogue, the second engineer, who stayed in touch, supplied the finishing chapters. The new plane commander didn't seem to realize that weather didn't mean anything to a live lobster, and canceling trips wouldn't work. At any rate, there were only a few trips before the whole enterprise collapsed. One of the PBMs ultimately became a hot dog stand at the Ellsworth Airport. The other serviceable one was a little more fortunate. Later she left her bones during an Antarctic expedition where she came to grief in the hands of an inept crew. So, over the past! On to the future!

Down at Squantum, while getting ready to take the Corsairs to Cherry Point, a chance meeting changed my whole approach to life. An ex-navy pilot friend had done something quite commendable. When the war was over he had put the pieces together and graduated from Harvard Medical. He was giving up on the reserve to start his internship. When the ongoing affliction of the Solomon Islands–induced malaria was discussed, he proved that he was ahead of his time. His prescription for reccurring malaria was a career in the outdoors requiring rigorous exercise. It was his theory that any passive and/or sedentary career would surely shorten life.

Very shortly the squadron took off for Cherry Point but got only as far as Willow Grove, Pennsylvania. In command of the reserve squadron there was Hank Miller, the Harvard Man, who was also a prominent attorney in the area. The conversation went long into the night, and that was fortunate, since it was to be the last meeting. He, despite his inevitably charitable and forbearing attitude, did voice some concern about the direction that peacetime marine aviation was taking. After the Korean War started it was reported that he became the first, and possibly the only, reservist to command a combat squadron there. When it was over he came home and, without comment, turned in his wings and commission.

The maneuver at Cherry Point was unremarkable but supplied an answer to the question of what to do next. The transport squadrons from El Toro had been used to fly the enlisted troops from the various squadrons to the maneuvers. One of these R5Ds was flown by an old fighter squadron comrade from the Solomon Islands, so there was no problem in hitching a ride to the West Coast. The convertible was left with a friend in Boston to be sold.

At El Toro, some more friends were flying an R4D up to Seattle, and so it seemed that the adventure would end where it started. When the airplane stopped at the Alameda Naval Air Station en route, I made a quick decision. Why not get off here and do what had seemed so appealing when San Francisco had been first encountered during the war? Live here; after all, life was going to begin again.

In next to no time, residence was taken up in "Marvelous Marin", the county which lay just north of the Golden Gate Bridge and was still rather bucolic. With no social onus present, and heeding the young Harvard doctor's advice about hard work, I found employment in the construction industry, which, after all, had been the family's business.

Once in a while I visited the Marine Reserve squadron at Oakland Airport, just to go joy riding in a Corsair. This activity was headquartered in the very same hangar where Amelia Earhart kept her Lockheed before taking off on her around-the-world flight that didn't quite get all of the way around. Fortunately, there were no openings in the squadron—"fortunately" because the ill-fated Korean War had begun and, although volunteering and feeling some lingering sense of duty, the Threadbare Buzzard got turned down. Promotions had bestowed too much rank to be called, unless already in a squadron. Shortly after Harry Truman left office, the next administration promptly surrendered, and the disgruntled reserves came marching home. Their chief complaint was against the regular establishment, who wanted the reserves to do all of the shooting while they did all of the commanding. At any rate, even after the Korean War, the reserve squadron at Oakland was occasionally visited to do a little flying, but things were different. The really go-to-hell-type fighter pilots were only a memory. All of the new type called themselves fighter pilots but were no more entitled to do so than the regulation little old ladies in tennis shoes. Under the old definition, a fighter pilot had to strap on his machine and go out and kill somebody (or, heaven forbid, get killed). For the new breed it meant getting checked out in a fighter-type aircraft, and bragging about it. No place for a gentleman.

It was not realized at the time, but the United States was undergoing rapid and radical change. While flying had been a glamorous and exciting endeavor before, and even in the early stages of the war, that was all in the past. The rapid urbanization and newfound prosperity offered more exciting prospects and new adventures. It was observed that no longer would the products of Ivy League schools and the more affluent families participate in military adventures. The regular military had been returned to well-behaved, well-mannered, serious middle-class people with a firm fixation on the secure careers provided by this vocation.

They believed that their line of work, despite the war being long gone, was still the most significant aspect of U.S. life. This was certainly no place for a renaissance man. The romance and adventure of flying had sailed away. There had once been knights in shiny armor. Then there had been the cowboys of romance and myth, and now they were all gone. So be it with the flyers whose tales shall live after them—with an approximation of the truth somewhere in the mix. The airports no longer had the exciting smell of high-octane gas for the big reciprocators, just the stench of burning kerosene for the blow-and-go machines increasingly controlled by computers.

Having picked the right career to finally, and fully, recover from the malaria, and now becoming increasingly involved in business, I was developing a whole new outlook. Flying and the people involved were becoming increasingly tiresome. It was now an endeavor of high-tech and disciplined performance. The humorless participants were wholly dedicated to conformance, and any original thoughts or actions were regarded in the same manner as that employed by Carry Nation when inspecting a saloon.

The love affair with the sky didn't even die with a whimper.

It just faded away.

The following are transcripts from the logbooks of the USS *Essex* and the USS *Sea Devil* marking the loss and rescue of Captain Tomlinson's division of Corsairs (four aircraft). Misspellings, grammar, and inconsistencies in form and/or style have not been edited. Italics have been added by author for emphasis.

DECK LOG—ADDITIONAL REMARKS SHEET
[classified confidential]

United States Ship <u>ESSEX</u>   Saturday 7 April, 1945

ADDITIONAL REMARKS

12 to 16 [1200 hours to 1600 hours]
    Steaming as before. 1208 Enemy aircraft in the vicinity. Set Condition ONE in Gunnery Department. 1211 Changed course to 020°T, opened fire on diving plane. 1212 HANCOCK hit by KAMIKAZE plane, flight deck, port side forward. Many men were sighted in water. Ships position: latitude 27°-10.5 N, Longitude 129°-43 E. HANCOCK burning furiously, DesDiv 96 standing by to pick up men in water. TG maneuvered to remain with HANCOCK. 1222 Launched CAP. 1232 Fire under control, HANCOCK keeping station. 1244 Changed course to 210°T. Maneuvered on various courses to prevent attacking planes from gaining favorable position. One bogey shot down by CAP in sight of disposition. 1357 Changed course to 140°T and landed Tracking Team, less 2VF. 1400 Jettisoned F4U-1D, bureau No. 82491. *The following planes failed to return from mission as Communication Relay Team of Search No. 1, this date: F4U-1D, bureau No. 57912, piloted by Captain T.M. TOMLINSON, USMCR, (011273); F4U-1D, bureau No. 82488, piloted by Second Lieutenant H.M. SAGERS, USMCR, (032758); F4U-1D, bureau No. 76479, piloted by Second Lieutenant T.M. LEWIS, USMCR, (032688); F4U-1D, bureau No. 82525, Piloted by Second Lieutenant J.L. GARLOCK, USMCR, (032550).* 1412 Changed speed to 24 knots. 1413 Rotated TG axis right to 140°T. 1420 Changed course to 145°T 1421 Opened fire on a ZEKE diving on ESSEX and splashed him 50 yards abeam to starboard. Pilot parachuted. 1425 Turned into wind and landed 2VF of Tracking Team. 1441 Changed course to 130°T. 1456 Changed course to 145°T. Commenced landing Strike and TCAP. Landing is interrupted by emergency turns to prevent attacking planes from getting favorable position.

The following plane failed to return from Strike against JAPANESE Fleet this date: SB2C-4E, bureau No. 20738, piloted by Lieutenant (jg) K.Q. ELLIS, (A1), USNR, (251005); crewman, GUPTIL, F.E., ARM2c, USNR, (801-39-22). The plane caught fire enroute to base and both pilot and crewman were seen safe in a liferaft in a moderate sea. 1546 Completed landing Strike and TCAP. Changed course to 055°T. 1548 Changed course to 355°T. 1549 Changed course to 315°T. Average R.P.M. 192.5

/signed
J. L. Poucher
Lieutenant, U.S. Naval Reserve.

DECK LOG—ADDITIONAL REMARKS SHEET
[classified confidential]

United States Ship <u>SEA DEVIL</u> (SS400)   Saturday 7 April, 1945

ADDITIONAL REMARKS

20–24 [2000 hours to midnight]
    Underway as before. 2048 *Sighted red star flare bearing 020°T, distant 2000 yards.* 2050 C/S to A/A one-third, fired green Very shell, C/C to 010°T. 2051 Sighted life-raft carrying two (2) men. 2057 Maneuvered to pick up men. 2108 *Picked up two American aviators: 2nd Lt. H.M. SAGERS, USMCR and Capt. T.M. Tomlinson, USMCR.* 2122 Sank rubber life raft with gunfire. 2126 Secured #3 main engine from battery charge, put #3 main engine on propulsion. 2137 Secured #2, #3 and #4 main engines from propulsion, put #3 main engine on battery charge. Commenced search for other possible survivors. 2224 Sighted flashing light bearing 045°T, C/C to 045°T. Maneuvering on various courses and speeds to pick up survivors. 2240 *Picked up one (1) American aviator: 2nd Lt. T.M. Lewis, USMCR.* 2242 Put #1 main engine on propulsion and #3 main engine on battery charge. Commenced search for other survivors.

/signed
A.R. Smith
Lt. (jg), USNR.